Drivetime

Literary Excursions in Automotive Consciousness

Lynne Pearce

EDINBURGH
University Press

Edinburgh University Press is one of the leading university presses in the UK. We publish academic books and journals in our selected subject areas across the humanities and social sciences, combining cutting-edge scholarship with high editorial and production values to produce academic works of lasting importance. For more information visit our website: edinburghuniversitypress.com

Edinburgh University Press Ltd
The Tun – Holyrood Road
12 (2f) Jackson's Entry
Edinburgh EH8 8PJ

Typeset in 10.5/13 pt Sabon by
Servis Filmsetting Ltd, Stockport, Cheshire

A CIP record for this book is available from the British Library

ISBN 978 0 7486 9084 8 (hardback)
ISBN 978 0 7486 9085 5 (webready PDF)
ISBN 978 0 7486 9086 2 (epub)

Contents

This book is dedicated to my late father
who loved driving – and thinking

My father as a young mechanic.
Author's personal collection

Acknowledgements

Since this book has had such a long gestation – followed, it must be said, by a fairly speedy execution – I have ordered my acknowledgements chronologically. Hence:

Ignition: Apart from the personal circumstances that caused me to drive many thousands of miles between Lancaster, Cornwall and Scotland during the 1990s and early 2000s, the catalyst for this book was undoubtedly the positive reception of my essay, 'Driving North, Driving South', by colleagues at Lancaster. Particular thanks here – as noted in the Preface – go to my colleague, Imogen Tyler.

Re-ignition: In 2010, by way of preparation for the Research Excellence Framework (REF), our (then) Director of Research, Sally Bushell, gave me a strong steer to include an article of my own in a special issue of *Mobilities* that I was editing. Given that the issue was already well on its way to completion, this involved me writing the article 'Automobility in Manchester Fiction' (2012) in the space of a long-weekend. This was also my first encounter with a decade's worth of automobilities scholarship and – notwithstanding the pain of that particular weekend – Sally's directive was also the kick-start that reminded me how much I wanted to work on this topic. So, thanks to Sally, together with those colleagues who initiated the (auto)mobilities revolution, in particular: John Urry, Mimi Sheller and Tim Dant from Lancaster, as well as Tim Edensor, Nigel Thrift, Peter Merriman and Mike Featherstone (all represented in the double special-issue of *TCS* (2004) which was, itself, a landmark moment in the establishment of the field.

Motoring: The research – and thinking – which sparked the proposal for this book has its origins in a chapter for Jackie Stacey and Janet Wolff's edited collection, *Writing Otherwise: Experiments in Cultural Criticism* (2013). This essay 'Autopia: In Search of What We're Thinking When We're Driving' – which incorporates the auto-ethnography of a (failed) road trip to the north of Scotland in 2012

– was where I first determined on moving cognition and affect to the centre of my investigations. Therefore many thanks indeed to Jackie and Janet in commissioning this piece and for receiving it so enthusiastically. It should also be noted that, during this period, my knowledge of, and interest in, phenomenology was greatly enhanced by conversations with my PhD student, Eleanor Fitton: so, thanks too to Eleanor.

Road trip: It was Jackie Jones's immediate and enthusiastic response to a speculative letter I sent out to several publishers that caused this to become an Edinburgh book. Jackie was the publisher of my first two books (with Harvester-Wheatsheaf), way back in the late 1980s/early 1990s, and it has been wonderful working with her again. Her interest and involvement in this project, from beginning to end, has been second to none, while her personal research interests – literary Modernism and Henri Bergson – has meant that she also proved an excellent critical reader for Chapter 1. Thanks, also, to all those friends and colleagues who provided me with such excellent suggestions of books and films on the driving theme including Brian Baker, Catherine Clay, David Cooper, Laura Doan, Jackie Jones, Andrew Tate and – most especially – Hilary Hinds, who recommended not only the 'delightful' *Mrs Miniver* but also the redoubtable Neil Young.

Maintenance: As well as Jackie, there are several other colleagues at EUP to whom I would like to offer personal thanks: Adela Rauchova, James Dale and Rebecca McKenzie have all provided outstanding support and shown that, without doubt, EUP is one of the best publishers to work with. Thanks also to staff at the British Library and the National Library of Scotland for their help during my visits, and for Lancaster University, through its Faculty research grants, for funding my trips to these archives. More recently, Hazel Stewart (NLS), Richard Stenlake (Stenlake Publishing), Yvonne Seeley (Fotolibra) and Lesley Suart (Finance Department, Lancaster University) have been especially helpful vis-à-vis the book's illustrations, and Lee Horsley has – as ever! – been indispensable in helping prepare my personal photographs and the diagram in Chapter 5, and offering technical support generally. Lee – together with Bruce Bennett, Hilary Hinds, Jackie Jones, Colin Pooley and Christine Torney – also provided invaluable feedback on draft chapters on the book; given the time constraints everyone is working under, this help, advice and 'steerage' was greatly appreciated; thanks, likewise, to psychology PhD student, Rachel Burdett, of Waikato University, New Zealand, who – through our mutual friend and colleague, Cathy Coleborne – has brought me up to date with developments in automotive psychology. Thanks to you all – as well as to my own PhD student, Muren Zhang, who, in the final stages of the book's production, has proven an exemplary research assistant.

Fellow travellers: Finally, warm thanks to all those who have supported and/or shown an interest in this project more generally including (in no particular order): CeMoRe colleagues (especially John Urry, Pennie Drinkall and Monika Büscher); Department colleagues (especially the 'Landscape and Literature Reading Group' and 'Northern Theory Seminar' with whom I shared this work); Christine Torney, for her general interest in the project and for reading Proust for me (!); Ruth Wodak, for her astute career guidance at a critical juncture; my friends at the 'Robin's Nest' Teashop in Taynuilt (notably Anne Bowers, Roy Bowers, David MacCallum, Vivienne MacCallum, Margaret Reffen, 'Joey' Reffen, Mairead Sim, Vera Shaw, Sandra Bergant and Sandra Steel) whose good humour sustained me during the writing process; and, finally, Viv Tabner for her excellent photographs and companionship on our many road trips north.

Permissions: Thanks to Palgrave Macmillan for granting me permission to reproduce some short sections from my chapter 'A Motor-flight Through Early Twentieth-century Consciousness: Capturing the Driving-event 1905–1935' (Pearce 2014). Photographic permissions are included with the illustrations.

Postscript: John Urry's untimely death on 18 March 2016 just before this book went to press demands one further acknowledgement. As many of you will be aware, John played a leading role in developing mobilities scholarship into the dynamic and interdisciplinary field it is today and to which this book speaks. His interest in, and enthusiasm for, this project meant a huge amount to me, and I am so pleased he got to see the proofs before he died.

Preface

It is my hope that this book will make a small but distinctive contribution to the rapidly expanding field of automobilities research. As the introduction to Chapter 1 explains, my own relationship to this new body of scholarship is shadowed by a sense of belatedness inasmuch as there has been a twelve-year delay between the publication of the essay – 'Driving North, Driving South' (2000) – that first put the idea of this book in my head and its realisation. It was, of course, during this very period that mobilities research emerged as a field in its own right, a good deal of it led by colleagues at my own institution where the Centre for Mobilities Research (CeMoRe) was launched in 2003. While this hiatus in my project meant that I had a vast amount of scholarly 'catch-up' to do when I was finally able to return to it in 2012, I also benefited from the groundbreaking work that had already been done on the 'car system' (e.g. Dennis and Urry 2009), car cultures (Sheller and Urry 2000; Miller 2001; Wollen and Kerr 2002; Merriman 2007, 2012) and the history of motoring (e.g. Scharff 1991; Jeremiah 2007; Clarsen 2008) during this time, not least in sourcing many of the primary texts that are the focus of my discussions here.

When I characterise my own contribution to this vibrant and, of course, politically urgent, new field as 'small' I do so advisedly inasmuch as my highly specific focus on automotive consciousness – literally, 'what we're *thinking* when we're driving' – notionally goes against the 'holistic' vision of the field's leading researchers such as John Urry, Peter Merriman and – most recently – Gijs Mom (2014). All these theorists, in their different ways, have emphasised the complexity and interconnectedness of the 'car system' and its attendant cultures as well as within/ between mobilities themselves. Further, my reintroduction of a 'mind/ body split' in a theorisation of the driving process may, on first inspection, appear to ignore all the important work that has been done over the past decade – and across the wide-ranging disciplines of sociology, psychology, geography and literary studies – in bringing the 'embodied' or 'haptic' experience of driving/passengering to the fore. As the discussions that follow will hopefully demonstrate, this was very much not my intention since the work of scholars like Danius (2002), Thrift (2008), Dant (2004), Sheller (2004), Duffy (2009), Merriman (2012) and Garrington (2015) – to name but a few – has arguably put beyond doubt the view that driving is both learnt and experienced 'through the body' as well as cognitive skill-sets (even if experimental psychology is, understandably, taking its time to endorse this).

However, acknowledging that driving is a profoundly embodied practice does not, in itself, address the fact that it also presents drivers with a unique opportunity to think about things *other than driving*, and it is with these things – in the form of perceptions, memories, reveries, fantasies, meditations and problem-solving – that this book concerns itself. In terms of this specific remit, the book has – as far as I'm aware – few obvious antecedents, although the work of Eric Laurier (2004, 2011), Peter Merriman (2004, 2007, 2012), Iain Borden (2013) and Gijs Mom (2014) all acknowledge, in their different ways, the role of cognitive and affective consciousness in the enduring appeal of motorised automobility. There is, however, one text which appears to have been inspired by a perspective on driving almost identical to my own: Tim Edensor's article 'M6 – Junction 19–16' (2003) which includes an auto-ethnography of the author's own journeys up and down the M6 at this time. Although Edensor's article references my own essay (cited above), I'm ashamed to say that I did not pick up on his until earlier this year, and would consequently like to thank him for his generosity in wishing this project well.

The fact that Tim Edensor and I share so many similar reflections – both personal and theoretical – on the practice of driving may also be read as welcome evidence that our experiences are not entirely idiosyncratic, even if – as this book repeatedly acknowledges – there will be many readers who refute the special pleasures and privileges of which we write. As well as those who inherently dislike driving/passengering as a mode of transport and/or use of their time, there is a growing international community of citizens opposed to 'the car system' on (entirely legitimate) environmental and political grounds. The introduction to Iain Borden's *Drive* (2013) – a book whose overall project is not dissimilar to mine but whose textual base is film rather than literature – anticipates and addresses such criticism by arguing that 'the private car cannot simply be replaced by improved forms of public transport without first understanding, and responding to, the various pleasures and experiences offered by automobile driving' (Borden 2013: 1). This view is also implicit in Gijs Mom's awe-inspiring 800-page comparative study, *Atlantic Automobilism* (2014), which answers his own opening gambit – 'why the car?'(p. 1) – with the conclusion that it is 'the car's transcendent, sublimating affordance' (p. 650) that explains its longevity. For readers who have been working in the field of automobilities research from a sustainable transport perspective – including many of my friends and colleagues at Lancaster University– such arguments will doubtless have the ring of tired excuses: for how much longer are 'car enthusiasts' going to justify the indulgence of their personal and/ or idiosyncratic passions by these means? Rather than respond to this challenge by a further lame attempt to defend my personal pleasure in driving, it is probably more useful if I explain, instead, that this book – like all my publications on automobility thus far – has been inspired by a recognition that motorised automotive transport – at least, as we know it – *is* facing the demise forecast by Dennis and Urry in *After the Car* (2009) and that we have most likely entered not only the second but the final 'century of the car'. It is in the light of this probable future that I have thus argued for the need to imagine and anticipate what the disappearance of the car will mean in terms *other* than transportation, in particular the loss of a dedicated and protected space in which to think (and 'be') given that such a high premium is placed on this facility in ethnographic surveys of driver-experience (e.g. Garvey 2001; Bull 2001; Redshaw 2008). Thus, while many readers will doubtless remain unconvinced that the loss of 'sanctuary' (Bull 2001) afforded by the car will have a widespread impact on our individual and social well-being as we glide from the twentieth to the twenty-first century, this book is committed to capturing the fast-receding horizon of 'automotive' twentieth-century consciousness before it disappears forever. In this regard, *Drivetime* is an avowedly *historical* project, focusing on the literary texts of the long twentieth century in order to investigate a 'phenomenology of driving' that Nigel Thrift, way back in 2004, recognised that we were only just – and, indeed, belatedly – beginning to recognise and understand (Thrift 2008 [2004]: 75).

This mention of 'phenomenology' returns me to another of this book's starting points, and also serves to introduce the somewhat eclectic theory and methodology in which it is grounded. When I presented an early version of my chapter 'Driving North, Driving South' to a seminar group at Lancaster in the late-1990s, my colleague Imogen Tyler described it as 'a sort of phenomenology of driving'. This observation stuck with me, and when I returned to the project in 2012 – and soon after attempted an auto-ethnography of a road trip (Pearce 2013) – I initially contemplated focusing the book entirely on the ways in which driving may be seen to *facilitate* specifically phenomenological insight.

What my new auto-ethnography revealed, however, was that – fresh, intuitive and profound as the thinking occasioned by driving sometimes is – such insights necessarily take their place alongside many other less intellectual thought streams and reveries. I soon realised that I wanted to make these the object of my study also, not least on account of the wide diversity of automotive consciousness recorded in the literary and other texts I had begun to survey. This moment was also a recognition, of course, that this was to be a project which would have its disciplinary roots in psychology as well as philosophy and literary and cultural theory, with a particular focus – spanning all these disciplines – on perception, memory and affect. Chapter 1 attempts to bring some of the most important frameworks from these disciplines together in a theorisation of the category I have designated 'automotive consciousness', as well as what has become the basic building block of my enquiries, the 'driving-event'. My secondary critical and theoretical sources, meanwhile, are mostly drawn from the recent debates in (auto)mobilities scholarship which has, itself, emerged from departments of sociology and historical/cultural geography, with literary criticism (particularly within the field of Modernism) and social history also providing invaluable contexts for my textual analysis.

In addition there is, of course, the question of the rationale for my selection of literary texts from across the twentieth century. Benefiting greatly from all that has now been written on the subject of motoring and car culture, it was not difficult to establish a substantial and fascinating library of relevant texts from Britain, America, Australia and (more occasionally) continental Europe. I also spent time consulting the vast automotive periodical archives held in the British Library and National Library of Scotland, and a good deal of the early twentieth-century literature with which I engage derives from these sources. From a methodological point of view it is, however, important to recognise that I consider myself as a cultural theorist rather than a literary critic, and that my final selection of texts was therefore based on their usefulness in helping me to model the different kinds of thinking drivers and passengers are engaged in. This, then, is very emphatically not a book that employs the thematic of driving – or cars/motoring in general – in order to better understand the texts themselves, but one that draws upon literature as a means of contributing to and advancing recent debates in automobilities research. This said, I nevertheless hope that the book will also prove of interest to literary scholars given that the theorising is built around close readings of texts that aim to be fresh and interesting in and of themselves. While on the subject of my methodology and textual rationale, I feel that I should also address the slightly uncomfortable question of whether this study might not have done more to address and challenge the weight of gender bias and prejudice that still circumscribes motoring discourse (including academic discourse). This is a difficult call since, notwithstanding the fact that I am typically cast as a feminist scholar, the nature of my enquiry here – with its focus on the *mechanisms* of consciousness as facilitated and structured by driving (and passengering) – would have run the risk of essentialism had I also sought to gender the process. In Chapter 1 I do, nevertheless, draw attention to the implications of women's historical exclusions from driving for my theorising, and vis-à-vis my textual materials I have endeavoured to ensure that both women writers – and female protagonists – are well represented.

The use of literary and cultural texts by the social scientists working in the field of automobilities research has arguably been one of the means by which this research has been able to reach, imaginatively, beyond more utilitarian transport studies approaches. Peter Merriman's two books (2007 and 2012) have been especially groundbreaking in this regard, while the recent publication of Lesley Murray and Sara Upstone's *Researching and Representing Mobilities* (2014) and Gijs Mom's *Atlantic Automobilism* (2014) clearly signal that the Humanities have now begun to contribute to mobilities research in a major way. It is, of course, my hope that this book will be seen as part of this trend, in particular by bringing the type of theorised close reading that has long been popular in literary and cultural studies to bear upon a practice (i.e. driving) that, until recently, was the province of scientific research. In this regard, my recent conversations with a scholar working on driving and cognition in a psychology department has been especially encouraging. While such science will, of course, always seek to base its conclusions on experiential evidence, it seems that work such as mine might well prove useful in the modelling of experiments in the future.

The book's contents are organised as follows: after the opening chapter which, as noted above, attempts a theorisation of 'automotive consciousness' by drawing upon and introducing the cross-disciplinary theories and debates that inform the project, the book is divided into four chapters, each one dealing with a different expression of automotive consciousness: 'searching', 'fleeing', 'cruising' and 'flying' (the last of these featuring six 'altered states of consciousness' which driving may be seen to induce). Between Chapter 1 and the subsequent chapters there is also a short 'Interlude': this comprises extracts from my latest auto-ethnography – 'Driving South, Driving North' – which re-enacts my 1999 journey (detailed above) and, in the process, sheds interesting light on the changing conditions of motoring in Britain. While every effort has been made to ensure that each of these chapters coheres and is of interest in its own right, it will be obvious that this is a book that was conceptualised as a unity and whose thesis necessarily becomes clearer – and, I hope, more compelling – as the various modes of automotive consciousness are set alongside one another and compared.

Finally, it worth mentioning that – as for other female academics who have taken to writing about automobility in recent years (I am thinking, in particular, of Georgine Clarsen and Sarah Redshaw) – cars, and driving them, are integral to my personal past. Born into a garage-owning family (see the photograph of my father as a young mechanic), cars were both the theme tune to my childhood and the 'economic base' that supported me through university and beyond. Indeed, were it not for my father providing me with a succession of cars – all of them old, none of them costing more than £400 – during the decade it took me to secure an academic job, the experiences which have inspired this book would never have happened. Like Neil Young (2014), I therefore owe a great deal to 'my life in cars' even if, like him, I also know that their time is almost up.

Argyll (Scotland)
November 2015

'Glencoe village and garage (1930s)', Guthrie Hutton, *Old Glencoe and Ballachulish* (2011). Courtesy of Stenlake Publishing Ltd.

Chapter 1

Theorising Automotive Consciousness

It is my aim, in the first chapter of this book, to demonstrate how driving is paradigmatic as well as formative of the way we think. By this I am suggesting that the way in which the mind travels through time and space on its everyday cognitive journeys – encountering a novelty here, a memory or an obstacle there – is figuratively similar to the way in which cars and their drivers engage with the temporal and spatial environments through which they pass: probing, pausing, advancing, reversing and, of course, changing direction with the flick of an indicator light.[1] The automobile, long regarded as a prosthesis of the human body (Thrift 2008 [2004]; Dant 2004), may thus also be thought of as a prosthesis of the human mind.

The rapid succession of thoughts that present themselves to a driver's consciousness – directed now towards the past, now towards the future, and prompted, in both cases, by a perceptual encounter with the present – first occurred to me when I was working on my essay 'Driving North, Driving South' in the late 1990s (Pearce 2000). Although, at the time of writing, I never thought of this as an essay 'about' driving, its publication coincided with the birth of the Mobilities research centre at Lancaster (CeMoRe)[2] and a seminar presentation to this group caused me to reflect that this was an area of research that I might pursue further. Sadly, other commitments meant that I was unable to do so for another decade: indeed, it was 2010 before I wrote about driving again and 2012 before this book was conceived. Such time lags are, of course, unremarkable in academic scholarship: the wide-ranging professional duties of academics mean that the gestation, writing and production of books often take this long. However, what lends this anecdote a thought-provoking edge is the extent to which the experience of driving in Britain has, itself, changed during this fifteen-year period.

Throughout the 1990s, when my parents were still alive and I had first started working at Lancaster University, I made frequent trips 'down the road' to Cornwall. From the mid-1990s onwards, I also started driving up to Scotland on a regular basis and, in 1998, bought a small cottage there which meant that all vacations and several weekends also involved a drive in that direction. As for many of us, my relationship to my family and birthplace was a complicated, sometimes painful, one and my drives south were marked by a good deal of anxiety and what I now perceive to be rather desperate anticipation that things might be better; by contrast, my drives north were more emotionally straightforward if no less intense. My 'destination home' (Pearce 2000: 25–6) evoked powerful feelings, but they were not complicated ones.

Yet what is remarkable, looking back, is the extent to which the material circumstances of driving (that is, the impact of the volume of traffic and/or the road infrastructure) were largely the same in both directions. Driving south was not that much different to driving north in these essentials. While the traffic must have been heavier going south, even then[3] – and although I do have memories of occasional marathon journeys when an accident or breakdown clogged up the M5 to such an extent that it took ten hours to get home – the majority of trips up and down the road were fast, smooth, straightforward. Even in old, low-performance cars I regularly covered the 360 miles, door-to-door, in six to seven hours (including stops). The section of the M6 from Manchester to Birmingham was always the busiest stretch of the road, and the merger of the M6 and the M5 the one place where (travelling north, especially) you might expect some queues, but the M5 itself (excluding national holidays) was frequently half-empty; likewise the A30 from Okehampton through to Truro, apart from the summer when holiday traffic could cause a problem getting out of the county. The crucial factor here, however, is that such hold-ups were largely unpredictable; I never set out expecting them.

This qualitative change in the driving experience on Britain's major auto-routes (see note 3) is, of course, one that will be familiar to all frequent road users and one which has prompted a complex range of responses from the government, highway agencies and various transport action groups (some demanding more and better roads; others campaigning to stop further road expansion).[4] However, my own interest in these changes – now as then – is not simply focused on how the increase in traffic and changes to the road infrastructure in the UK has impacted upon our journeys at the functional level of speed and convenience, but rather how they – together with the advent of mobile technologies (the mobile phone and its attendant social media) – have transformed the cognitive and affective dimension of the driving experience: that is to say, the ways in which what we think and feel when we drive has qualitatively changed (Pearce 2013).[5] The long journeys I have described making in the 1990s and early 2000s – both north and south – instilled in me a love and need for driving as valuable (indeed, exceptional) thought-space: a longed-for, ring-fenced slice of time which nothing would intrude upon or interrupt. Many of the things I had to think about in both my professional and personal life were unravelled, and sometimes resolved, in the course of my drives in both directions.

In 2015, by contrast, the meditative thought-space that arguably depends upon a sustained and comfortable cruising speed (see Chapter 4) is no longer possible on many British motorway routes: where once it used to be just the M25 and some sections of the M1 that were synonymous with gridlock, the problem now extends to erstwhile rural motorway routes such as the M5. As all long-distance drivers are aware, the sheer volume of twenty-first century traffic is such that the nation's arteries are liable to clog at any moment.[6] True, this is not always the case, but the threat of the motoring equivalent to sudden cardiac arrest is always there. Indeed, what my most recent experience of 'driving south, driving north' confirms is that now you always have to anticipate the worst on a journey south. The automotive equivalent of the flap of a butterfly's wing can bring the flow to a standstill in an instant.

For drivers who are habitual users of mobile technologies, meanwhile, quality thought-time has arguably been excluded from the driving experience for reasons that have nothing to do with the traffic. Recent sociological research into work and mobility has revealed the extent to which organisations now expect their employees to be working (i.e. making calls, doing deals, setting up meetings) while they are simultaneously on the move, including when travelling by car (Laurier 2004; Hislop 2012: 220–37).[7] Bluetooth technology has rendered the car, the van, the lorry as effective a mobile office as the train or plane, notwithstanding serious safety implications.[8] Further, although we must assume that there are plenty of long-distance journeys still undertaken for recreational purposes, mobile devices are now rarely switched off with the consequence that very few drivers or passengers will complete a long journey uninterrupted.[9] For even if we choose not to pick up our calls and texts until the next stop, the interruption has occurred: to whatever we have been thinking has now been added the expectation/concern of what the message(s) contain (Pearce 2017).

Those less interested than myself in the changes in the qualitative experience of driving will, of course, observe that the post-millennial explosion in mobile technologies has impacted on all aspects of our personal and professional lives, not merely our use and experience of transport. But what my own personal experience tells me is that long-distance driving is one of the last bastions of ring-fenced 'thought-space' in the modern world. While this opportunity to think while driving will be perceived as a privilege by only some drivers,[10] for those of us who have valued the car's 'sanctuary' (Bull 2001; Edensor 2003)[11] the qualitative changes underway represent a significant loss (Laurier and Dant 2011). In a world where more and more of our activities – including, of course, thinking – are computer-mediated and centred on information retrieval rather than non-referential speculation and/or the independent generation of ideas, the pristine thought-space of the driving-event (see note 9) is, or was, an oasis in the rhythm of daily life. Walking, cycling, rail and air transport arguably present similar 'third-space' opportunities for contemplation (Solnit 2001), but these mobilities were intruded upon by mobile devices even sooner. As part of this discussion, it is of course important to remember that many drivers actively dislike, and feel threatened by, the loneliness of a long journey by car, with the consequence that the loss of uninterrupted thought-space may, indeed, matter to only a minority of the population. But it is certainly a change that has mattered to me and which, combined with the changes in the road conditions, means that the long drives to Cornwall, which used to represent such an important interlude in my cognitive life, would no longer be available to me in the same way were I still driving in that direction. This said, any retrospective of Britain's roads needs to avoid romanticising the past; as historians, geographers and cultural theorists (Jeremiah 2007; Merriman 2007; Moran 2009) repeatedly seek to remind us, queues, jams and even gridlock were a feature of many British towns and cities from the 1930s onwards, as discussed here in Chapter 5. In this regard, it would be more appropriate to figure the mounting pressures on motorway driving today as analogous to what happened to the A-roads before the motorways opened and be reminded that congestion was a symptom of motorised transport from its earliest days (Pooley 2013; Keir and Morgan 1955).

To extend analysis of the cognitive processes associated with car driving to thoughts other than those needed to safely negotiate the road is, to the best of my knowledge, something that has only been briefly touched upon by other scholars (Edensor 2003; Sheller 2004; Merriman 2004, 2007, 2012; Trigg 2012; Laurier 2011; Laurier and Dant 2011; Mom 2014), even though there is a rich repository of literary texts – from the early twentieth century to the present (some autobiographical, some fictional, some philosophical) – which reveal, often in a self-consciously phenomenological manner, the altered states of consciousness[12] to which driving (and, indeed, passengering)[13] gives rise. Psychologists interested in driving as a 'complex everyday task' (Groeger 2000; Van Lennep 1987; Charlton and Starkey 2011) have undertaken research to account for the way in which drivers are able to 'think of other things' and enter into conversations with their passengers while driving, but largely from the perspective of road safety. Yet all drivers will, at some time, have thought thoughts of the kind featured in the pages of this book: thoughts that connect the things we see through the car windscreen with things that have happened in the past, or might happen in the future; thoughts of events, and people, lost to time; thoughts of things that might have happened but never did. As Tim Edensor (2003: 161), writing specifically about the 'relaxed awareness' enabled by motorway driving, similarly observes: 'According to recent events, drivetime may become a period in which we can celebrate or grieve.' And all this maelstrom of cognitive activity will have been taking place alongside our perception of the random phenomena that present themselves to us through the windscreen as we surge, ineluctably, forward: looked at this way, Groeger's 'complex everyday task' (2000) becomes very complex indeed, even allowing for the fact that more recent psychology and neuroscience is better placed to understand the mind's capacity for multi-tasking (see Thompson 2015 (also Merriman 2007: 8) on the ways in which the visual, sensory, somatic and social combine in the practice of driving).

Nevertheless, it can also be argued that the meandering consciousness that I present here as exemplary of the driving-event is really not that different from the rabbit-runs and detours of everyday thought. Walking across the car park at work, waiting in a queue, sitting at a desk are all activities that permit the mind to wander at will along routes whose final destination is rarely known (see Edensor (2003: 155) who likens driving to other 'everyday activities' whose 'rhythms' and 'rituals' have only recently been given the attention they deserve). What driving does – or, rather, what a phenomenological reflection upon the driving-event may achieve – is to render the cognitive dimension of such everyday practices newly visible, and seemingly on account of the way in which the defamiliarising act of driving a car typically sharpens perception, speeds up cognition and stimulates all manner of thought-association.[14] As Bart Kennedy[15] in his 1919 article on 'The Magic of Speed' for *The Car Illustrated* observes:

> You are gripped with the might of a strange potent wine. The magic is about you. It surrounds you . . . To your eyes have come a sharper vision. And these pictures that flash through your consciousness as this magic of speed is enveloping you. Pictures from the past, and pictures out of that time that is upon you now, and pictures perhaps of things to come. (Kennedy 1919a: 115)

What exactly counts as 'speed' in terms of cognition (i.e. it is evidently something that has been, and can still can be, experienced at 20mph as well as at 60mph), and to what extent other aspects of automobility contribute to the experiences Kennedy describes here, is something I return to at the end of this chapter. What is certain, however, is that – in the early twentieth century – motoring was widely regarded as a sport with the capacity both to enlighten and to render insane (Pearce 2014: 78–81) and this, in turn, prompted a good deal of self-conscious reflection on exactly *what* we are thinking when sat at the wheel of a car.

Before proceeding with more substantive discussion of the ways in which driving may be seen to lend itself to phenomenological reflection, I wish first to probe further the mimetic and metaphorical similarity between driving and thinking per se. There is, as I have already suggested, a somewhat uncanny similarity between the roving of our 'mind's eye' and an automobile's progress through the world that may provide some further insight into why driving has proven such a pleasurable and compelling activity for large sectors of the population – worldwide – for over a century. True, there are those who have rejected this love-affair with the car on many grounds since its inception (and these voices will also be heard in the course of this book), but my own interest is guided by what *besides* the utility of transportation, the thrill of speed and the status symbol long associated with car ownership, has made driving so popular, so difficult to relinquish (see also Borden 2013: 9; Mom 2014: 649–50). From their very earliest days, both motoring and cycling[16] have afforded complex cognitive and affective[17] pleasures resultant upon a qualitatively new sense of agency that was not simply about a choice of destination but, more profoundly, a relishing of the ways in which one's vehicle both mimics – and may be put into the service of – the vagaries of one's mind. As will be demonstrated by many of the literary texts featured in the chapters which follow, the car's movement through the physical (and spatial) landscape is often strikingly evocative of the mind's journey through the figurative (and temporal) landscape of internal consciousness. In other words, even as the view from the car window may be likened to the thoughts that 'flash' through a subject's mind, minute by minute, so too does the driver's ability to reverse, detour and generally explore the road network appear to simulate the journeys of our minds into the past or, through projection, into the future.[18]

And yet it is perhaps the persistent, repetitive nature of our journeying – in particular, the way in which we have used our mobility (by foot, by cycle, by car) to *probe* our environment – that seems best to capture the analogy between automobility and thought. In common with nonhuman animals, everything would seem to depend upon our being able to test, map, learn and, ultimately, expand our territory in a spatially specific way: for centuries humans did this by foot and by horse, then by cycle and by car. Figured thus, the automobile may be seen as a prosthetic not only of the human body but also of the human mind. With this paradigm in mind, my project here thus seeks to draw upon literary and other texts not only to explore the ways in which car driving gives rise to heightened and/or altered states of consciousness that excite psychological and philosophical enquiry (Chapters 4 and 5), but also to reveal the ways in which the behaviour of the 'driver-car' (Dant 2004) resembles the behaviour of the mind in the most mundane and habitual of ways (Chapter 2).

Having established this close correlation between the spatial/temporal explorations of everyday consciousness and the 'to' and 'fro' of automotive transport, it is also not difficult to see why driving can, on occasion, prove therapeutic. Beyond the widely held acknowledgement that cars are synonymous with 'escape' (see Chapter 3), there are a few scholars (myself included) who have reflected on the way in which a driving-event can positively reorient the direction of our thoughts. The psychological inference here is that it is precisely *because* the behaviour of the moving car mimics that of the human brain that a change in one is felt as a change in the other. In the analysis of my 2012 road trip (Pearce 2013), I remark upon the way in which both acceleration and determining one's own route through a myriad of potential pathways seemingly spills over into one's thinking in an empowering way, and something similar is noted by Dylan Trigg (2012) in his phenomenological account of a journey to, and from, a service station:

> Enlarging the body beyond its own objective edge, things in the world take on the sensibility and nervous system of one's own being.
>   Coupled with this embodied emergence, the interior of the car simultaneously gives itself over to an imagined landscape. By using the phrase 'imagined landscape', the role the passing landscape plays in forming the continuity of the self and the car becomes central. This twofold temporality, between self and landscape, in time, leads to the dynamic production of an internal landscape . . .
>   [I]nstead of simply being a transportation device, the car's constant sense of becoming-toward leads to the formation of place as being a retreat from the immediate present and a projecting towards the unmapped future. (Trigg 2012: 140)

As will be discussed in the next section of this chapter, Trigg is one of the few contemporary theorists to have self-consciously performed a sustained phenomenology of the driving-event. Here, his reflections on the way in which the driver's perception of the landscape outside the car maps itself onto the 'camera roll' of his or her inner consciousness is similar to my own thoughts on the way in which the movement/ viewpoint of mind and car mimic and inter-animate one other; further, we are both profoundly impressed by the 'future-oriented' ('becoming-toward') nature of all driving-events and how they have the capacity to direct ('project') our thoughts and fantasies in that direction. Trigg consolidates his own point with reference to Paul Auster's novel, *The Music of Chance* (2006), observing:

> The experience of driving through place, disrupted only by the intensifica-tion of traffic, means that different places emerge as a residue, or a stream of discontinuous fragments, taken in by the driving-subject and simultaneously left behind in a horizon of disappearances ... the car's becoming-toward structure has the consequence of emphasizing the notion of the car as an escape, from place and time. (Trigg 2012: 141)

Trigg's own mixing of the landscape with the driver's consciousness captures brilliantly the ways in which what we see and what we think/ feel feed off one another and how – in existential terms – the discarding of places passed through at speed can prompt the jettisoning (or, at least, the rearrangement) of things stored in our 'internal landscape'.

Trigg's Deleuzian[19] encoding of the inherently 'becoming-toward' character of car travel invokes the vision of another philosopher whose work is central to Chapter 5 of this book, namely Ernst Bloch. Although Bloch's work has never enjoyed more than a minority following since his death in 1977, *The Principle of Hope* (in three volumes) is arguably the most future-oriented philosophical project of the twentieth century (if we count Filippo Marinetti's 'Futurist Manifesto' (1909) as aesthetics/ politics rather than philosophy).[20] Rejecting, in particular, the logic of Freudian determinism which explains all aspects of the human psyche – including desire – in terms of its past, Bloch sought to show how both individuals and societies are, on the contrary, inherently oriented towards the future. In this regard, and following on from the previous discussion, what driving 'gifts' the driver (and passenger) is an enthu-siastic steer towards the 'not-yet-conscious' dimension of thought. As will emerge in the chapters that follow, driving is an activity, or event, that indisputably promotes futuristic daydreams as well as retrospective memories and, in this regard, Bloch's focus on 'anticipatory conscious-ness' in *The Principle of Hope* is an immensely important supplement to phenomenological models of consciousness discussed below (see also Edensor 2003: 154, 161).

Driving and phenomenology

Having proposed a mimetic likeness between driving and thinking, it is necessary that I now offer a rather more informed rationale for the ways in which the practice of driving may be seen to facilitate the practice of phenomenology given that this is the branch of twentieth-century philosophy to which the embodied experience of automobility most obviously speaks. First, however, I need to establish my own critical distance from phenomenology and reinforce the point made in the Preface that my own interest in driver-consciousness is by no means restricted to the phenomenological.

This is, in essence, because the first principles of the movement as characterised by Edmund Husserl and Maurice Merleau-Ponty[21] – and allowing for the modifications introduced later their careers (most notably Husserl's 'transcendental reduction'[22]) – remain broadly committed to the primacy of perception and the 'givenness' of the phenomenon in a notional present, unsullied by memory or anticipation, as the key to philosophical enlightenment. These foundational principles are, indeed, explicit in most attempts to define phenomenology as a movement: for example, Moran and Mooney's opening gambit 'Phenomenology may be characterised initially in a broad sense as the unprejudiced, descriptive study of whatever appears to consciousness, precisely in the manner in which it so appears' (Moran and Mooney 2002: 1). While the polluting 'matter' of memory is not named as an obstacle here, the notion of 'unprejudiced description' arguably presupposes it. Whatever he or she is attending to (and this might be an abstract thought as well as something that is materially present in the material world), the phenomenologist must give it his or her undivided attention and, in particular, resist any practice of association which might rob it of its specificity (conceived by Husserl first as *eidos* and later as *essence*: see note 22). While such a characterisation fails to recognise the complex evolution of Husserl's ideas in particular, it nevertheless remains the popularly held view of what defines phenomenology. I return to the significance of this stance in my exposition of E. H. Gombrich's theory of the relationship between 'seeing' and 'knowing' below, but suffice to say that the requirements of phenomenology, as practised by Husserl and Merleau-Ponty, not to mention others associated with the movement such as Martin Heidegger,[23] are too rigorous to entertain the heterogeneity of the states of consciousness I explore in the representations of driving featured in this book.

The practice of driving most certainly has the capacity to startle us into fresh perceptions of all manner of phenomena – to reveal their intentionality[24] – and hence prompt intuition; however, inasmuch as the driving-event is also a mental space in which not only present perception but also memory, anticipation and daydreaming hold sway, it is clear that – on many, if not most, occasions – it will be incapable of delivering the sustained purity of thought associated with dedicated phenomenological practice. In the course of a typical journey we are arrested both by the fresh and 'original' phenomena of the immediate present and, through the agency of memory, by what Husserl describes as 'symbolic' (i.e. reconstructed) images and thought processes.[25] For Gombrich and the Gestalt school of psychology, as we shall see below, this is an unrecognisable distinction (there can be no perception without a prior 'schema', which is a memory of sorts), and, vis-à-vis my project here more generally, it is precisely the dynamic interaction between present and past – and, in Husserl's terms, perception and 'phantasy' (see note 25) – that has revealed itself as the most fascinating aspect of driving as a cognitive event (Pearce 2013).

Stepping back from these philosophical exigencies, there is, of course, no good reason why the driving-event *should* deliver sustained phenomenological reflection. The fact that it facilitates it partially – or at all – as evocatively as it does is wonder enough. To be clear, then, although, the chapters that follow explore the textual representation of a wide range of thought processes and states of consciousness that are far from phenomenological in character, there are numerous other occasions when we see the car driver (or passenger) following the 'intentional object' they have seized upon with an attention akin to the 'phenomenological method' and achieving the deepest philosophical insight.

To illustrate this point, I now turn to two extracts – one elucidating the visionary experience of driving, the other 'about' the phenomenological method – which reveal a striking similarity between the two practices *as practices*. First, A. B. Filson Young on 'The Open Road':

> But the road . . . restores to our journeys their true value and importance, making them not a matter merely of departure and arrival, but of deliberate and conscious progress, in which every mile, every yard, is of equal importance with the beginning and the end . . . by motor-car we lose the extremely minute detail of the road, but cover it in spans so much greater that the sense of passage is vastly increased. And this, I think, is the supreme charm of this kind of travel; that it takes us from one world to another, not as the railway takes us sealed up in an envelope containing ourselves and our environment, but open to, and conscious of, the things that connect those worlds with each other, so that we see the change coming and know how it has come. (Filson Young 1904: 312)

And second, Jean-Luc Marion in *Being Given* (2002) as paraphrased by Dylan Trigg:

> Above all, then, phenomenology as a method is marked by its reliance on things taking course, giving full weight, not to the perception of things in advance, but, in Marion's words, to the work of 'travel[ling] in tandem with the phenomenon, as if protecting it and clearing a path for it by eliminating roadblocks. (Trigg 2012: 23)

In the same way, then, that driving and thinking may be presented as paradigmatic of one another in general terms, so too may the practice of driving and the practice of phenomenology. While the chance serendipity of Marion's metaphor can hardly be used to proclaim this a universal principle, the analogy is compelling: in the same way that the movement of automobiles may be seen to mimic that of the human mind, so too does the car's ability to travel not only through, but *with*, the passing landscape, liken it to the phenomenologist's commitment to travel with and alongside his/her phenomena. Moreover, the role that mobility plays in both practices is crucial; indeed, it is the act of *following* the phenomena, and of gaining new perspectives on them, that characterises phenomenology as an intellectual process rather than the epiphany it is sometimes mistaken for. According to Marion, we get to see into the life of things only by *staying with them*, observing them on their own terms and clearing away the mental obstacles that stand in the way of their apprehension.

The notion that all insight depends upon such 'travelling with' is also at the heart of Filson Young's eulogy to motoring: an activity that is lauded precisely because of its intellectual stimulation and analysed, as here, in distinctly phenomenological terms. A. B. Filson Young is a name that will feature on several occasions in the pages that follow, and this extract serves to illustrate why. In anticipation of literary modernists like Virginia Woolf, Filson Young was not only inspired by what he saw from his moving vehicle (i.e. the novel experience of seeing the world at speed) but also what this new mode of perception had brought to bear upon consciousness itself. As may be seen in this extract, of particular fascination is the way in which motorised automobility – in contrast to other forms of transport – enables a self-conscious observation of one's passage from 'a' to 'b' in much the same way as the phenomenologist is taught to observe, or 'follow', the orbit of his or her thoughts. As is the case for the student of Husserl or Merleau-Ponty, an 'unprejudiced' attention to detail is key ('deliberate and conscious progress'), as is the perspective, delivered by speed and distance which enables the traveller to ultimately grasp the whole of his or her journey as the sum of its parts. This ambitious prescription – that we attend both to the particulars of the journey and what they add up to – looks forward to my own definition of the 'driving-event' (see below), but also resonates with the objective of Husserl's phenomenological reduction which is to relentlessly pursue a phenomenon to the point that we can glimpse its essence (Trigg 2012: 17–25).

For Filson Young, the 'thought' being pursued is, of course, the automobile journey itself, and the author is at pains to contrast the steady, attentive 'passage' of the car with the 'sealed envelope' of the train that delivers us to our destination even more quickly, but at the expense not being able to witness what *connects* 'a' to 'b'. This view is, of course, in signal contrast to Marcel Proust's frequently quoted observation in *Remembrance of Things Past* (1941: 693; see also Danius 2002: 91–146) on the railway's 'magical' ability to transport the passenger from Paris to 'Balbec' without his knowing anything about it. For Filson Young, by contrast, the magic of the journey lies in its lengthy exposition and in the active, attentive thought processes that make us open to, and conscious of, the things that connect those worlds with each other, '*so that we see the change coming and know how it has come*' (my italics). The future tense of Filson Young's closing sentence lends a final, metaphysical flourish to this vision but also, arguably, marks the limit of its phenomenology.

The practice of driving, then, may be seen to map onto the practice of phenomenology in a highly suggestive way; but only to a point. As will be demonstrated repeatedly in the textual analyses that follow, drivers and passengers may indeed be 'travel[ling] in tandem with the phenomenon' (Marion 2002) – be that an object of perception or an abstract thought – for part of their journeys, but typically become distracted by other, less elevated, thought-processes sooner or later. This is not to say that the effort expended on such phenomenological enquiry is entirely lost – indeed, as we shall see in the section on the driving-event following, we would expect it to feature in the journey's reckoning – but it must be remembered that a motor car is the quintessential 'dream-machine' and, as such, lends itself to all manner or unregulated thought and fantasy.

Finally, it is worth observing that the arrival of phenomenology as a new philosophical method at the cusp of the nineteenth and twentieth centuries (Brentano's lectures on 'descriptive phenomenology' took place in 1888–9 and Husserl's *Logical Investigations* was first published between 1900 and 1901) coincided, almost exactly, with the manufacture of the first automobiles (*c*.1888 (Karl Benz) – 1908 (Henry Ford's Model-T)) and the rapid expansion of motoring for sport and recreation. As Stephen Kern observes in his definitive study of the changing cultures of time and space in the Modernist period (Kern 2000 [1983]), virtually all of the scientific/intellectual movements of the time – from psychoanalysis to Einstein's special theory of relativity to Futurism (see note 20) – may be sourced to the mechanical and technological innovations of the day, and while Kern does not link his discussion of Husserl, William James and Henri Bergson (2000: 37–44) explicitly to the reorientation of time and space engendered by automobility, the evidence is surely to be found in the literary representations of motoring featured in this book. In particular, and as will be discussed further in the section which follows, the 'speed' of both transport and communications meant that 'the present' had become a hotly contested category.

Memory matters

In this section I expand upon those features of phenomenology which are of most relevance for the chapters that follow, as well as introduce some productive complications originating in Gestalt psychology[26] in order to demonstrate the limitations, as well as the appeal, of thinking about automotive consciousness in phenomenological terms. In the course of these discussions, my own position on the mechanisms of perception-cognition, which owes a good deal to E. H. Gombrich's theory of 'schema and correction', will also emerge. As acknowledged in the Preface, this collision of academic disciplines will doubtless jar for some readers; however, inasmuch as they have an object of enquiry in common – namely, the relationship between perception and cognition – the conversation seems justified. On this point it is also worth remembering that phenomenology, via Franz de Brentano, has its roots in early psychology (*Psychology and the Empirical Standpoint* (2002b [1874]: 32–4), even if those who followed in its wake, such as Heidegger, subsequently drew clear lines between their efforts to establish it as a radical new way of understanding 'being-in-the-world' (see note 23) and the mere workings of the human mind.

As already intimated, the most significant disagreement within the various philosophies and psychologies of perception/cognition (including phenomenology itself) which has a direct bearing on my own project is that which concerns the primacy (or not) of perception. Although Husserl and Merleau-Ponty address this issue rather differently (and, indeed, modify their ideas throughout their careers), both are broadly in agreement that the act of perception (in the present) precedes, or precipitates, the act of memory rather than the other way round. Further, that which presents itself to consciousness in this notional present is of far greater *value* (i.e. more capable of generating new knowledge/enlightenment) than our 'symbolic thoughts' or 'secondary consciousness' (i.e. memory). In 'Time and Internal Consciousness' Husserl accounts for the difference thus:

> Perception, or the self-giving of the actual present, which has its correlate in the given of what is past, is now confronted by another contrast, that of recollection, secondary remembrance. In recollection, a now 'appears' to us, but it 'appears' in a sense wholly other than the appearance of the now in perception. This now *is not perceived, i.e. self-given, but presentified* . . . The phantasied now presents a now, but does not give us a now itself. (Moran and Mooney 2002: 116 (italics in the original))

Although the objective of Husserl's article on 'Internal-Time Consciousness' (first published in 1966) is actually to acknowledge the necessary intrusion of the recent past (in the form of a 'primary retention') on our comprehension of the present (Moran and Mooney 2002: 110), a rhetorical analysis of the preceding extract reveals a latent hostility towards 'recollection' or 'secondary remembrance' which (in contrast to primary retention) is seen as perception's inauthentic 'other'. Similarly, Merleau-Ponty – in setting forth his own theory of perception contra various 'associationist' models from the first half of the twentieth century – is adamant that, in the 'chicken and egg' of perception vs. memory/schemata, perception must always come first:

> From this can be judged the worth of accepted formulas about the 'role of memories in perception'. Even outside empiricism there is talk of 'the contribution of memory'. People go on saying that 'to perceive is to remember' . . . But on what basis have we this belief? What is it, in present perception, which teaches us that we are dealing with an already familiar object, since *ex hypothesi* its properties are altered? If it is argued that recognition of shape or size is bound up with that of colour, the argument is circular, since apparent size and shape are also altered, and since recognition here too cannot result from the recollection of memories but must precede it. Nowhere then does it work from past to present, and the 'projection of memories' is nothing but a bad metaphor hiding a deeper, ready-made recognition. (Merleau-Ponty 2002 [1945]: 22–3)

In contrast to those philosophers (he footnotes Léon Brunschvicg and Henri Bergson) who incline to the view that we see only what we already know, Merleau-Ponty's logic insists that, on the contrary, without the perception *of something* in the notional present there can be no 'shape' to prompt memory. Hence his resolute conclusion: 'nowhere then does it work from past to present'. Further, his reference to 'ready-made recognition' in the final sentence quoted above would seem to indicate an even greater hostility to all theories, like those of Karl Popper, the Gestalt school of psychology and E. H. Gombrich, who posit not memories but *schemas* as the a priori of perception. Given the emphasis placed on the necessary 'purity' of perception required for the effective practice of phenomenology it is therefore not surprising that any theory of perception predicated on 'ready-made' shapes or gestalts would be anathema.

While it is, thankfully, not the objective or responsibility of this book to solve the riddle of 'which comes first', it has been essential for me to negotiate a model of perception-cognition which values both the enlightening properties of the perceptual present and the equally fascinating properties of the 'recollections' or 'secondary remembrances' dismissed by Husserl, inasmuch as the driving-event facilitates, and is defined by, both. In my attempts to figure such a model I have also been repeatedly reminded of the philosophy-psychology fence on which my own research sits. The reason that Husserl and Merleau-Ponty perceive memory as such an undesirable and contaminating aspect of consciousness is arguably because they are dedicated to an 'unprejudiced description' of phenomena as a means to philosophical, rather than psychological, insight. And inasmuch as driving does, indeed, seem to prompt and promote such phenomenological practice, it is important that this stance is respected. However, the literary sources I work with have demanded that I also pay attention to the more banal preoccupations of driver-consciousness, in particular those distracting 'phantasies' (Husserl) and memories that are a disturbance to the dedicated attention to 'the present' that mainstream phenomenology requires. In this regard, the work of Henri Bergson and E. H. Gombrich has proven an immensely helpful theoretical supplement.

Although Bergson's philosophies of consciousness can, and have been, compared and contrasted with the precepts of phenomenology in many different regards (see, for example, Kern 2000: 44; Trigg 2012: 49–50), it is at the contested interface of perception, cognition and memory in his work that I have found most food for thought as far as automotive consciousness is concerned. As well as his most widely touted concept, *durée* (widely and variously translated but denoting, for my purposes, the 'real-time' of subjective consciousness (Trigg 2012: 49–51)), to which I shall return below, Bergson's attempt to theorise how memories are made is a useful bridge between phenomenological and psychological accounts of how the mind is seized upon by certain phenomena and what this might owe to memory as well as to perception. One of the most useful of his texts in this regard is his short essay, 'Memory of the Present and False Recognition', which demonstrates – through the intriguing phenomenon of déjà vu – several of the key principles laid down in his longer works (e.g. *Matter and Memory* 2010 [1896]). On the intimate relationship between memory and perception Bergson here writes:

> Indeed, when we speak of our memories, we speak of something our consciousness possesses or can always recover by drawing in, so to speak, the thread which holds it. The memory, in fact, passes to and from consciousness to unconsciousness, and the transition from one to the other is so continuous, the limit between the two states so little marked, that we have no right to suppose a radical difference of nature between them ... On the other hand, let us agree to call 'perception' the consciousness of anything that is present, whether it be an internal or an external object. Both definitions being granted, I hold that *the formation of memory is never posterior to the formation of perception, it is contemporaneous with it.* (Bergson 2000 [1908]: 47 (italics in the original))

For Bergson, then, perception and memory arise simultaneously, although much of the information thus consigned to the unconscious will only ever be actualised if they serve a purposeful cognitive function:

> But the forward-springing one, which we call perception, is that alone which interests us. We have no need of the memory of things whilst we hold the things themselves. Practical consciousness, throwing this memory aside as useless, theoretical reflection holds it to be non-existent. Thus the illusion is born that memory *succeeds* perception. (Bergson 2000: 48 (italics in the original))

This idea – the notion that 'everyday' perception is strategically *restrictive* and mainly directed towards our preservation in the present – features widely in Bergson's work, including the essay I draw upon here (Mullarkey 1999: 52). The unconscious, accordingly, takes the form of a vast repository of 'pure' or 'virtual' memory (Mullarkey 1999: 34–5), but this material is accessed only when needed to help make sense of the present in a particular way. Crucially, similarity or likeness alone will not create a memory:

> Thousands and thousands of memories may be evoked by resemblance, but the memory that tends to reappear is the one which resembles the perception in a particular way, the one which may illuminate and direct the action in preparation. (Bergson 2000: 56)

Further, although such statements may initially give the impression that, for Bergson, memory is a *secondary* characteristic of consciousness (notwithstanding its co-simultaneous production at the moment of perception), this is far from the case once we have grasped the model as a whole. While memories may, indeed, be actualised for strategic purposes, the fact that this vast repository of unrevealed matter is forever lurking, primed to *combine* with new perceptions in the present as and when it is called upon, renders the relationship between perception and memory fully dynamic.

For Bergson, the psychological phenomenon which most clearly evidences the contemporaneous manufacture of perception and memory is déjà vu. About the way in which these so-called 'false recognitions' are formed he writes:

> Step by step, as perception is created, it is profiled in memory, which is beside it like a shadow is next to a body. But, in the normal condition, there is no consciousness of it, just as we should be unconscious of our shadow were our eyes to throw light on it each time it turned in that direction. (Bergson 2000: 47)

It is, then, this coincidence of active perception and latent memory that will, on occasion, create the sensation of déjà vu: that uncanny experience of having been somewhere before or knowing what we are going to think, act or say next. According to Bergson's model, these presentiments are, in fact, things we have *already* thought – but only just. They belong, as it were, to our shadow-*present* and, rather than waiting be actualised years later, come into being a heart beat after they have been formed.

In the context of my project here, Bergson's model may certainly be used to help explain why driving, specifically, evokes so many memories. The flux of the landscape as seen from a moving vehicle makes all manner of familiar things strange and, following Bergson, arguably requires us to call upon past perceptions in order to make sense of them ('what was *that*?'), at the same time as awakening a crowd of associated memories and affects. As I have posited elsewhere in my work on romantic love (Pearce forthcoming), this slippage between the past and present perceptions both enhances the vividness of the conjunction and its strangeness: memory provides us with enough information to make strategic sense of our current situation but also, simultaneously, registers the extent to which the two things/events differ from one another. Bergson himself registers the importance of this gap or slippage when he writes: 'Reflective perception is a circuit in which all objects, including the perceived object itself, hold each other in a state of mutual tension' (Bergson 1959: 249). As John Mullarkey expands:

> Attentive recognition, then, is a set of circuits of reverberations within perception caused by the disturbance of some novel event. Conscious awareness

is amplified by shock, resistance or disorder interrupting our habitual actions, following which perception is more and more enhanced with memory-images in an attempt to reintegrate the object or dissipate the shock of the disturbance. (Mullarkey 1999: 50)

In other words, it is the process of *defamiliarisation,* as construed by the Russian Formalists in relation to artistic practice,[27] that ensures a (once) familiar phenomenon remains alive for us, and memory that makes what is strange recognisable. For Dylan Trigg (2012), meanwhile, an almost identical mechanism is at work in Husserl's phenomenology inasmuch as 'disturbing the familiarity of what has been taken-for-granted . . . becomes emblematic of second seeing' (otherwise known as the transcendental reduction: see note 22) (Trigg 2012: 25). Here, the search for the 'essence' of the phenomenon in question deploys the practice of 'bracketing' (i.e. the suspension of all existing beliefs about a phenomenon) (Trigg 2012: 18) to make visible its specificity. Therefore, although notionally opposed in their 'first principles' (i.e. the a priori of perception vs the 'always already' of memory), Husserl and Bergson concur that 'familiarity' is the enemy of the 'attentive recognition' required for a fresh and unprejudiced apprehension of the phenomenon.

As previewed, I now cross disciplines to consider how another group of scholars – working in the middle decades of the twentieth century – grappled with perception. My own first encounter with E. H. Gombrich's theory of 'schema and correction' was as a student of art history and this, indeed, is the arena in which – and on behalf of which – he investigated the relationship between 'what we see and what we know'. Gombrich's interest in the work of the philosopher Karl Popper, the psychologist J. J. Gibson[28] and the Gestalt School (see note 26) arose from his attempt to theorise the history of (Western) art: namely, how the styles and conventions of pictorial representation change and evolve. It was the was the way in which each new generation, or school, of artists developed a style that was similar to, yet different from, that which preceded them which fascinated him (Gombrich 1980 [1960]: 55–78), and which he finally explained through his model of 'schema and correction'. According to Gombrich, in order to 'even describe the visible world . . . we need a developed system of schemata' (Gombrich 1980: 76), but when we triangulate such schemata with *both* the representations of our predecessors *and* what we see with our own eyes (i.e. the 'correction') a wholly new schemata emerges:

My point is rather that such matching will always be a step-by-step process – how long it takes and how hard it is will depend on the choice of the initial schema to be adapted to the task of serving as a portrait . . . He [the draughts-man] begins not with his visual impression but with his idea or concept . . .

Having selected such a schema to fit the form approximately, he will proceed to adjust it . . . Copying, we learn from these experiments, proceeds from the rhythms of schema and correction. The schema is not the product of a process of 'abstraction', of a tendency to 'simplify'; it represents the first approximate, loose category which is gradually tightened to fit the form it is to reproduce. (Gombrich 1980: 62–4)

Gombrich's draughtsman, then, is compelled to repeatedly reconfigure what he *knows* in the light of what he *sees* even though, without his initial schema as a point of reference, he would have been unable to even begin his task. 'Matching' might 'come before making' (Gombrich 1980: 99), for sure, but the lasting achievement of the artist is in wresting a new and fresh perception from the disjuncture of the percept and its schema. Those who do best at 'seeing with fresh eyes' will therefore become the 'great artists' of their generation, in contrast with those mere 'follow-ers' who struggle to move beyond their inherited schema (Gombrich, 1980: 247). Although this theory of artistic innovation has since been widely disputed (for example, Mitchell 1995) – and is, on first principles, diametrically opposed to the anti-cognitivist principles of Bergson and the phenomenologists discussed above – the dynamic between seeing and knowing which fascinated Gombrich has always fascinated me. Notwithstanding the logic of Merleau-Ponty's proposition (cited earlier) that without a percept in the present there can be no schema for it to refer to, everyday life furnishes us with numerous examples of both humans and animals *mis*recognising what they see (or, indeed, hear) because of its close resemblance to something else they are familiar with. (Hence the reason I spent the best part of a month thinking that the two conductors on the telegraph pole seen from my study window were collared doves and my dog's insistence that empty bin-liners are black cats!) Gombrich, meanwhile, drew upon Ludwig Wittgenstein's famous duck-rabbit experiment to illustrate this point (i.e. the outline of a shape that may be seen as a duck or a rabbit depending upon which concept the observer first brings to bear on his/her interpretation) (Gombrich 1980:4), and I would argue that such slippages in perception/cognition remain utterly compelling and thought-provoking in and of themselves regardless of whether they are used to prove or disprove that cognition precedes perception.

As the chapters which follow will, I hope, demonstrate, the relation-ship between what we see and what we know – between 'matching' and 'making' – is integral to the experience and practice of driving at many levels. First, the ability to 'read the road' swiftly and correctly is widely regarded to be one of the essential skills of driving, and most automotive psychologists – from J. J. Gibson through to John Groeger and colleagues (2000)[29] – have researched and debated how this is achieved. One key point of contention in these debates is the extent to which drivers depend upon a pre-existing 'road-schema' in order to negotiate the multiple demands upon their attention; in other words, is it the broad similarity between road/traffic scenarios – notwithstanding the generic differences between motorways, A-roads and country lanes – that ultimately enables us both to deal with the unexpected (e.g. a child running out in front of the car) and think/speak about other things while we drive? This debate speaks to, yet differs from, other recent automotive research – considered here in Chapter 5 – on the ways in which embodied knowledge (of the kind identified by Merleau-Ponty in *Phenomenology and Perception* (2002)) or pre-cognition (Laurier 2011) is instrumental in rendering the practice of driving habitual (i.e. because it is learnt by and through the body we do not have to 'think' about it). However, the skills needed to *handle* the car are still, arguably, of a different order to the explicitly visual skills needed to 'read' the road and, while the texts I draw upon vividly demonstrate the extent to which all phenomena in the driver's perceptual field slide in and out of view, there would seem a strong argument for schema playing at least a partial role in enabling us to switch focus as easily as we do. Although very much writing with the assumption that the driver is paying full attention to his (*sic*) immediate road conditions at all times, automotive psychologist D. J. Van Lennep nevertheless captures something of the way in which different features come to the fore:

> One can watch everything at the same time. For the driver of a car this is not at all necessary, nor even desirable . . . At a single glance he must survey what is happening on his left and his right and what is happening in front of him and farther ahead. But he sees all of this in a determinate structure in which what is important and what is unimportant is divided according to the *meaning* which the things have for him in his situation and which he gives them on the basis of his own judgment. As is always the case, we have perception only if the data of the perceptual world become structured according to the schema figure and the ground. Against the horizon of houses, road-surface, trees, and so on, certain objects force themselves upon him as figures on which his attention becomes focused; or formulated in a better way with which he keeps up a kind of 'interview' which is sometimes short, sometimes long, now dull, now sharp. (Van Lennep 1987: 219)

Implicit here are assumptions discussed elsewhere in this section: for example (following Bergson), the way in which 'memory' supports perception in a strategic way: we see only what we need to; and (following Gombrich/Wittgenstein), the alternation of 'figure' and 'ground' in the production of the schema. What Van Lennep categorically does not allow for, however, is the possibility that a specific 'house' or 'tree' (or, indeed, the *recollection* of a very different house, tree or something unrelated to the road situation altogether) might also come into focus for a 'short' or 'long' period of time and become part of the driver's 'interview'. This, in turn, relates to the question of how driving can 'safely' accommodate reverie and notional 'altered states of consciousness' (see Chapter 5) but, for now, this brief discussion will, I hope, have helped explain why cognitive psychology can be usefully placed alongside phenomenological accounts of perception in an exploration of automotive consciousness.

With respect to the literary texts I am dealing with as part of this project, moreover, Gombrich's account of how the fresh and 'original' image/conceit emerges from the old and conventional one speaks directly to the way in which mobility transformed many drivers' (and passengers') apprehension of the world in the early years of the twentieth century. Chapter 2, for example, features examples of how seeing the world 'flash by' at 20 or 30mph transforms two travel writers' potentially generic accounts of the landscapes through which they pass into ones that are vivid and distinctive. In such instances, the pre-existing schema is radically 'corrected' and a new impression formed. At the same time, there are other occasions when drivers appear to be in urgent *need* of familiar schema to make sense of an unaccountable 'shock of disturbance' (Mullarkey 1999: 50) in their perceptual field. One subgenre of early motoring literature in which such 'disturbances' abound are the widespread and evocative accounts of driving at night: an activity that not only demanded new and challenging skills on the part of the driver, night-driving also opened the door on a strange and magical new world (see Gordon Crosby's illustration, Figure 1.1).[30]

Nowhere is this better captured that in Dixon Scott's[31] remarkable essay from 1913, 'Motoring by Night':

> The transformation begins with the very road. The vaguely glimmering track, along which the pedestrian softly fumbles, suddenly stiffens out into a harsh, blanched beam – a spectral gang-plank thrust into the emptiness. The motorist's road is never mere dead macadam; by daylight, for instance, it leaps towards him like a twitching tide, a white lasso uncoiling as it comes. But at night its direction is reversed. It moves with you, seems a part of your machine; you seem to make it as you go . . .
>
> And when you have got accustomed to it there are any number of other thrills to take its place. You run for a time between hedgerows – and every dim bush seems to burst into a piece of branching coral; you might be sitting in a submarine . . . You live in a circular world, in the centre of a leprous wreath. Oaks, elms, and beeches all part with their identity and submit to be woven into this haunting hoop – as white as a hoop of hawthorn. It always

Figure 1.1 'A wet night on the Bath Road', Gordon Crosby, *Autocar*, 15 March 1929. Courtesy of the National Library of Scotland.

seems the same wreath. It quivers and fluctuates, making a weak rustle as it shivers; but it never falls back. With nothing to measure your pace by, all sense of motion disappears. You seem to sit in a kind of numb trance with nothing but the drone of your engine and the whisper of this mesmeric arch. Perhaps you are not altogether unrelieved when it is wrenched aside and tossed behind, and you are out on your naked gang-plank once more with the stars tumbling and twirling overhead . . . (Scott 1917: 42–4)

As is evidenced by the author's persistent recourse to simile, almost everything encountered during the course of this singular driving-event is made sense of only by reference to something else: the road becomes a plank, the trees become coral, the tunnel of hedgerows becomes a 'leprous wreath'. Indeed, the mighty cognitive effort required to effect even these rudimentary connections is enough to send the driver into a 'numb trance': he *sees*, both literally and conceptually – *but not quite*. In affective terms, the experience is both thrilling and frightening: a confusion of emotion that is central to the narrator's observation that one is not 'altogether unrelieved' when it comes to an end. So extreme, indeed, is the defamiliarisation of the landscape that it can only really be captured in supernatural terms: as one of the marginalia instructs, the experience is 'as fantastic as a fairy tale' (p. 44). Through examples such as this, I would argue, we see that there is nothing mechanical or reductive about the process of 'schema-correction', should we choose to understand the driver's attempts to make sense of his or her environment in these terms; rather, we witness the extent to which both the phenomena and the schema (or 'memory-image' (Mullarkey 1999: 50)) called upon to make sense of it (e.g. the road which becomes a 'spectral gang-plank') are startled into new life by their chance and manifestly uncanny encounter.

Finally, and in conclusion, I would propose that what all the theories I attend to in this section share – despite some profound foundational differences – is a model of consciousness in which perception and memory (however construed) exist in *dynamic* relation to one another. This, too, is a defining feature of a great many of the literary texts dealt with in the chapters that follow. Whether practising a quasi-phenomenological investigation of the world as 'seen from the car' (Kennedy 1919b), or indulging in nostalgic reminiscences on a return journey to a 'special place' – as in Mrs Miniver's sentimental attachment to her 'memory flags' (Struther 1989: 49)[32] – what the driver or passenger sees is rarely unsupported by what he or she remembers, be this a shape, shadow or a full-blown narrative.

The Driving-Event

The experience of coming to a halt at the end of a long car-ride is described with memorable disgust by Margaret Schlegal in E. M. Forster's *Howards End*:

> 'The motor's here to stay,' he [Mr Wilcox] answered. 'One must get about. There's a pretty church – oh, you aren't sharp enough. Well, look out, if the road worries you – right outward at the scenery.'
>
> She looked at the scenery. It heaved and merged like porridge. Presently it congealed. They had arrived. (Forster 2012 [1910]: 206)

'Congealed porridge' is what the landscape becomes when it has finally stopped 'heaving' and 'merging': a sticky, mangled mess of the perceiver and the perceived that could hardly be further from phenomenological enlightenment. And yet, for other writers and commentators, the moment of congealing is clearly an intrinsic part of the driving experience and, for my purposes here, defining of what I have named 'the driving-event' (Pearce 2017). The text which encapsulates what I understand by the term 'driving-event' more perfectly than any other is Virginia Woolf's 'Evening Over Sussex: Reflections in a Motor-Car' (Woolf 1942 [1927]), but it would be helpful if I first explain why the need for this item of vocabulary has arisen.

During the past two decades, a good deal of research has been undertaken by sociologists interested in why the Western and, indeed, developing world remains in the grip of 'car culture' at a time when economic, environmental and logistical factors all point to the fact that we should have already moved on to other forms of transportation (Williams 1991; Zuckerman 1991; Böhm et al. 2006; Dennis and Urry 2009; Mom 2014). Although – as this book will, I hope, demonstrate – there are a great many pleasures associated with driving that have yet to be identified (most notably, cognitive ones), the work of automobilities scholars like Miller (2001), Bull (2001), Edensor (2003), Thrift (2004), Dant (2004), Sheller (2004) and Redshaw (2008) has already gone some way to explaining the social, psychological and affective appeal of driving for a range of demographic groups, and the field, in general, concurs that car-ownership and use has tangible social and existential as well as practical benefits (see the section on 'Contexts' which follows).

When I first began to review recent automobilities research I was, nevertheless, struck by the fact that the experience of driving was generally taken to be a reproducible event: in other words, neither in the theory nor in the ethnographic analysis did the scholars tend to distinguish between *specific* driving-events. While there is widespread acknowledgement that the commute is a different mode of driving from the long motorway journey or road trip – and that driving to work is very different to driving for pleasure (Laurier 2004; Redshaw 2008) – within those categories the driver's experience is assumed to be the same. As a consequence, the possibility of one drive being ontologically very different to another – even when they are undertaken for the same social purpose or in similar traffic conditions – is entirely lost. Such an approach ultimately defines and categorises driving-events according to their utility and function (generic and reproducible) rather than how they were experienced by their driver (unique and non-reproducible). By demonstrating the specificity of each and every journey for the drivers (and passengers) concerned, the literary and other texts I explore in the following chapters productively challenge these generalisations and offer new insights into the psychology of driving. True, the daily commute to work may involve all manner of detours and delays, but a long jam on the day the driver has had a good time at work and/or has plenty of positive thoughts to preoccupy her will represent a very different driving-event to that which she experiences in equally bad traffic the day she has just heard that her father has been taken ill. In neither case are the material circumstances of the traffic jam irrelevant (in the first scenario, the delay allows the driver time for pleasurable and productive thought; in the second, the length of time it takes the driver to get to the hospital promotes terrible anxiety), but it would clearly be wrong to define or characterise the drive purely in terms of external markers such as journey time or even a generalised psychological association of congestion with stress (a point that will be developed in my discussion of driver-anxiety in Chapter 5).

At this point in the discussion it is worth noting that, even before I have begun to define it, I have already been prompted to use the term 'driving-event' on several occasions. As I quickly discovered when embarking upon this project, there is no existing term to distinguish a specific drive from a type of drive that might have taken place on several occasions. As I observe in my article on this subject (Pearce 2017), the *first* defining feature of the driving-event, therefore, is its capacity to be both habitual and unique. We may make the same journey to work every day for fifteen years, but the combination of external and subjective factors that cause us to entertain a different sequence of thoughts on each and every journey means that no two journeys will be exactly the same.

How I have come to think about the driving-event nevertheless extends beyond this baseline recognition. What my reading of literary and other texts has revealed is the need to calibrate the nature and duration of the material journey with that of the driver's consciousness more dynamically. Indeed, we need to recognise that it is unusual for the temporal-spatial parameters of a journey to coincide with a single, pre-occupying chain of thoughts. True, such occasions do exist: for example, on a short commute, the driver may spend the whole journey thinking about a work matter that needs his urgent attention. In this case, material and cognitive journeys combine to deliver a very straightforward and easily classifiable driving-event. More typically, however, a driver will experience or pursue multiple thought-chains (each with an attendant emotional register) in the course of his or her journey, making it impossible to equate that journey with a single thought or mental preoccupation: this, therefore, may be seen to be the *second* defining feature of the driving-event.

As will be seen in the subsequent chapters of this book, meanwhile, there is plenty of evidence to suggest that specific car journeys form themselves into a consolidating set of thoughts as and when the car draws to a halt (see also Pearce 2012: 100) where I first reflected on this 'congealing' moment and likened it to a shuffled set of cards settling back into a single pack). As I set out below, with reference to Virginia Woolf's story, the fact the driver's (or passenger's) mind wanders widely in the course of a car journey does not mean that it is impossible to ascribe a distinctive cognitive/affective character to a particular drive. On the contrary, a great many of the autobiographical and fictional texts considered in the subsequent chapters 'sum up' the journeys they describe in just these terms. Hence, I have proposed the driver's/passenger's tendency to retrospective consolidation as the *third* and final defining characteristic of the driving-event. And while in some cases, such as Woolf's account of her evening drive through Sussex, this characterisation of the driving-event takes the form of a self-conscious reflection, most of us will know it as casual and fleeting observation: a passing sensation, perhaps, of feeling newly confident and optimistic as we step out of the car because a set of issues have been resolved along the way. In the chapters that follow, I identify several such 'congealing' moments in the rich archive of motoring stories from across the twentieth-century.

In 1927, Virginia Woolf wrote an essay called 'Evening Over Sussex: Reflections in a Motor Car' (Woolf 1942 [1927]) in which she appears to make a connection between the dizzying succession of impressions encountered on a 'motor-flight'[33] (notably as a passenger, not as a driver) and the equally alarming dance of everyday consciousness in which the present, past and future are whirled mercilessly together. Acknowledging, first, the split within her psyche between the 'self' who wishes to enjoy the beauty of the evening as it is and another, 'stern and philosophical', who wants to account for its meaning (and passing), she paints a colourful picture of the Sussex landscape as it rushes by:

There they [her two selves] sat as the car sped along, noticing everything: a haystack; a rust red roof; a pond; an old man coming home with his sack on his back; there they sat, matching every colour in the sky and earth from their colour box, rigging up little models of Sussex barns and farmhouses in the red light that would serve in the January gloom. (Woolf 1942: 12)

Superficially similar to many other early twentieth-century accounts of landscapes seen from cars (for example, Edith Wharton's *A Motor-Flight Through France* (2008 [1908]), Woolf's depiction – on closer inspection – nevertheless bears the brush marks of a painter's abstraction. Like her sister, Vanessa Bell, and like Lily in *To the Lighthouse* (1978 [1927]), Woolf's third persona (the narrator of the essay) reveals herself to be an artist intent on subduing all she sees to abstract forms, colours and (inasmuch as her medium here is *writing*) symmetrical patterns of words. Understood thus, as an artistic representation of landscape, mobility and the driving-event, this story possibly comes as close as any pre-1930s text to explaining the peculiar synergy that exists between thinking and driving and, in particular, our profound need to fix the fast-fleeting images of what we see and what we think in order that we do not drown in an endless sea of impressions. In other words, it is a text which positively embraces the notion of a congealing landscape: the very thing that caused Forster's character (admittedly some two decades earlier) such disorientation and distress.

In Woolf's text, indeed, the protagonist's 'two selves' are seen looking for ways to consolidate the landscape – and the fragmented self – before the car has reached its final destination (by 'rigging up little models' of all they see), and the story concludes with a passionate declaration that such fixing, such 'art', is the *only* way to manage the overloaded consciousness, especially when overabundant beauty excites the nerves:

> The sun was now low beneath the horizon. Darkness spread rapidly. None of my selves could see anything beyond the tapering light of our headlamps on the hedge. I summoned them together. 'Now,' I said, 'comes the season for making up our accounts. Now we have got to collect ourselves; we have got to be one self. Nothing is to be seen any more, except one wedge of road and bank which our lights repeat incessantly. We are perfectly provided for. We are warmly wrapped in a rug; we are protected from wind and rain. We are alone. Now is the time of reckoning. Now I, who preside over the company, am going to arrange in order the trophies we have all brought in. Let me see; there was a great deal of beauty brought in today: farmhouses; cliffs standing out to sea; marbled fields; mottled fields; red feathered skies; all that. Also there was disappearance and the death of the individual. The vanishing road and the window lit for a second and then dark.' (Woolf 1942: 13)

Reflecting, in quasi-phenomenological fashion, upon those things that have 'intuitively' (Moran and Mooney 2002: 2) pressed themselves upon the traveller's consciousness in the course of the drive, Woolf's narrator – her 'presiding self' (Woolf 1942: 12) – calls for a 'reckoning' that will resolve the myriad past impressions into *one* defining thing that will somehow sum up and memorialise the event.

The fact that Woolf's alter ego is herself a passenger rather than a driver nevertheless raises some interesting questions for my definition of the driving-event as set out above. Implicit in my three-point summary is the assumption that the driving-event 'belongs' to (solo) drivers and not passengers on account of the fact that all its key characteristics presuppose dedicated thought-space (i.e. the privacy and lack of distraction essential for extended contemplation, even if on mundane matters), and also the special ways – widely demonstrated in the chapters which follow – in which the embodied practice of driving steers and clears the mind. What the Woolf extract – like other early accounts of motoring (Wharton 2008; Parker 1919) – therefore reminds us is that passengering *can* accommodate/promote contemplation in favourable conditions (i.e. if your fellow passengers are not unduly distracting) and, seemingly, without the need to be behind the wheel. Historical and social factors do, however, apply; the fact that Woolf's protagonist may well have been sitting behind a chauffeur – or, alternatively, a close family member[34] – would have obviated the need for polite conversation and the noise of the engine, wind and tyres seriously impeded it. Returned to the historical present, what this would therefore seem to suggest is that – now as then – the automobile journeys of passengers, as well as drivers, may be characterised as driving-events, but only if they are granted sufficient privacy in which to process and reflect upon their thoughts. Since drivers – even when transporting a car-load of passengers – can intermittently 'tune out' from the conversations of others (due to their need to concentrate on the road), the situation is rather different. Thus, while solo driving undoubtedly affords the greatest opportunity for the sort of reflection that will render a drive – or a portion thereof – a memorable 'event', journeys with friends and family should still include intervals in which the driver can attend to his or her personal thoughts, even if these are no more than a keen attention to the world beyond the windscreen. This, certainly, is my own experience. Although, as a passenger, I may think and dream a little as well as chat with my companion(s), the things that present themselves to my consciousness rarely stay with me; such journeys are merely journeys – they are not 'events'. At the same time, it is important to acknowledge that, for couples, a car journey can be a site/occasion of special intimacy – see Chapters 3 and 4 – and important, sometimes life-transforming, conversations may render a particular stretch of road memorable and distinctive.

This theorisation of driving *as* an event also resonates with the work of the recent cultural geographers (e.g. Doel 1996; Thrift 2008; Cresswell 2006; Laurier 2004; Merriman 2007, 2012; Cresswell and Merriman 2011; Laurier and Dant 2011). As discussed below, their reconceptualisation of space and place in terms of our movement through and within it overthrows conventional notions of landscape as fixed, static and a-temporal, and counters all those philosophical traditions which privilege 'place' over 'space' (e.g. Heidegger's 'dwelling' (Cresswell 2004: 29–32)) or – *pace* Marc Augé (1995) – lament the steady advance of 'non-place' across the map of Western culture. Like Edensor (2003) and Merriman (2004, 2007, 2012), I have found little evidence either in my research or my personal experience of driving spaces being empty ones. Quite apart from the overwhelming evidence that both roads and the vehicles that inhabit them are dynamic social, cultural and multi-sensory sites that drivers and passengers inhabit in any number of ways (Merriman 2007: 10–11), my own account of the driving-event – as an occurrence defined, in part, by the consciousness that the driver brings to bear upon it – demonstrates that *no* place is a non-place if the traveller imbues it with meaning (of whatever kind) from his or her reservoir of memories. Habit and repetition play an especially important role in granting roads and motorways such significance (see Edensor 2003: 155), supporting a counter-argument that the generic spaces of restaurant and motel chains are evocative precisely because one space can conjure up another – and the memories associated with it – so readily. Stopping for a break on a long journey is a time-out that I always look forward to and which is filled with memories of previous travels along that road (see Interlude). Inasmuch as what always accompanies us during the driving-event is our consciousness, it is hard to conceive of these purported non-places as 'voids' other than because something within us refuses to engage with them. As Merriman astutely observes in his critique of contemporary artists like Julian Opie and Andrew Cross[35] who have sought to represent the 'detached yet engaging visual experience of motorway driving' (Merriman 2007: 212), the dystopian mythology of modern motoring (monotonous, perfunctory, alienating) has caused us to overlook the 'individualized, embodied, multi-sensory and kinaesthetic ways in which drivers and passengers inhabit both the car and the motorway, shifting their gaze, listening to music, singing, daydreaming, working or talking to passengers'. Similarly, my own focus – on the expressly cognitive aspects of driving – suggests that no road can ever meaningfully be considered a non-place unless (as will be explored in Chapter 3 entitled 'Fleeing'), the driver is nihilistically intent on leaving all fixed coordinates behind.

What my identification of driving *as an event* has therefore sought to achieve is an appreciation of the potential meaningfulness of each and every automobile journey we make; this is not to suggest that all drives will yield profound personal or philosophical insight, but the possibility is there. Further, while the type of journey we are making and the motoring environment will, undoubtedly, influence and direct our thoughts in a particular way, a focus on driver-consciousness (as revealed by the literary and other texts I deal with in the following chapters) makes it clear that it is impossible to extrapolate generalisations. As I discuss in my article on this subject (Pearce 2017), driving is best understood as an 'event' on account of its *non-reproducibility* and, following Slavoj Žižek, its undoubted capacity to effect 'a change in the way reality appears to us' (Žižek 2014: 5).

Contexts

Although many excellent books, both academic and popular, have been written on the history of motoring (e.g. Sachs 1992; Kirsch 2000; Thorold 2003), the majority are more interested in the history of car design, the sociology of motoring and what is now typically spoken of as 'car culture' (e.g. Wollen and Kerr 2002; Volti 2006; Heitmann 2009; Morrison and Minnis 2012) rather the history of driving per se. This has consequently involved me in some challenging yet productive reading between the lines of many of the key scholarly texts in the field in an effort to glean how, for example, changes in car design impacted specifically upon the driving experience; likewise, developments in road building and road regulation (Jeremiah 2007; Moran 2009; Merriman 2007, 2012). This said, the field of (auto)mobilities studies has, over the past fifteen years, been both radical and imaginative in the way in which it has repeatedly crossed and stretched disciplines in its attempt to capture the many aspects of automobility – including driving – that, together, constitute the 'car-system' (Dennis and Urry 2009). The leading figures who have insisted upon this holistic approach to automobility – its practice, its history, its economics, its function, its culture – include: the geographers Nigel Thrift (2008 [2004]), Tim Edensor (2003), Tim Cresswell (2006), Peter Merriman (2007, 2012 – see also Cresswell and Merriman 2011) and Peter Adey (2010); the sociologists Daniel Miller (2001), John Urry (2007 – see also Urry and Dennis 2009; Sheller and Urry 2000), Mimi Sheller (2004), Tim Dant (2004 – see also Dant and Martin 2001) and Sarah Redshaw (2008); as well as scholars, like myself, who originate in the Humanities (Iain

Borden (2013), Ian Davidson (2012), Neil Archer (2013) and Gijs Mom (2014)[36]).

What all these scholars have in common is a belief that no one part of the car-system can be understood in isolation from the other factors that play into it, even if each of us must necessarily foreground particular interests and concerns in the course of our research. Merriman's summary, reproduced below, is indicative of the profoundly interconnected way in which the performance of mobilities of all kinds – including, but not prioritising, automobility – are now understood:

> Movement and mobility explode … fracture … shatter … into an array of embodied movements with … machines, bodies and engineered infrastructures which have distinctive histories and geographies, are marked by particular sensations, socialities, political debates and all manner of social, cultural and spatial differences. Movement and mobility are qualitative emergences, molecular becomings, molar effects, embodied apprehensions, sensations and affects, and the past decade or so has seen an explosion of interest in its social and spatial formations. Mobility has been approached in terms of practices, embodiment, emotions and feeling, affects, gender, politics, rhythm, stillness, meeting, networks, governmentality, scale, place, biopolitics, exclusion, ethics, banal and mundane mobilities, and much more. (Merriman 2012: 13 (ellipses in the original))

Implicit in Merriman's overview is a recognition that it is ultimately problematic to consider the mobile subject as separate from the mobile world: a position that delivers a particular challenge to my own focus on automotive consciousness which draws what, for some, would constitute an artificial distinction not only between subject and world, but between the subject's mind and his/her body. As Merriman asks: 'where do we "draw the line" or "make the cut", for these bodies also travel with countless other things, performing turbulent movements, becoming passage, becoming landscape …' (Merriman 2012: 13). Viewed in this way – as the proverbial 'wheel within a wheel' – (auto)mobility is arguably not best served by the line of enquiry I have adopted here, not least because my focus on the philosophical/psychological mechanisms of automotive consciousness has meant that issues of class, gender, ethnicity and economics have often been laid to one side. In the remainder of this chapter I therefore acknowledge some of the most important contextual factors that frame my theory of automotive consciousness, at the same time as previewing the literary-historical case studies in the subsequent chapters which will, I trust, restore this chapter's more abstract considerations to their material context(s).

Sociological

There are plenty of sobering statistics available to remind us of who has, and who has not, had access to the sorts of automotive experiences this project is concerned with. For instance, while by 2014 *c*.40 per cent of cars in the UK were registered with a female keeper, in 1994 the figure was only *c*.23 per cent; meanwhile, in terms of licence holders, the RAC statistics for England show that in 1975/6 only 29 per cent of women in England held a full driving licence, compared to 69 per cent of men (RAC Foundation 2015).[37]

These figures, not from the early years of the twentieth century where my research begins, but from the recent past, inevitably place a question mark over the cognitive processes and practices I have been exploring from a gender-neutral perspective. 'What we're thinking when we're driving' (Pearce 2013) was, until very recently and in one of the wealthiest nations in the world, an issue of relevance to only a relatively small proportion of women: an observation that sits somewhat uncomfortably alongside all those descriptors (my own included) of driving as a habitual, mundane, 'everyday' social practice. Thus, although women and other 'excluded'[38] groups may experience cognitive and affective responses similar to those explored in the following chapters of this book by other means, such experiences will not then be simulated, aggravated, intensified or, indeed, relieved through the experience of driving. This is not to imply that all those who have never had access to a car are socially and culturally impoverished; for many citizens the world over – and perhaps increasingly – the decision not to drive and/ or own a car is a positive and liberating one; however, their everyday cognitive and affective encounters will not be mirrored by or mixed with their automotive consciousness in the way it is for many drivers. So-called 'road rage' is sadly the best known illustration of what I am hinting at here, namely a now widely held recognition of the way in which the stresses of contemporary living can spill over, and be replicated (or, following Jack Katz (1999: 60–73), 'acted out') in our driving.

In line with the work of automotive historians such as Laura Doan (2006), David Jeremiah (2007) and Georgine Clarsen (2008), sociologists have nevertheless paid close attention to the ways in which marginalised and/or vulnerable social groups have benefited from becoming drivers. Sheller's 2004 article 'Automotive Emotions', for example, focuses on what car use has meant for young mothers and cites several earlier scholars (Gilroy 2001; Stradling et al. 2001; Stradling 2002; Carrabine and Longhurst 2002) who have demonstrated the ways in which young people, the poor and ethnic minorities also exhibit a particular investment in becoming drivers. It is noticeable, however, that such investments are often explained in terms of social status rather than the 'practical freedoms' afforded by the car and/or the sorts of cognitive/affective pleasures that are the object of my own investigations. Stradling's interpretation is typical: 'Different kinds of persons obtain different kinds of psychological benefit from car use. Driving a car is particularly attractive to the young and the poor because of the sense of displayed personal identity that it conveys' (Stradling 2002: 11). This, I would suggest, reveals a certain class bias of its own, and it is my hope that the following chapters will reveal that drivers from all social groups share in the distinctive experiences of driving as well as the status associated with car ownership. On this point it is especially important to recognise that not all cars convey status – the past twenty-five years have seen the actual and symbolic value of old, second-hand cars collapse across the first world – and, as essays in Wollen and Kerr (2002) exploring car use in Cuba (Narotzky), Romania (Otoiu) and South Africa (Addison) reveal – this can often help us to understand the qualitative experience of driving *qua* driving more clearly. Indeed, it is the very fact that poor people in their 'bangers' can derive as much pleasure and utility from their automobiles as business executives in their 'top-of-the-range' saloons that reminds us of how little the car figures as a status symbol for many drivers the world over. As James Dunn observes:

> It is . . . true that there is a very large economic gap between the driver of a battered 1980 Chevette and one who owns a brand new Mercedes. But when they both are on the open road, or stuck in a traffic jam, or circling the block looking for a parking spot, there is a fundamental equality in their condition as automobilists that unites them across class, racial, ethnic, and religious lines as few other aspects of our society can. (Dunn 1998: 2)

While the association between the car and US-styled neo-liberalist notions of freedom and equality that grounds Dunn's observation will be anathema to the politics of most mobilities researchers today, the implication that the experiences – cognitive, embodied and otherwise – of driving are available to all drivers, regardless of whether their car cost £600 or £60,000, is an important and necessary one if we are to distinguish the cultural/psychological pleasures of car-ownership from those associated with driving itself. Indeed, a number of excellent post-millennial ethnographic studies have contributed important new understandings not only to car culture and car use but also the likes/dislikes of driving per se, complicating deeply entrenched stereotypes vis-à-vis the age, class and gender of drivers. The conclusions that have been drawn from such projects function as useful and important correctives to existing stereotypes (such as the notion that women are typically nervous drivers and/or only interested in the car for getting from 'a' to 'b'), and provide invaluable insight into the specific conditions that facilitate different modes of automotive consciousness.

Pauline Garvey's work with young female drivers from the small Norwegian town of Skein in the late 1990s is especially groundbreaking in its focus on the counter-cultural ways in which driving empowers women and all those in the lower-income bracket. There is little interest in the car as a status symbol among Garvey's female respondents, for example, but widespread evidence that driving provides the young women concerned with 'time for themselves', a sense of purpose (even if illusory) and transgression, as well as emotional release. The following extract, from Kari (a 25-year-old kindergarten worker) reveals the profoundly therapeutic role played by the car:

> A problem seems worse because you are so used to sitting here [at home] . . . but when you take your car you can always pretend to go somewhere the car is taking you from A to B and then back to A again but when you sit at home you are just staying at A . . . (Garvey 2001: 140)

In line with recent psychological research on driving and cognition (Groeger 2000) and my own analysis of the driving-event, Kari demonstrably benefits from the 'channelling' of her thoughts necessitated by driving; it is not that it 'zones out' entirely, but rather that her thoughts, like the car, are steered, directed and *moved on*. As anyone who has suffered from depression will know, one of the most disabling features of the condition is the sense of mental and physical stagnation. What Kari's reflection appears to tell us is that even a short, routine journey by car can help alleviate the sense of being stuck; as she observes, travelling from A to B even if it is to return to A again, is very different to 'just staying at A'.

On other occasions, the empowerment afforded by the car is more obviously transgressive. Garvey recounts the story of setting off for a quiet Sunday afternoon 'cruise' with Kari and Hilde – in Kari's 'battered Ford' – and ending up creating mayhem on the streets of Skein:

> The excitement gradually mounted and with it Kari and Hilde grew more daring. Kari began driving on the wrong side of the road, each complimenting the other on being 'crazy' while swerving suddenly in the direction of oncoming cars. 'This is Norwegian humour' she quipped to me in the back seat, suddenly changing direction at a T-junction and near-missing a Volvo. (Garvey 2001: 134)

While such 'oppositional' (Koshar 2008) driving practices have long been associated with young males (see Chapter 3), instances of young women getting their 'kicks' in this way remain rare in the literary texts I have worked with[39] and, for this reason, the significance of Garvey's study cannot be underestimated. Not only does it provide evidence that young women as well as young men find transgressive pleasure in driving, but also that the empowerment provided by the car (therapeutic, anti-social) is consequent upon *driving* it rather than simply *owning* it; further, it confirms that for young people (of both sexes) seemingly 'trapped' in lower-income employment, the practice of driving is a powerful emotional release and means of channelling, correcting and alleviating negative thought-processes. Therefore, although Garvey's study does reveal that young men appear to have an additional investment in cars as a means of 'display' and self-performance (Garvey 2001: 142–3), she is clear that mobility per se – variously expressed – defines the car's appeal for both sexes (Garvey 2001: 143).

Although the ethnographic studies of driving habits and behaviours that Maxwell (2001) and Redshaw (2008) draw upon are focused upon the more mundane utility and empowerment provided by car use, their analyses point to a similar complication of stereotypical gender roles as well as the generally unpredictable nature of which driving-events constitute a pleasure (typically figured as a 'time-out' for thought and reflection) and which are not. In some cases, as in the first extract below, this is tied to the type of journey the driver is undertaking (e.g. a long, weekend drive is contrasted with a short, city commute) but for other drivers (see the second extract) it is precisely the drive to work that provides this thought-space:

> I think when I've got to go somewhere, like to work and uni . . . I hate driving because it's just annoying. It's just something you have to do to get there, and it wastes your time. I'd rather be doing something else. But then, if I'm at work, like I said before, and I jump in a brand new Commodore with sequential gears I love it. The power and . . . I don't know. It's just nice. It's nice to get out on the road. (Male 1, Shellharbour) (Redshaw 2008: 57)

> I enjoy driving. Most of my driving's done by myself. I do a lot of driving with work . . . I just like driving and listening to music. I find I reach a point in my journeys where I really just take in my surrounding, 'it's good to be back sort of thing'. (Female 2, Blacktown) (Redshaw 2008: 58)

If any general conclusions can be drawn from the interviews featured in this particular chapter of Redshaw's book ('Boredom and Pleasure on the Roads'), it is the unsurprising one that drivers of both sexes become most 'bored' and impatient with driving when they are stuck in traffic on the way to work. As will be explored further in Chapter 5, there can be little doubt that the traffic jam is both a cause of stress and paradigmatic of *the form stress takes* in late-capitalist societies in which (well-)being is so closely associated with 'doing'. Indeed, all the evidence – both textual and ethnographic – suggests that in many, perhaps most, instances, traffic jams are anathema to thought: rather than opening up a space for contemplation, the stress of the situation ('I should be somewhere else by now') stalls the flow of thought and reduces consciousness to a state of fixed anxiety, rage or – to invoke the mindset explored here – boredom.[40] Leaving this particular feature of urban driving to one side, however, the interviews would seem to confirm that there are few straightforward correlations between car use and the aspects of automotive consciousness that my own book is concerned with. While it can be assumed that certain modes of driving (e.g. touring and cruising) facilitate characteristic cognitive states more readily than others (i.e. enquiring and reflective), opportunities for contemplation and/or feelings of elation may also be had on a drive to or from work.

Working alongside and often entangled with social scientists' environmental concerns with the car-system – and, within that, a need to better understand car use – is a critique of late-capitalist neo-liberalism. Popularly understood as a brand of (non-party) politics that 'asserts the power and importance of private entrepreneurship, private property rights, the freeing of markets, the freeing of trade' (Dennis and Urry 2009: 141–6), as well as the minimal interference of the state in the lives of individual citizens, the discourse of neo-liberalism has become a key critical target for the socialist Left and few things have served to illustrate the West's investment in its values more spectacularly than our unrelenting 'love affair' with the motor car. Regarded from this critical viewpoint, everything about the car – its manufacture, its material and symbolic capital, its non-sustainability as a means of transport, the type of selfish or individualistic pleasures it gives rise to – are seen as anathema to more social or collectivist notions of freedom and well-being. For Dennis and Urry, meanwhile, the 'flexible freedom' associated with the car as a means of transport has become inseparable from the politics of personal freedom (Dennis and Urry 2009: 40–1) The private motor car, then, by delivering 'freedom' quite literally to the hands of those individuals who are able to afford one, has arguably done more than any other invention (until, perhaps, the widespread availability of personal computers and mobile phones) to make individuals believe they can direct and control their own destinies without state interference. The fact that this is an illusion (cars cannot function without state-maintained roads; the safe and speedy flow of traffic requires drivers to abide by all manner of state-imposed rules and regulations) is, of course, further testament to the power of the discourse *qua* discourse; very few people can have driven a car without at some time experiencing a thrill of liberation even though most cultural theorists (as discussed in the following section) would argue that this sensation is itself, in part, ideologically manufactured.

Yet such insights are hardly new. One of the most striking features – indeed, one might even call it a 'trend' – of middle-brow motoring fiction from the early-to-mid twentieth century is its relentless ridicule of drivers who become 'egomaniacs' as soon as they get behind the steering wheel of a car. One indicative example is Aldous Huxley's 'Lord Hovendon' (1959 [1925]). This pitiful tale of an unattractive and unaccomplished young man (with a speech impediment) who undergoes a personality transformation every time he steps aboard his trusty 'Vauxhall Velox' is clearly written out of a deep (if comic) contempt for what cars – even in the 1920s – had come to represent in social and economic terms:

> But when they turned into the flat highway along the western shore of the lake, his face brightened. 'Vis is more like it', he said. The wind in their faces increased from a capful to half a gale, from half a gale to a full gale, from a full gale to very nearly a hurricane. Lord Hovenden's spirits rose with the mounting speed. His lips curved themselves into a smile of fixed and permanent rapture. Behind the glass of his goggles his eyes were bright. 'Pretty good going', he said. (Huxley 1959: 118)

For while Lord Hovendon's fantasies and delusions may, at first, appear to be a private matter, a close reading of the text as a whole (especially when placed alongside others in the genre) reveals its wider target to be the brash new individualism (both personal and economic) of the times. Lord Hovendon might well be a member of the aristocracy, but his dependence on a motor car to bolster his sense of personal sense of self-worth reveals the extent to which bourgeois values, a conspicuous display of wealth and a hedonistic pleasure in the power of speed have stitched him into an early incarnation of the 'car-system' (Dennis and Urry 2009).

This brief survey of the sociological research that has shaped our recent (i.e. post-millennial) understanding of car use has exposed what would seem to be a problematic slippage between the idiosyncrasy of driver-experience (i.e. no two drivers and no two driving-events are the same) and the discourse of individualism. The fact that driving is often – though by no means always – a solitary practice does not mean that the driver is necessarily concerned with the performance of social status *or* the expression of personal freedom. Although driving may include an element of self-conscious 'display', for many drivers this is an irrelevance. Further, while the recent psychological/sociological ethnographic research on driver-experience – in particular, the insight it has provided into the contending pleasures and frustrations of driving – has been of huge importance in bringing to light the wide variety of feelings drivers have about the time spent in their cars, there has been a tendency to interpret the data in a rather utilitarian way. For example, while the mapping of drivers' moods onto journey type and road conditions is, of course, of sociological (and environmental) interest, the need to draw conclusions from such research has arguably obscured just how potentially unique each journey made by car actually is.

Cultural

While the historical and sociological research which frames my project reports upon and analyses automobility as a 'lived' phenomenon, a good many recent books and articles in the field are also at pains to emphasise the extent to which this is a materiality which is inseparable from the discourses that surround its practice. Inasmuch as this book is, itself, concerned with the cultural representation of the experience of driving throughout the course of the twentieth century it may, at first, appear that this is a given rather than an issue. For the cultural theorist, the practice and representation of driving exist in circular and dynamic relation to one another: our experience of driving depends, in part, upon our cultural awareness of the practice and the discourses associated with it (such as 'freedom' and 'escape', for example) which will have its source in all the books, magazines, films and television programmes we have imbibed from childhood while the textual representations themselves will refer both to other texts/discourses and the author's ontological experience of driving/riding in a car (itself – as noted – culturally mediated). Conceived of in this way, the phenomenon that is driving may at first appear easier to negotiate for the cultural theorist – already safely situated within his or her circuit of meaning-production – than for the historian or sociologist who must always negotiate the tensions between the material and the representational.

Unfortunately the situation is not quite that simple. Notably, there is the complication that many of the conceptual tools I use to describe and analyse the driver-experience are themselves culturally produced, none more so than 'emotion'. This is something that Mimi Sheller also observed in her article on 'Automotive Emotions' (2004):

Emotions are felt in and through the body, but are constituted by relational settings and affective cultures; they are shared, public and collective cultural conventions and dispositions . . . Emotions, in this perspective, are not simply 'felt' and 'expressed', but are rather elicited, invoked, regulated and managed through a variety of expectations, patterns and anticipations. (Sheller 2004: 226)

It is precisely the cultural and discursive – or, if you prefer, ideological – nature of the thoughts and feelings (themselves, arguably inseparable: see note 18) that attend and are consequent upon our experience of driving/ passengering that has caused me to expand this project's focus beyond the phenomenological to include consideration of the full spectrum of cognitive and affective registers inherent in automotive consciousness. It is for this reason, too – as well as the practical, methodological necessity of holding on to a model of subjectivity that recognises the mediation of consciousness and memory – that I have resisted wrapping the cultural model of 'automotive emotion' within a phenomenological one predicated purely upon embodiment (see the discussion of Dant (2004) in Chapter 5).

Emotion is, however, but *one* of the 'foundational' categories I draw upon which may, itself, be seen as a product of discourse and culture. With the lens of methodological scrutiny tilted in this direction, it is possible to see a great many of the defining characteristics of automobility as, in part, discursively-produced: from the 'skills' we need to drive a car safely and competently; to the sensations we feel while motoring; to the speed at which we travel; to the experiences of different types of motoring (touring, cruising, making a road trip, sitting in traffic). For each of these commonplace driver practices and experiences, there is an ideological backstory. Since the discursive constructions of the different types, or modes, of driving will become evident in the chapters that follow, I restrict myself here to a brief but, I hope, indicative discussion of the first three: skills, sensations and speed.

While 'skill' may, superficially, appear to be a gender-neutral, a-political requirement of driving, its textual history reveals this to be far from the case. Quite apart from the crude gender-stereotyping that has, for over a century, presented women as inherently lacking in the physical and psychological characteristics needed to be skilful drivers (e.g. strength, concentration and spatial awareness), the early history of motoring literature reveals the astonishing degree to which the 'handling' of cars was aestheticised and classed. Across the many handbooks and manuals written during the first three decades of the twentieth-century (by women as well as men), an enormous emphasis is placed on the driver's ability to 'feel' the car. These instructions, from the Times Motoring Correspondent, are typical:

Steering should never consist of definite movement but a continuous 'feel' should be kept on the wheel and a sympathetic guidance accorded to the car. It is suggested in a subsequent chapter on gear-changing that the driver should handle the lever as though it were something of which he was fond. The steering wheel should be regarded and treated similarly. Never wrench or be rough with the wheel. (Times Motoring Correspondent 1929: 44)

Yet what is most remarkable about these recommendations, penned almost a century ago, is not merely that they invoke the language and sensibilities of the connoisseur (the classical music buff, the art collector, the wine taster) but that they translate into material *practices* that, even today, we associate with 'good' and pleasurable driving. The gendering of this particular discourse is, moreover, a complex one since the requisite quality of a 'delicate' handling of the car was and is regarded as more typically feminine than masculine – a factor seized upon by many female authors of the early motoring guides such as Dorothy Levitt[41] – even if (as in the extract quoted above) the instructions themselves are sexualised (see also Merriman 2012: 98):

Even at its most functional, then, the act of driving may be shown to be a profoundly cultural practice and one in which the written text – even and perhaps especially in the form of practical instructions – has impacted upon our relationship with the car. And this, in turn, will play its part in how thinking and bodily action cohere in automotive consciousness: our competence in handling steering wheels and gears lightly and deftly is a competence that translates readily into the cognitive realm. As is seen repeatedly in thrillers and crime fiction featuring heroic drivers (Ian Fleming's 'Bond' novels, for example), driving 'cleanly' has long been associated with thinking clearly (Fleming 2012 [1955]: 221–35).

The sensation of travelling in an automobile – of which a good deal was written in the first decades of the twentieth-century – is another feature of automobility that may not, at first, strike us as being culturally inscribed. As I and other scholars have observed (Urry 2007: 126; Merriman 2012: 73ff.; Pearce 2014: 81–2), the visceral experience of being moved at speed by noisy and juddering machinery was the overwhelming impression of automobility for most early car owners, and to the extent that thinking about 'other things', or even attending to the world as seen from the car, was out of the question. As soon as the literature(s) of motoring took hold, moreover (and here it is important to remember that motoring periodicals came into existence virtually as soon as cars became available to the general public),[42] a discursive circuit of expectation and experience was quickly established with novice drivers and passengers evidently discovering, in their motor expe-

Figure 1.2 'The lubrication of the De Dion is extremely simple', Dorothy Levitt, *The Woman and the Car* (1909). Nabu Public Domain Reprints.

ditions, the very thrills and sensations they had read about. This is especially noticeable in early female motorists' accounts of their adventures where the kinaesthesia is typically overlaid with discourses of daring and – often implicitly sexual – loss of control (see Mrs Aria 1906: 53–5, 57–8, discussed in Chapter 5).

As is evident in many of the extracts featured in this chapter, at the heart of the sensations associated with driving – then as now – is the notion of speed. More than any other aspect of motoring, speed is the phenomenon that has characterised both the visceral experience of driving and automotive consciousness, and which – from the Futurists (see note 20) through to more recent philosophers like Baudrillard (2010 [1986]) and Virilio (2008 [1984]) (see Chapter 3) – has functioned as an expression of modernity. Until more recent interventions by literary critics and cultural historians such as Sara Danius (2002) and Enda Duffy (2009), however, the possibility that speed, itself, is both relative and culturally constructed has nevertheless been largely overlooked. Indeed, Baudrillard's characterisation of speed as a 'pure object' (pp. 5–6) (see epigraph to Chapter 3), as well as something that necessarily denatures perception and confounds cognition, may be seen as indicative of how far the concept has travelled as a cultural phenomenon since the first decades of the twentieth century. By placing Edith Wharton's 1908 account of driving through the French landscape at approximately 20mph – a speed that was not inconsiderable then – alongside Baudrillard's and Virilio's descriptors, we grasp not only the relativity of speed (what is fast to Wharton would seem like crawling to Virilio) but also the fact that, in the course of the century, it has been valued very differently in terms of perception and cognition (see also Moran 2009: 166).[43] In the chapters that follow, for example, we see, first, how the 'speed' of motor transport in the 1920s and 1930s enabled drivers to search out and synthesise a multitude of landscapes in the course of a single day (Chapter 2), while, by the 1950s, speed had become a means (for some) of *dis*connecting people and places – i.e. a means of escape (Chapter 3). Chapter 5, meanwhile, returns us to the 'magical' mind-expanding properties of speed identified by Bart Kennedy (1919a) (see extract cited above).

What I have sought to capture in this brief discussion of the cultural contexts in which any book concerned with driving and automotive consciousness must operate is the extent to which historical discourse may be seen to construct or mediate every aspect of the practice. We are all aware of the ways in which certain types of driving – for example, the road trip – are profoundly ideological, but it is easy to overlook the fact that virtually all the details that have come to be associated with driving, passengering and car-culture in general have a discursive history also, from the emotions we feel when driving, to the sensations that (in part) engender the emotions, to the speed that summons up the sensations.

For those committed to accessing meaningful data on the experience of driving as a material and historical practice, this deference to the role of culture and discourse might at first seem problematic. My response, in line with a good many discourse theorists before me, would be to argue that simply because an experience is culturally mediated at every level does not render it any less 'real' or 'meaningful' to the subject concerned. Indeed, as a cultural theorist, my objective in the pages that follow is to use literary and other textual materials to explore what forms automotive consciousness takes in ways that will be of interest and value to all those historians, geographers, psychologists and social scientists that share a fascination with automobility, past and present. Across a rich and colourful archive of texts, that span the length of the twentieth century and, on occasion, a little beyond, we will encounter many different 'types' of driver and passenger, and many different categories of 'driving-event', all bearing testimony to my thesis that it is our capacity to think while we drive (of so many different things, in so many different ways) that defines this unique if (for some) outmoded form of mobility.

Conclusion

In 1919, the MP Sir Gilbert Parker made a motor tour of Ireland and later recorded his impressions in an article in *The Car Magazine*. In many respects the piece is typical of the sort of features the magazine published during this period. Alongside the practical guides to car ownership (how to drive them, how to repair them), reviews of new models, race and hill-trial reports, editorials on the latest spats between the motoring organisations and the police, touring information and humorous short stories, you find columns such as these: the autobiographical impressions of motoring by someone distinguished enough to be considered worth printing.

What is striking about Parker's column, however, is the freshness and enthusiasm with which he communicates his experience and – as seen in the extract following – his insight into all that is distinctive about automotive consciousness:

> The mind is bemused by a myriad impressions, and yet, contrary to my previous contentions and beliefs, real pictures remain, real records are printed on the mind. It had always seemed to me that the traveller by motor car was so engaged in thinking of speed and of his machinery, of the nature of the dusty road and the next objective, of the sharp curve and the 'pig on the highway', that he had no time to observe and enjoy, to note and ruminate. The railway traveller had appeared at an immense advantage on an even rail and a steady course . . .
>
> I am not quite so sure now. Over one of the toughest courses a car could travel, and frequently hurled like a catapult into the arms of my fellow travellers, I saw and observed, enjoyed the countryside, took in the wide picture as I never had done in a railway carriage; that much I will say. (Parker 1919: 15)

As I have observed elsewhere (Pearce 2014: 85–6), it is striking how 'modernist' this non-professional's writing becomes in his attempt to capture the quick succession of phenomena that flash upon his retina. Further, like Woolf in the essay discussed earlier, Parker is moved to reflect on the surprising vividness of the visions ('real pictures', 'real records') that this new mode of transport affords and hence acknowledges that motoring – contrary to his expectations – has enabled him to 'observe', 'enjoy', 'note' and 'ruminate' in ways he would never have imagined.

The value of such writings for automobilities scholarship today is immeasurable; in returning us to the early days of motoring, texts like Parker's offer instruction into what a 'true' phenomenology of driving might look like were we able to escape our twenty-first-century habituation to mobility in its many forms. As Nigel Thrift (2008:75) presciently observed, 'driving is sinking into our "technological unconscious" and producing a phenomenology which we increasingly take for granted but which in fact is historically novel.' The fact that this is a way of seeing and experiencing the world that is both novel and – according to Dennis and Urry's 'future scenarios' in *After the Car* (2009: 160–4) – in imminent danger of extinction focuses the mind even more. Without suggesting that any representation, literary or otherwise, can be mistaken for a window onto what drivers and passengers saw, heard, felt and thought during their motor-flights through the decades of the previous century, it is hoped that the chapters which follow will go some way to capturing this 'historically novel' way of apprehending the world and our relation to it.

Notes

1. The distinctive qualities of motorised automobility – as opposed to other forms of transportation – for 'thought production' will become clear in the course of the chapter; also, the qualitative differences between driving and passengering (see note 13).
2. CeMoRe had its tenth anniversary in 2013 and is now one of the world's leading research centres for mobilities research. See http://www.lancaster.ac.uk/fass/centres/cemore/ (last accessed 20 September 2015).
3. Statistics from the Department of Transport reveal that the number of licensed vehicles in the UK rose from approximately 22 million in 1995 to 36 million on 30 September 2013: an increase of 64 per cent. Twenty years prior to this, in 1975, there were only *c*.12 million vehicles on British roads. See the RAC Foundation Q&A factsheet for statistics on changes in travel speed, traffic flow and congestion: http://www.racfoundation.org/motoring-faqs/mobility#a1 (last accessed 1 April 2015). Especially noteworthy is

the fact that motorway traffic has increased by *c*.9.6 per cent over the past ten years and that motorways and major roads together account for *c*.65.6 per cent of total road traffic. Britain's minor roads constitute *c*.87.3 per cent of total road length but carry only *c*.34.5 per cent of total road traffic. In 2013, the average traffic flow for motorways was *c*.76.7 thousand vehicles for each motorway mile compared with *c*.10.8 thousand vehicles for each mile of rural A-road per day. Taken together, these statistics confirm my impression that it is the long-haul motorway drive that has changed most over the past twenty years.

4. In December 2014 the Department of Transport announced a new £15 billion 'Road Investment Strategy' including plans for another 1,300 new lane miles to be added to motorways and trunk roads. The Campaign for Better Transport responded: http://www.bettertransport.org.uk/sites/default/files/Roads_Retrofit_Proposals_FINAL_Sep2014.pdf (last accessed 1 April 2015).

5. See Pearce (2013), 'Autopia: What We're Thinking When We're Driving'. This essay, which includes my auto-ethnography of a road-trip to the north of Scotland, was the springboard for this book.

6. The likening of Britain's road system to the arteries of the human body dates back to the designation of the key routes out of the capital as 'arterials' in the 1920s (see Jeremiah 2007: 134). See artist Susan Stockwell's recent work on this theme: http://www.tate.org.uk/context-comment/blogs/art-maps-project-blog (last accessed 2 April 2015).

7. At the CeMoRe symposium (16 March 2015), 'Work on the Move', Donald Hislop (Loughborough, UK) and Reinhard Gressel (IFSTTAR-SPLOTT, Paris) presented papers on the impact mobile technologies are having on employer expectations for 'work on the move'.

8. There are now regular reports in the media of drivers texting and using other mobile technologies while driving, as well as reading documents for work purposes (Laurier 2004). In 2014 one woman was photographed reading a book while travelling at 70mph on the M1: see http://www.dailymail.co.uk/news/article-2643934/Woman-photographed-driving-ten-miles-busy-motorway-reading-BOOK-wheel-smiled-waved-furious-driver-beeped-her.html (last accessed 2 April 2015).

9. In my endeavour to (re)define journeys made by car in terms of the driver's subjective experience it has become clear that rest stops play a crucial role in fragmenting the driver's cognitive and affective mindset and hence the potential for medium–long drives to be figured as multiple 'driving-events' (see below and Pearce 2017).

10. A significant number of respondents interviewed as part of the 'Transforming Drivers' project (NSW, Australia: 2000–2006) nevertheless confirm how important 'thinking time' is (Redshaw 2008: 74).

11. Drawing on Richard Sennett's (1990) work on the changing nature of 'sanctuary' in contemporary life, Bull (2001: 199) observes: 'Automobiles appear to operate as symbolic "sanctuaries" in which drivers operationalize strategies of "centredness". This sanctuary represents a physical zone of "immunity" between the driver and the world or space beyond. Historically this zone was thought to be imbued with qualities not attributable to the world beyond, as in the spaces of a church ... Following Sennett, the

automobile might constitute one of the last, albeit problematic, refuges of a retreating public subjectivity.'

12. 'Altered states of consciousness': the use of this umbrella-term to denote the various practices and events which can induce elevated states of consciousness was popularised by the American psychologist, Charles Tart, in the late 1960s (Tart 1990 [1969]). Tart's work with psychoactive drugs aided the understanding and classification of mind-altering practices more generally, and those grouped under this banner now include meditation, fasting and adrenalin-fuelled 'highs' as well as drug use and involuntary causes such as sleep deprivation, oxygen deficiency and traumatic experiences.

13. The distinction between driving and passengering (a term coined by Laurier et al. 2008) is a crucial one for this book and I have endeavoured to use both terms advisedly throughout, i.e. when I use the term 'driving' it is with specific reference to the person behind the steering-wheel, while 'driving/passengering' recognises that the event/experience under consideration may be shared by both the driver and the passenger. The psychologists D. J. Van Lennep (1987) and Jack Katz (1999: 32–3) write in illuminating detail about the differential perception/embodiment of drivers and passengers. For my purposes here, the most crucial distinction lies in the ways in which the concentration needed to drive the car often constrains, directs and/or liberates our thinking in ways that are significantly different to the passenger experience.

14. Iain Borden writes about the 'defamiliarising' properties of driving in similar terms, including the aesthetic dimension: 'Objects can assume a purposeless beauty, being divorced from their original function' (2013: 71).

15. Bart Kennedy (1861–1930) was a self-taught writer – novelist and journalist – whose early travels across America and Europe were the subject of several novels on 'tramping'. He also wrote for a number of periodicals including *The New Age* and *The Car Illustrated*. Kennedy's writing style was evidently influenced by the Modernist and Futurist movements (see Chapter 5).

16. See Chapter 2 for discussion of the commonalities shared by early motoring and cycling.

17. Although the post-millennial groundswell of interest in 'affect' in academic research has (re)enforced a division between cognitive and emotional experience, most schools of psychology recognise this to be an artificial distinction: emotions present themselves to us through cognition. In my own exploration of driver-consciousness I have nevertheless found it useful to maintain a distinction between analytic/intellectual mentation (e.g. problem-solving) and the scrutiny of one one's 'feelings' (e.g. desire, grief). See Chapter 4.

18. To be clear, my figuring of our thought patterns as a 'journey' is not predicated upon neurological science but rather the tropes and discourses that are commonly used (by psychologists as well as the public) to capture the subjective experience of the movement of our thoughts – including, of course, William James's 'stream of consciousness' (Kern 2000: 24–8).

19. Although Trigg does not directly invoke Deleuze in his conceptualisation of the driver's condition of 'becoming-toward' it is implicit, as it is in the

work of many automotive theorists for obvious reasons (see Deleuze and Guattari 1992; Cresswell 2006: 17; Merriman 2012: 6–9).

20. The discourses surrounding the early history of the car are intimately connected with Italian Futurism (Humphreys 1999: 6–11), and its celebration not only of 'speed' but of a dynamic and radically mobilised world has informed the representation and theorisation of automobility ever since. The car is one of the icons of futurism – see, for example, Giocama Bala's 'Abstract Speed – The Car Has Passed' (1913): http://www.tate.org.uk/art/artworks/balla-abstract-speed-the-car-has-passed-t01222 (last accessed 20 September 2015).

21. Edmund Husserl (1859–1938) and Maurice Merleau-Ponty (1908–61) are but two of many philosophers who worked under the banner of phenomenology in the first half of the twentieth century. (Moran and Mooney (2002) is an excellent source text.) Husserl and Merleau-Ponty are of particular importance here on account of their focus on the relationship between perception and cognition (allowing for the fact that Merleau-Ponty's later work on embodied knowledge questioned the role of consciousness in our 'haptic' apprehension of the world).

22. 'Transcendental reduction': the term commonly used to account for Husserl's move from an insistence on 'eidetic' perception to a focus on the 'essential structures' that intentional phenomena reveal; this transcendental move – from the phenomenon in its 'thingness' to the phenomenon in its essence – breaks faith with what many phenomenologists, even today, see as the benchmark of their discipline, i.e. 'an unprejudiced, *descriptive* study of whatever appears to consciousness' (Moran and Mooney 2002: 2 (my italics)).

23. For Heidegger, the understanding of a subject's existence as a condition of 'being-in-the-world' discounts the mediating role of consciousness (Moran and Mooney 2002: 17). However, Thrift's book on *Non-Representational Theory* (2008: 6–7) includes a useful discussion of why we may strategically wish to protect a notion of 'consciousness' even when working with models of perception and consciousness which test its limits.

24. 'Intentionality': phenomenology recognises intentionality (i.e. the process whereby we are directed to the significance of the phenomenon in question) to be both a feature of consciousness ('the intentional act') and the 'object' under consideration (which reveals its significance to us).

25. For Husserl, the distinction between 'primary retention' (i.e. the images stored during the *process* of perception) and 'recollection' (whereby memory presents us with 'secondary images' predicated on former events) is absolutely key to a proper understanding of perception and its rootedness in the present. For Gaston Bachelard (1971), however, fantasy – in the form of the imagination – was integral to the successful practice of phenomenology (see Chapter 5).

26. *Gestalt* translates from the German as the 'essence or shape of an entity's complete form'. The key principle that underpins the theory, as it was developed by the Gestalt 'school', is that the eye sees objects in their entirety before identifying their individual parts, hence Kurt Koffka's maxim 'the whole is other than the sum of its parts' (see King and Wertheimer 2007).

27. 'Defamiliarisation': translated from the Russian, *ostranenie* ('making strange'), this term refers to the ways in language/tropes are employed to

present 'the familiar' in a strikingly new way that will reveal its essence ('to make the stone stony'). See Hawkes (1977): 62.

28. By coincidence, J. J. Gibson was one of the first twentieth-century psychologists to investigate the role of perception in driving (Gibson 1982 [1938]); see also Tim Dant's (2004) critique of Gibson in Chapters 4 and 5. It should be noted that Gibson was, himself, opposed to the core principles of Gestalt – i.e. that perception is initiated and organised according to abstract shapes and forms. Gombrich's own work remains largely indifferent to (or ignorant of) the fundamental differences between his theoretical sources, allowing his own context-specific enquiry (i.e. perception and style in the visual arts) to determine his standpoint.

29. John Groeger is a cognitive psychologist who has headed up several funded research projects on driving with different teams of scientists. See http://www2.hull.ac.uk/science/psychology/ourstaff/academics/johngroeger.aspx (last accessed 20 September 2015).

30. Dixon Scott died of dysentery on a hospital ship at Gallipoli in 1913 and his literary ambitions were never realised. This collection was compiled, posthumously, by his friend, Bertram Smith.

31. Jan Struther was the pen name of Joyce Maxtone whose *Mrs Miniver* (1989 [1939]) was based on a column which appeared in *The Times* in the period leading up to the Second World War. The 'memory flags' were the means by which Mrs Miniver and her husband marked memorable incidents on their motor tours.

32. Gordon Crosby was the most famous automotive artist/illustrator working in Britain during the first decades of the twentieth century. Given the difficulty of capturing speeding objects in photographs, Crosby's fine illustrations were preferred by periodicals and enthusiasts alike (Jeremiah 2007: 70–1). Crosby's 'Auto-suggestions' series appeared in *Autocar* in 1929 and includes some strikingly 'defamiliarised' images as reproduced in Figures 1.2 and 5.4.

33. 'Motor-flight': a term used widely in early twentieth-century motoring to describe motor touring; see especially Edith Wharton's *A Motor-Flight through France* (2008 [1908]; Pearce 2014).

34. See Leena K. Kore-Schröder's (2007) insightful chapter on this text which draws upon Woolf's diaries to further contextualise the author's experience of automobility as well as Merleau-Ponty in its discussion of the embodied perception of time and space; see also Garrington (2015: 119–23).

35. Julian Opies's *Imagine You Are Driving* (a series of screenprints depicting stylised and 'affectless' motorway landscapes) dates from 1998–9 (see http://www.tate.org.uk/art/artworks/opie-imagine-you-are-driving-p78311/text-summary: last accessed 17 September 2015). Andrew Cross works across several media (his 2002 essay is discussed in Chapter 4), including the film/book *An English Journey* (2004) which re-enacts J. B. Priestley's tour (1984 [1934]): see http://andrewcross.co.uk/site/index.php?page=index (last accessed 17 September 2015).

36. Gijs Mom, who works across the disciplines of literature, technology and engineering, insists upon the need for a cross-national, trans-continental appraisal of automobility if we are fully to understand its cultural impact and legacy (Mom 2014).

37. See http://www.racfoundation.org/motoring-faqs/mobility (last accessed 1 April 2015). Following Mom (note 36), it is arguably distorting to deal with UK statistics of this kind in isolation. Dennis and Urry (2009: 44–5) include some eye-watering figures for the seemingly exponential growth in car ownership/production in the USA and China from the first decade of the twentieth-first century.

38. While evidence suggests that women the world over have had delayed access to driving/car ownership, the same cannot be said of other socially/economically disadvantaged groups. See Clarsen (2008: 5) on the multiple ways in which black 'minorities' have participated in the history of driving.

39. Exceptions to this are to be found in American literature and film. See Deborah Clarke (2007: 111–39) on Barbara Kingsolver and Erika Lopez, and Iain Borden on *Thelma and Louise* (2013: 105–11).

40. Redshaw, following Barbalet (1999), offers this definition of 'boredom' vis-à-vis an automotive context: 'In repetitive action as a means to an end there is minimal involvement and no feeling of boredom. It is when repetitive action loses its function or purpose, that boredom, involvement of a negative type, arises' (Redshaw 2008: 76).

41. As well setting the ladies' world land-speed record in 1906 and competing in numerous other motoring trials and competitions, Dorothy Levitt (1882–1992) published a practical guide on motoring for women entitled *The Woman and the Car: A Chatty Little Handbook for All Women Who Motor or Want to Motor* (1909). See https://en.wikipedia.org/wiki/Dorothy_Levitt (last accessed 21 September 2015).

42. See Jeremiah (2007: 249–50) for a helpful list of British motoring periodicals from the early twentieth century. Remarkably, the weekly publication, *Autocar*, which began life in 1895, has remained in circulation up to and including the present day.

43. Historical research has revealed that speed is not only 'relative' but a phenomenon that was of little importance to human society before the nineteenth century: 'The word "speed" derives from the Old English *spowan* meaning to "succeed" or "prosper" [as in 'God speed'] . . . but the idea of speed as a natural, instinctual state emerged fairly recently' (Moran 2009: 166). See also Kern (2000: 156) and Duffy (2009).

Driving South, Driving North
Extracts from a journey made in March 2015

Driving south

The nature and extent of the change hits me almost as soon as I turn onto the M6.

It has always been the case that Preston is a limit-point as far as traffic is concerned: head north and the cars, vans and trucks melt away; head south and the opposite is the case. Within a short distance, one or two lanes of traffic quickly become a solid three – and, for a short stretch, just south of Preston – four. For as long as I can remember, academics, politicians and comedians have been debating where, exactly, the north begins; from a mobilities perspective, I would draw the line just *here*, 15 minutes south of Lancaster.

My journey to Cornwall on Friday, 20 March 2015 is my first trip south for the best part of four and a half years. It is also the day of a solar eclipse and – by coincidence – I was in Cornwall for the last one, sixteen years ago. Today I'm pleased that I caught a glimpse of the crescent-sun, shrouded in cloud, as I set out from Cockerham but the thick stream of traffic I now join is arguably the more jaw-dropping spectacle of the day. I am rolled into a flow that I am unable to extricate myself from until I'm within five miles of my destination. For 350 miles I am surrounded by other vehicles and road users and, to a greater or lesser extent, my mobility is dictated by theirs.

The stretch of motorway between Preston and my first stop, at Wolverhampton Services, has few 'memory flags' (Struther 1989: see note 32 to Chapter 1). The junction for the M61 to Manchester prompts a raw, but recent, flashback inasmuch as my best friend's mother died just before Christmas and my last journey to this point was for her funeral. Thereafter, there is little, past or present, to catch my attention and I reflect, instead, and with cautious satisfaction, upon the juncture in my life and career that this journey represents. (I am moving to a part-time contract in the autumn.) These ruminations are, however, brought to a sudden halt when I hit the first wave of heavy congestion. Such is the anonymous nature, for me, of this stretch of motorway – and so frequent are the subsequent hold-ups – that I now struggle to locate precisely where the first problems started. There are major road works near Stoke-on-Trent, for sure; but there are also several enforced 50mph speed restrictions before that. The jams merge in my memory, as does the traffic. A few somatic 'body-memories' nevertheless make themselves felt; for example, the rise and dip of the road as I approach Sandbach Services. Similarly, the brown 'heritage' direction sign for Stapeley Water Gardens, near Nantwich, activates a schema stored deep in my memory.[1] But mostly this stretch of my journey is grey (the tarmac, the concrete central reservation, the sky), dusty and unremarkable; what distinguishes it from all my past journeys is nothing I perceive through the windscreen but rather what surrounds me as I edge slowly along: a solid column of HGVs on my left, a jostling throng of cars and vans on my right. We accelerate for a minute or two, then brake, then stop, before lurching forwards again. In this ungainly way we do, nevertheless, make progress, and at a rate that would be the envy of motorists a few decades' back. Therefore, when I eventually pull into Wolverhampton Services I discover I'm only about 45 minutes 'late'. However, in terms of driver-consciousness, it has been a very different journey to the ones that I remember. [. . .]

My visit to Wolverhampton Services is very reassuring. Unlike others who have written on the subject (Augé 1995; Trigg 2012), I have never found service stations especially alienating places – or, at least, not the ones I use regularly – for the good reason that they have become familiar *to me*. The generic anonymity typically associated with motorway facilities is mixed with a rich store of memories of where I was – in my job, in my relationships – when I passed through them five, ten, fifteen, twenty years previously. Associated with each of them is the widest possible spectrum of emotions, ranging from the wildest euphoria to the deepest despair. Moreover, and as I have discussed elsewhere (Pearce 2013), some of these moments have subsequently been memorialised in my consciousness to such an extent that they greet me like a piece of public sculpture the moment I turn into the car park. On this occasion, I take particular pleasure in the fact that the Moto Services at Wolverhampton remain largely unchanged from at least a decade ago. [. . .]

As I creep closer to the exit for the M5 I am on the lookout for another familiar landmark: the 'space-age' profile of RAC headquarters. It is still here, but my perception is that it is surrounded by rather more buildings than it used to be. Shortly afterwards, I've joined the M5; however, instead of bursting from an impacted column of vehicles onto an open road, as used to be the case, I simply become part of another three-lane, slow-moving, stream. True, I am travelling more quickly than I was on the M6, but my speed – once again variable – is set by the traffic about me. And so it continues through Birmingham, past Worcester and on to Gloucester. For short periods, the phalanx achieves 70 or 80mph, but we do so collectively. The driver's speed is set by the lane in which she travels and the frequent lane closures mean that what is ostensibly the fast lane may suddenly become the slow one. I drive for another couple of hours, reaching Sedgemoor Services by about 2.30 p.m. This is reasonable progress – the traffic eases past Bristol without any significant hold-ups – but, in the old days, I would have made Taunton Deane before taking a second break. Now I'll have to make a third stop, for sure. During this phase of the journey, my thinking has been rather less focused. I'm doing what I'm doing – 'getting there' – rather than thinking about anything in particular. Listening to music nevertheless keeps me relaxed and upbeat, even if I can feel some tiredness creeping in. [. . .]

The unfamiliar business of the road notwithstanding, I am still unable to suppress my excitement as I make the final sweep west. The sun is getting low in the sky and sunglasses are essential. It seems a long time since this morning's eclipse and, because of the distance I have travelled subsequently, what I witnessed already feels a part of history; I could be remembering it from another fifteen years hence rather than as something that happened today. Once through the long flat of dual-carriageway between the M5 and Okehampton, the A30 – however busy – redeems itself as a road on account of its undulations. Although retaining the superficial character of a two-lane motorway, after twenty miles or so it begins to dip and climb repeatedly, granting the driver the thrill of sudden downhill acceleration and uphill flight. At some point on this roller-coaster we cross the border ('Kernow') and I am back in Cornwall. However, even at this juncture there is still another sixty miles or so of driving to go. [. . .]

Several roundabouts later, with the traffic still heavy, I finally turn off at 'my' junction (Scorrier Crossroads) and embark on the final five miles of my long drive south. After the shock of seeing what was once the 'Crossroads Motel' now converted into a care home, I enter a familiar warren of tiny lanes where – with relief – I note that pretty much nothing has changed. The Methodist Chapel at Crofthandy is up for sale and there are a couple of new-builds here and there, but nothing on the scale of what I have been witnessing in both Lancaster and in Scotland. I make my usual, favourite detour across United Downs (a derelict mining area), remembering how passionate I was about the bleakness and desolation of this place when a teenager: it was a small corner of moorland and industrialisation that fed into my dreams of 'the North' even then. From here it is only a couple of miles to where my parents are buried, half a mile more to the family home, and less that another mile to my friend's house. From this point on, the 'memory flags' are so dense it is no longer possible to see or respond to them individually and, interestingly, I don't even try. Instead, all my attention is focused, once again, on the visible, physical landscape: what's changed, what's not. The fact that so little has perhaps quells the need for memory. If everything is still here, everything intact, then perhaps the past is, too.

Rapidly, now, I encounter the final bends, final road signs, final junctions, final fields and buildings that stand between me and home. In seconds, I fly past the house (much gentrified) that was once my home and find myself minutes from my friend's. This is the point at which my social self kicks in, and the deeper thoughts that have accompanied me on this long journey – as they did on all those journeys in the past – get gently placed to one side. Significantly, there has been hardly a car in sight since I turned off the A30 and onto these country lanes, leading me to the conclusion that even if the nation's main auto-routes are now clogged, the tributaries are clearer than one might have hoped or thought (see note 3 to Chapter 1).

Driving north (1)

Two days later, and I am heading North again: from Cornwall, back to Lancaster. It's Sunday and I'm somewhat concerned about my late start. In the summer months, Sundays – and Saturdays – can be bad days to get out of the county on account of them being 'changeover' days for the hotels and self-catering businesses. Even in the 1990s, there was one memorable occasion when I got as far as Fraddon, saw the queues of traffic, and headed back to my parents' again. Today, however, the road is mercifully clear (even though meeting, first, a horse, and then a group of cyclists, on the narrow lanes causes me to alter my route and join the A30 at Truro rather than Scorrier).

As soon as I am on the dual carriageway, I breathe a sigh of relief and accelerate to 70–80mph: a speed which I am able to maintain, on this occasion, for most of the journey home. It is a beautiful spring morning in Cornwall, and with the sun behind me throwing glancing rays across the land, I am flying once more. This was often my mood, it must be said, when I left Cornwall in the past since – much as I looked forward to seeing my family and needed to see them – they were not always easy visits. Today I am reliving that mood and that moment, and at a time in my life when it feels like I have much to look forward to. The lightshow over Bodmin Moor is particularly spectacular, with the 'big' hills – Brown Willy and Rough [pronounced 'Row'] Tor – picked out sharply. I am by no means the only car on the road – indeed, I am part of a steady and composite flow north – but there are few HGVs and I am able to maintain a steady cruising speed all the way to the M5, a distance of approximately 100 miles. In the old days, when my parents were travelling up and down the road to car sales or the Speedway, Exeter was presumed to be a two-hour drive, but all the while I've been making the journey, it has been more like an hour and a half. It is still a long haul out of Cornwall, nevertheless, and this reminds me of what was different about growing up here. The traffic pours from the A30 onto the M5 seamlessly, and without any perceptible change of speed. The contrast with the slow shunt from the M6 to the M5 at the motorway's other end could hardly be more striking.

Because I am making good time I push on to Taunton Deane Services before stopping; this is my preferred break in the journey. For 130 miles I have driven in complete silence, totally preoccupied with processing the experience of my visit. I rarely drive without music, but sometimes I have so much to think about I don't even notice it isn't on. While my mood is upbeat (I am flying home, term has ended, I shall soon be up in Scotland for a good long time), my cognitive faculties are intent on savouring, evaluating, capturing my encounters with the people and places I haven't seen for a long time. Interestingly, these are things that have little direct bearing on my own life any more, but they are a compelling distraction nevertheless. [. . .]

Taunton appears to have represented a cognitive limit-point as far as my preoccupation with Cornwall is concerned, and for the next stretch of the journey I return to my music and range more widely in my thoughts. It's about three o'clock by the time I pull into Wolverhampton Services and, still concerned about the traffic I might encounter around Manchester, I don't tarry long. I take Star for a short walk in the rather less scenic woodland of the northbound service area and forgo getting myself a hot drink. It has been an excellent journey so far, but it won't do to be complacent. There is another 100 miles of my journey still to go.

As it happens, the congestion that has floated like a mirage before me the whole journey never materialises. The traffic is pretty much a solid three lanes from this point on, but we cruise along together at a comfortable 70–80mph. Such is the cohesiveness of the flow to which I, too, belong it is hard to think about this mobility as *auto*-mobility (my direction is governed by the straight lines of the road, my speed is governed by that of the vehicles about me), but at least the privacy of the experience remains intact and the thought-time is my own. And so, tucked snugly alongside, and between, several hundred fellow travellers, eating up the miles at a speed that (ridiculously) now feels no more than 'steady', I make it back to Lancaster by 5 p.m. after an exemplary seven-hour journey. This is how I remember it to have been – at least on most occasions – in the 1990s and early 2000s, and so it was today.

Driving north (2)

Given the momentousness of this particular journey, I am pleased to report that the drive north does not disappoint. It is a bright, sunny morning, if cool, and I experience familiar relief and elation as I pull the car door shut and fasten my seatbelt. The car is full, but not as full at it might be, since I moved several boxes of books and papers on my last visit. Altogether, I feel sorted – in mind and matter – and ready to go. I let out the clutch, check the mirror, and pull away from the curb outside my front door as I have done so many times before: an act of repetition, indistinguishable from any other, except to the part of my consciousness that registers this as a defining moment in my life.

As if to remind me that no future is guaranteed, I come within inches of an accident as I join the M6 northbound. There are road works on this stretch, and the inside carriageway of the motorway has been made into a temporary slipway. This is far from obvious, however, and the car in front of me brakes suddenly. I am far enough behind the vehicle to avoid a collision, but a faster driver would not have been. Once on, I negotiate my way through a band of slow-moving traffic until I reach the outside lane and can accelerate to 70mph enjoying, once again, the sensation of the other vehicles falling away as I glide up the hill out of Lancaster. The motorway end of the long-awaited Heysham link road is under construction at Junction 34, and the surrounding countryside has been landscaped beyond recognition. [. . .]

The M74 from Gretna to Glasgow is also fast, open and blissfully quiet. I listen to music and think about all the things I am writing about now as well as my project on driving more generally. The swoop through the Clyde Valley has been especially enjoyable ever since the M74 became a motorway (not long after I started coming to Scotland), and is now enhanced (at least, for some of us) by the Clyde Wind Farm which stretches across the undulating hills hereabouts like a vast twenty-first-century forest. As I near Glasgow, a travel flash comes on the radio telling me that there are potential delays at the Raith interchange. I wonder if this will mean an end to my hubris, but when I get to the junction the motorway is unaffected. I consequently fly onto and through the M74 extension that now bypasses the city to the south, feeling a familiar pang as I pass the old M8 junction. For years, *this* was my turning, but now – seen from the far reaches of 2015 – it is one that emphatically belongs to another phase of my life. The fact that it was a phase I never really wanted to end means that this will probably always feel like a turning of missed fortune for me, which subsequently leads me to reflect upon what a road-use survey could reveal about the affective, as well as the functional, fabric of our lives. [. . .]

When I make my next and final stop at Inveruglas, I realise how damp and chill the weather is up here. For a moment, the distance I have travelled the past few days collapses, and when I step out of the car it is with the balmy warmth of Cornwall still on my skin. Walking Star even the short distance to the pontoon is uncomfortable, and I feel myself shrink from the wind's edge. I nevertheless buy myself a drink at the cafe, and look forward to being home soon. At Pulpit Rock, where they have been widening the road for the best part of two years, there is still no suggestion that the works will be completed by Easter. Securing the rock face is clearly presenting as great an engineering challenge as constructing the pontoon over the loch, and – as has been the case for months – men and vehicles swarm over the site without evidence of much happening. There is no great delay at the lights, however, and I'm soon on my way again, hanging tight around Loch Lomondside's treacherous bends, past the 'Drover's' hotel at Inverarnan, through the tree-lined shelter of Glen Falloch before bursting onto the fast, uphill straight towards Crianlarich. Most of my friends up here avoid this road – they dislike the eight miles of bends that slows you down to 30mph—but I love it with my whole heart: it is the ever-magical 'road home' for me. [. . .]

Soon after this, I am through Tyndrum and making my final turn-off of the day: from the iconic A82 which, from here, tracks north across Rannoch Moor, onto the A85 – the road to Oban. This turning is the literal highpoint of my journey (in terms of altitude) and is frequently snowy in winter. Looking south, the road offers magnificent views of Ben More and the Glen Falloch mountains. It is also the gateway to the most wild and desolate section of road on my whole journey, with some very fast stretches.

Typically, this is the most thrilling section of my journey: the point at which tiredness has dulled complex thought and the simple, emotional pull of home takes over. Today, however, I am a little less sanguine: for whatever reason – possibly the simple change of weather and temperature: it is still grey and cold and wet – I experience a few sick waves of anxiety. I'm aware that I've been away from my house for three weeks and start focusing on what mail might have landed, what state I shall find things in given than the re-roofing has begun. There is a degree of self-protection in all this, of course, and it could be that I am purposefully steadying myself, dispelling the euphoria in preparation for the new life I am now committed to.

Another 20 minutes or so sees me braking sharply as I enter my village. Once again, my antennae are up, checking out anything different or unusual. Almost as soon as I register a new 'For Sale' sign, however, I am past the hotel and swinging up my own driveway. I suddenly I feel exhausted and – possibly for the first time – glance up at my new house with a sense of familiarity rather than wonder. I step out into the chill, damp air

'Tyndrum, looking south' (2013). Photo by Viv Tabner.

and observe that mountains are white with snow down to 1,000 feet. Two days and 680 miles since leaving Lancaster, I am here, and, for a moment, everything stalls and I don't know what to think or feel. Then Star lets out a howl, explaining it for me. We are home, and we are home for good. I open the front door, switch on the lights and turn on the heating. In Cornwall it is spring, but this is Argyll and there is a way to go. I nevertheless note with satisfaction that the daffodils here, unlike there, are just beginning: by driving north, I have bought myself extra time (or so it seems).

Note

1. Tim Edensor (2003) writes about this very same heritage sign for the gardens at Stapely in his own M6 auto-ethnography. An Internet search has nevertheless revealed that the gardens were closed to the public some time ago, making my recognition of the sign especially poignant.

Chapter 2

Searching

I begin with a photograph (Figure 2.1) that evokes the focus and sentiment of this chapter, namely the distinctive yet largely overlooked aspect
of driving that I have termed *searching*.

In contrast to the chapters which follow in which my concern is with
the complex exchange of perception, thought and feeling that characterises the practice of driving, this chapter recognises the signal role of the
car in providing access to places that would be largely inaccessible by
other means on account of their remoteness and/or distance from home.
For while, as will be discussed further in the conclusion, 'searching' is the
aspect of driving that comes closest to the benefits of cycling (Pooley et al.
2005; Horton et al. 2007; Pooley 2010; Bennett forthcoming), what the
early motoring literature reminds us repeatedly is that it was the ability
of the car to bring distances in excess of 100 miles within the realm of a
'day trip' (Jeremiah 2007: 73–4) that transformed personal mobility so
fundamentally at the beginning of the twentieth century.[1] Further, and in
contrast to cycling, motor vehicles were welcomed as a means of travel
and exploration that older and less fit individuals could also enjoy (not to
mention, of course, 'ladies' (see Murphy 1908 quoted below)).

Yet if the conceptual focus of this chapter differs from the others in
that it investigates driving as a means rather than as an end in itself,
this is not to suggest that the means is irrelevant. Although for some of
the authors surveyed the 'real' search for a place, person or fragment
of history begins when they step out of the vehicle that has taken them
there, for others the quest and the discovery are inseparable from their
means of transportation. Picking up on the trope introduced in Chapter
1, there are, indeed, many instances where the car in question may be
likened to a *probe* or prosthesis which the drivers use to investigate the
landscape that moves steadily towards them. In this regard, speed is
clearly a crucial factor in distinguishing 'searching' from, for example,
the sort of 'cruising' Neil Young is seen practising in Chapter 4: both

Figure 2.1 'Glencoe village and garage (1930s)', Guthrie Hutton, *Old Glencoe and Ballachulish* (2011). Courtesy of Stenlake Publishing Ltd. See page xiv for a larger reproduction of this image.

types of motoring value the car's ability to deliver them to unknown as well as known destinations ('searching' arguably implies both), but the relationship drivers and passengers have with the environments through which they pass at speeds rarely in excess of 30mph – in contrast with speeds of 50, 60 or 70mph – is substantively different and renders the car an integral part of the discovery (see also Pooley forthcoming).

But I begin with my photograph which, at first glance, might seem an odd choice for the process I have begun to describe. In contrast to the many other evocative shots included in Guthrie Hutton's fascinating book (2011) – including a companion piece which shows a large number of vehicles drawn up in front of the Glencoe Hotel (Hutton 2011: 29) – my photograph features only one small stationary car and two – possibly three – motorised charabancs (two parked on the left-hand side of the road; the third tucked away behind the AA box). Yet despite the fact that no conspicuous searching is taking place at this peaceful crossroads, what drew me to the image is the fact that it represents a place that I know well from my own travels but at a precise, and recognisable, moment in motoring history: the moment, arguably, when driving-*as*-searching was in its heyday (i.e. the early–mid 1930s).[2]

Set against the backdrop of two of Scotland's most iconic hills – the Pap of Glencoe and Sgorr nam Fiannaidh, the first summit (looking south) of the Aonach Eagach – the photograph depicts the road junction soon after the 'new road' through Glencoe had been completed in 1933.[3] The annotation that accompanies it in my source text (see note 2), also draws our attention to the garage and petrol pumps (at the intersection of the new road and the old road to Kinlochleven) and the AA box in the right foreground of the picture. While both the AA and the RAC had been established for over thirty years by the time this photograph was taken (Keir and Morgan 1955; Jeremiah 2007: 20–1), what both the box and the garage signify is the extent to which automobility was establishing itself as the preferred means by which people now travelled to more remote tourist destinations. Glencoe Village may have been one of the most popular stopping-points on the tourist map of Scotland since the days of Cook's Tours (Cook's 1861),[4] but what this photograph tells us is that it was now within the reach of independent travellers as well as parties (look closely, and you will see at least a dozen people, most of them visitors, moving through the village). Both the garage and the AA box would have performed a crucial role in this last regard, since the relative unreliability of motor vehicles at this time meant that no individual or company could undertake a tour of any distance without provision for possible breakdowns. What the photograph thus confirms is that, by the mid-1930s, the 'car-system' (Dennis and Urry 2009) had accommodated this fallibility to the extent that drivers could risk long-distance travel to the far flung corners of the British Isles: to take themselves to regions where they could *search* the byways as well as *travel* the highways of the road network.[5]

In an article from 1930 describing a journey made from London to Edinburgh in a single day, Alec Maclehouse draws a particular distinction between motor touring and what he calls 'stern travel', observing – vis-à-vis the latter – that 'the experience is rounded and complete, and the emotional pitch, in consequence, greatly heightened' (Maclehouse 1930: 59). I explore Maclehouse's delight in his 'stern travel' in Chapter 3 (in the context of motor sport), but here its chief value lies in the distinction it draws between 'motoring for motoring's sake' (see also Chapter 3) and driving that has absolutely nothing to do with speed and little to do with utility. As will be seen in the case study which follows, neither H. V. Morton nor Edwin Muir care how long their journeys take them as long as their modest vehicles get them to their destinations – eventually.

Yet important and fascinating as this historical context is, it is still not the prime reason I chose this photograph above all others. My first attraction was that it is an image of somewhere both familiar and loved (I have climbed both the peaks featured in the picture and driven through the village many scores of times), but tweaked just enough by time to be new and unfamiliar. Indeed, the full-frontal shot of the junction is such that it reproduces almost exactly the driver's-eye perspective of entering the village today, with the consequence that – on first viewing – I found myself instantly plunged into a process of compare-and-contrast, 'schema-and-correction', as outlined in Chapter 1. Following E. H. Gombrich (1980), this is very evidently a case of the disturbance of the schema enabling us to see things freshly, though, in this case, a scene from the past rather than a landscape in the present.[6]

This, therefore, was an image I found myself returning to repeatedly in an effort to make sense of the slippages between 'what I see and what I know' (Gombrich 1980: 76): the recognisable but slightly skewed lay-out; the garage and its pumps; the AA box; the road surface; the kerb-stones; the signpost to Kinlochleven; the traces of manure on the road (a visible reminder that, in the 1930s, the 'days of the horse' were far from over); the telegraph wires; the discrete groups of people; and, of course, the white dog stood in the middle of the road (near the charabancs). While most of the people located on the New Road and in front of the garage are fully conscious of the fact they are being photographed (the man next to the car, the group by the charabanc, the two mechanics stood on either side of the Kinlochleven signpost), those strolling through the village appear to be unaware of what is happening. Passengers from one of the charabancs, most likely, they are almost certainly on their way to the monument to the 1692 massacre;[7] following in the footsteps of a century's worth of guide books, they have descended from their vehicle and begun their preordained search.

For myself, meanwhile, this vivid and somewhat uncanny encounter with the past enables me to fantasise what 'motoring-as-searching' involved in the 1930s. True, this particular schema is already well established in my mind on account of all the early motoring literature I have read, as well as the precious fragments of film footage that survive (Claude Friese-Greene's *The Open Road* (1925) being a stunning example),[8] but it is 'familiar' images like this that bring the moment – or, rather, the intersection of history and place – most fully alive and enable me to translate the thrill I still experience in using my own car as a means of searching out unspoilt solitudes into what it must have felt like then. Significantly, the bleak wilderness of Rannoch Moor (see Figure 2.2)[9] – which lies just the other side of the Pass of Glencoe – was little more of a motoring risk in the 1930s than it is now on account of the motoring services (AA box/'patrol' and garage)[10] featured here. The biggest difference between an expedition into this wilderness then compared with now would have been somatic – the different type and feel of the car, the rougher road surface, exposure to the elements (Urry

Figure 2.2 'Heading across the Rannoch Moor towards Glencoe (1930s)', Guthrie Hutton, *Old Glencoe and Ballachulish* (2011). Courtesy of Stenlake Publishing Ltd.

2007: 125–6) – and affective: for all but the most 'blasé' motor tourists (see Osmond 1929), the self-consciousness with which such driving-events were undertaken (to 'get off the beaten track', to experience 'true wilderness', etc.), would have engendered a frisson of excitement that is difficult to match today. And this, more than anything, is what I take from the photograph: a sharp, clear apprehension of the extraordinary thrill and privilege of what it would have felt like to pull into the garage, fill up with petrol and then head off towards Rannoch Moor (see Figure 2.2) through the breathtaking chicanes of the Pass.

Touring and searching

As most readers of this book will be aware, touring by motor car began surprisingly soon after the automobile's invention. Although the motoring periodicals from the first decade of the twentieth century are arguably more focused on motoring as a sport than a mode of tourism (see Chapter 3), the range and (reasonable) reliability of motor vehicles of all types (including electric)[11] meant that those who could afford them were soon persuaded to trial the new transport; indeed, an element of challenge and unpredictability (even if mitigated by the reassuring presence of a chauffeur/mechanic) clearly added to, rather than detracted from, the adventure.

The exciting and complex novelty of the earliest motor tours is attested by a welter of publications from the first years of the twentieth century including such delights as the American author Thomas D. Murphy's *British Highways and Byways from a Motor Car: Being a Record of a Five Thousand Mile Tour in England, Scotland and Wales* from 1908 and Edith Wharton's *A Motor-Flight Through France*, also 1908 (discussed in Pearce 2014, 2017). While most of these texts would now be classed generically as travel writing, it is important to register the variety of forms included under that umbrella: from factual tour guides on the one hand to autobiographies at the other – with the majority lying somewhere in between (the personal anecdote being a favoured feature of even the more didactic travel guides). What most of the volumes I have surveyed share, however, is a rationale for how and why touring by car is now to be preferred to all other modes of transportation, these two extracts from Murphy and Wharton being indicative:

> There are three ways in which a tourist may obtain a good idea of Britain during a summer's vacation of three or four months. He may cover most places of interest after the old manner, by railway train. This will have to be supplemented by many and expensive carriage drives if he wishes to see the most beautiful country and many of the most interesting places. As Professor Goldwin Smith says, 'Railways in England do not follow the lines of beauty in very many cases,' and the opportunity of really seeing England from a railway car window is poor indeed. The tourist must keep a constant eye on time-tables, and in many of the more retired places he will have to spend a day when an hour would quite suffice as well could he get away . . .
>
> For a young man or party of young men who are travelling through Britain on a summer's vacation, the bicycle affords an excellent and expeditious method of getting over the country, and offers nearly all the advantages of the motor car, providing the rider is vigorous and expert enough to do the wheeling without fatigue. The motor cycle is still better from this point of view, and many thousands of them are in use on English roads, while cyclists may be counted in their tens of thousands. But the bicycle is out of the question for an extended tour which includes ladies. The amount of impediments which must be carried along, and the many long hills which are encountered on the English roads, will put the cycle out of the question in such cases . . .
>
> The motor car affords an expeditious and reasonably sure means of getting over the country – always ready when you are ready, subservient to your whim to visit some inaccessible old ruin, flying over the broad main highways or winding more cautiously in the unfrequented country byways – and is, withal, a mode of locomotion to which the English people have become tolerant if not positively friendly. (Murphy 1908: 1–11)

The motor-car has restored the romance of travel.

Freeing us from all the compulsions and contacts of the railway, the bondage to fixed hours and the beaten track, the approach to each town through the area of ugliness and desolation created by the railway itself, it has given us back the wonder, the adventure and the novelty which enlivened the way of our posting grandparents. Above all these recovered pleasures must be ranked the delight of taking a town unawares, stealing on it by back ways and unchronicled paths, and surprising it in some intimate aspect of past time, some silhouette hidden for half a century or more by the ugly mask of railway embankments and the iron bulk of a huge station. Then the villages that we missed and yearned for from the windows of the train – the unseen villages have been given back to us! – and nowhere could the importance of the recovery have been more delightfully exemplified than on a May morning in the Pas-de-Calais, as we climbed the long ascent beyond Boulogne on the road to Arras. (Wharton 2008 [1908]: 10)

While both are extracts that invite extensive response, I shall assume that readers of this volume are generally familiar with this signal moment in transport history (including the classed and gendered prejudices discussed in Chapter 1), and focus on their shared vision of motor touring as searching. In common with many other pre-1939 authors and texts, both Murphy and Wharton extol the car's facility to take its passengers down forgotten byways and 'unchronicled paths' and, most importantly, to stop, browse and /or explore at will for as long (or, in Murphy's case, as speedily) as they wish. Together, the texts also pay tribute to the versatility of the car itself in terms of speed (it can 'fly', but it can also *creep*) and its capacity to deliver fresh and idiosyncratic viewpoints and perceptions which are contrasted with the restrictive frames offered by the train window. These authors, then, conjure up a picture of motorists engaged in a search of their tourist objective (typically the 'spirit' and 'character' of a nation, be this Britain, France or elsewhere) as 'seen from the car' (Kennedy 1919b), but also when the car is temporarily stopped in order to enable a stroll to 'some inaccessible old ruin'. This spontaneity, which is regularly contrasted with the tyranny of the 'railway clock' (Kern 2000: 313) – of stopping, starting and searching at will – is also the subject of several advertisements from the period, including the idyllic pastoral picnic promised by the 1919 Sizaire-Berwick (see Figure 2.3). Notable in the text accompanying this advert is the emphasis placed on the motorist's sensory contact with the countryside: 'It puts you in close, intimate touch with the things most desired.'

With the Sizaire-Berwick advertisement we have, of course, jumped forwards a decade from Wharton and Murphy, but the purpose of my opening here has been, in part, to demonstrate the continuity between

Figure 2.3 'Where the rail cannot take you', Sizaire-Berwick advertisement, *Autocar*, 17 September 1919. Courtesy of the National Library of Scotland.

the origins of the discourse and practice of 'motoring-as-searching' and its extension into the mid-twentieth century. Such was the widespread appeal of H. V. Morton's 'In search of . . . ' guides that one could be forgiven for thinking he invented this particular tourist ethos: in fact, as we have already seen, it was well established when he first took to the wheel in the mid-1920s. Further, as the Wharton extract acknowledges, it was a practice that itself looked back to journeys by horse-drawn coach and on foot (and later cycling) before the hegemonic intrusion of the railways. Here it is worth observing, however, that the notion of searching for something new and original was especially paradoxical in the case of Scotland where the main tourist routes have remained broadly the same across three centuries on account of a geographically determined road network.[12] This said, my reading across the first decades of the twentieth century certainly confirms the widely held impression that the 1930s were, indeed, the 'golden age'[13] of motoring-*as-searching*, not only, I would suggest, on account of the better roads, cheaper and more efficient cars and increased leisure time (for those wealthy enough to enjoy it), but because the manner of exploration that I have termed searching (spontaneous, modest, whimsical) had also peaked.

Before moving on to the textual case study for this chapter – a comparative reading of H. V. Morton and Edwin Muir – I would, however, first like to tighten my definition of motoring-as-searching a little more with reference to some British motoring periodicals from the decade 1919–30.

What is striking about the articles on touring from the start of this period is the extent to which they focus on the minutiae of the motoring landscape, sending drivers in search not of the spectacular view or historic landmark but rather the quiet and picturesque 'corner' of England, Scotland or Wales that is sufficiently 'off the beaten track' to give the driver satisfaction in finding it. Their titles alone capture what these pieces are about ('Motoring in West Somerset' (1919), 'A Beautiful Corner of North Wales' (E. J. B. 1919), 'A Motor-tramp in North Wales' (1919), 'Late Autumn Touring' (Phillip 1919)), and the emphasis on slow, probing progress through the byways and, indeed, 'backwaters' of Britain could hardly be further from the thrill-seeking that elsewhere characterises driving during this period (see Chapter 3). As the author of 'Motoring in West Somerset' observes: 'It is the touring motorist who prefers to go slowly and enjoy the views by the way that will be most pleased with West Somerset, for even when one knows them well there are few roads along which one is glad to hurry at top speed' (1919: 101).

Scanning the same periodicals across the ensuing decade, meanwhile, it is clear that although this notion of savouring the British countryside at a slow speed and of stopping to explore places of interest 'by the way' had not entirely disappeared, it was now competing with new models of motor touring where the emphasis is less on a detailed exploration of the countryside and its heritage than on 'taking in' as much of the region's character as possible. Hence we have the 1929 *Autocar* article, 'Motoring in Arran' – which warns prospective visitors to the island that '[d]istance is of the least consideration in Arran, and speed would be a slight on its generous resources. One must make one's way leisurely that the interest, spread lavishly to right and left, be not overlooked . . .' (1929: 1000) – juxtaposed with an amusing series of articles entitled 'Sightseeing in a Hurry'. Part II of the latter advises readers on how to '[Visit] as Much as Possible of Central Europe in a Limited Space and Time' (Davis 1929: 104–6). However, as Raymond Williams (1977) has shown, it is in the nature of social and cultural change for 'residual', 'dominant' and 'emergent' ideologies to coexist and driving-as-searching clearly remained a dominant discourse throughout the 1930s and 1940s, hence the popularity of H. V. Morton's formidable series of books that recognised the commercial value of using the word 'search' in their titles. At the same time, quietly creeping around country lanes was clearly no longer everyone's preference, and the periodicals mark a gradual subjugation of the discourse, especially when domestic holidays resumed after the Second World War.[14]

No mention has been made in the preceding discussion of what the 'searching' ethos meant in terms of driver-consciousness. While this will be central to my discussion in the case study that follows, it would be fair to say that the majority of the periodical articles on touring from this period tend not to reference the driving 'experience' as such. Rather than extolling the landscape as 'seen from the car', the assumption in many of these pieces appears to be that the exploration proper – as we saw in the Sizaire-Berwick advertisement (Figure 2.3) – will begin only once we 'dismount' from our vehicles, an objective made explicit in 'A Motor-tramp Through Wales' (1919) where the author describes how:

> [N]ext morning we shouldered our knapsacks and set forth on our first tramp across the mountains of Capel Curig by way of the lovely ravine that leads up to Llyn Crafnant, we forgot our trouble – ay, we even forgot the dear old car down there . . . as we watched the fleeting wisps of cloud sliding lazily across the higher slopes of hills, and our nostrils were filled with the pungent odour of the mountain firs. (1919: 36)

Such disregard for the vehicle that has enabled the salubrious activities that ensue is, indeed, a world away from the 'motoring for motoring's sake' to be explored in the subsequent chapters and marks a distinctive and paradoxical moment in the history of driving. While it is clear that many drivers '(dis)regard' their cars in a similar way today, it is perhaps surprising to observe that that this was also the case when owning a car was so much more of a privilege. Interestingly, both Morton and Muir fluctuate in this regard: sometimes the car is an integral part of the search; sometimes, as in the previous extract, it is simply a means to an end.

In search of Scotland with H. V. Morton and Edwin Muir

The little car

In his three-part television series on Scottish writers,[15] Andrew Marr described Edwin Muir – who featured in his programme on Hugh MacDiarmid (23 August 2014) – as 'a terrible driver'. I have no idea what sources Marr was basing his observation on, but it is certainly possible to infer from their books – *In Search of Scotland* (1929) and *Scottish Journey* (1935) – that neither H. V. Morton nor Edwin Muir was especially interested in cutting a dash as a motorist. Instead, both authors paint a portrait of themselves and their cars that is modest, tentative and, at times, vulnerable: adjectives that are unlikely to be associated with any motor manufacturer's promotion of drivers and driving today. Here, for example, is Morton's memorable third-person account of his early morning departure from London 'in search of Scotland':

> The early sunlight flung those strange shadows which are known only to milkmen. Everything looked snug and languid, and here was a man in a small car isolated by an adventure from his recumbent fellows going on alone into Scotland.
>   What would he find there? What new friends would he make? What new songs would he sing? Over what graves would he stand a moment in thought? . . .
>   There was an early start.
>   Newcastle.
>   And a road going on and on: the road into Scotland. (Morton 2008 [1929]: 1–2)

In striking contrast to the many other early twentieth-century accounts of motorists enjoying the power-buzz of streaming out of London via the Great North Road (Hissey 1902; Maclehouse 1930; Bowen 2006 [1932]; Struther 1989 [1939]), Morton chooses this distinctive 'bird's eye' perspective to emphasise the 'littleness' of the man and his car. This, of course, paradoxically intensifies the enormity of the adventure:

will this man and his small car really make it all the way to Scotland? What risks is he exposing himself to? What sensations? From page one, then, the emphasis is on the functionality and durability the car (in Morton's case, a Bullnose Morris) rather than its speed and power, the further implication being that by 1929 significant motoring adventures (i.e. round trips in excess of a thousand miles) were within the reach of 'ordinary' men and women – or, at least, those of them who *dared*.

Muir's vehicle, meanwhile, was even more modest than Morton's, being thirteen years old at the time he undertook his 'Scottish Journey'. Leant to him by a friend, Muir's car, a Standard 12, refused to travel at anything above 30mph: a speed constraint that I reflect upon positively in the next section:

> I left Edinburgh on a bright July Sunday in a 1921 Standard car. It had been given to me for nothing by an old friend, with the guarantee that if it could be made to start it would keep going. Its age and appearance excited a good deal of interest at the petrol stations where I stopped, but I found it skittered along the roads quite briskly, except for a trick of dancing like a high-spirited colt when I forced it to do over thirty-five miles per hour. At thirty, it produced a calm, loud snore, which had a pleasantly lulling effect in the windless bright weather. (Muir 1996 [1935]: 40)

However, towards the end of his tour (Ullapool, to be precise) the car develops a problem with its plugs which means that the remainder of Muir's journey (to Thurso – where he will take the boat for Orkney – his final destination) becomes a feat of extreme patience and endurance for the driver:

> The car went more and more slowly, seemed to waver for a moment and stopped. I was only two-thirds up the hill, hanging precariously at what seemed to me an angle of forty-five degrees. I started the engine again, speeded it up until it roared, slipped the clutch into first gear, jerked the car up a few yards, and then rested it. In this way, by a series of jerks, I got the car to the top, hoping this was the worst hill I would have to climb . . . As it was I was doomed to jerk myself up all the hill roads of the western and northern Highlands from Ullapool to Tongue, and sweat and curse amongst the strangest and most magnificent scenery . . . and this is all I intend to say about my troubles with the car. They filled my mind in the most curious way, nevertheless, creating a sort of little private Hell from which I looked out like Dives on the heavenly beauty of the north-western Highland mountains. (Muir 1996: 210–11)

Not only does this extract bring the experience of transporting oneself in an ailing car viscerally – and cognitively – alive, but it also echoes my own abortive road trip to the 'Far North' of Scotland in July 2012.

Like Muir's, my car developed an engine fault on the way to Ullapool but – in contrast to Muir's experience – the local garage would not even attempt to repair it because they lacked the necessary computer-analysis equipment. Consequently, my car, my dog and I were sent back to the VW garage in Inverness on a transporter. I have discussed this dispiriting, if amusing, end to my own 'Scottish Journey' elsewhere (Pearce 2013), but the further point I would draw out here is the profound shift in our relationship to the car. For Muir and the mechanics who assisted him, reaching his destination was all that really mattered – even if this meant the driver had to endure a 'private hell' along the way; in my case, nothing less than a fully functioning car was recognised as a permissible means of transport even though, as was later revealed, the fault was merely electrical and there would have been no risk at all in my completing the trip. This suggests that not only have we have gone backwards in automotive design – by manufacturing vehicles that are no longer repairable – but also that we have lost touch with the functionality of driving. In the spirit of some of the more basic electric vehicles that have recently come onto the market such as the Renault Twizy (discussed below), it is useful to remind ourselves that Edwin Muir's 'little car' was only a day behind schedule in reaching its destination; unrecognisably different from one another in so many ways, the distance between Muir's 1921 Standard and a contemporary car in terms of simple functionality – i.e. getting us there – is, in fact, minimal.

Such a utilitarian approach to motoring does not, however, undermine the car's value as a unique way of seeing the world. In the Preface to *In Search of Scotland*, Morton, like so many of his motoring predecessors, attempts to specify all that is distinctive about car travel, making particular links between motor tourists such as himself and pioneering travel writers like Thomas Pennant, James Boswell and Sir James Carr who surveyed Scotland's highways and, more particularly, *byways*, either on foot or by horse and carriage (Morton 2008: x–xi). At the end of this preamble Morton also observes that 'this is not primarily a book about Scotland: it is *an account of a journey through Scotland*' (Morton 2008: x–xi (my italics)), which, I would suggest, distinguishes it markedly from his earlier *In Search of England* (2013 [1927]). While the latter is manifestly about the places visited (as per the chapter headings), *In Search of Scotland* reflects self-consciously upon the process of journeying and, even though the car itself is seldom mentioned, its role is keeping the author moving through the landscape is very evident.

Muir also – and notwithstanding the challenging end to his journey – appears to have related to his modest Standard 12 with a mixture of affection and disregard. It is striking, for example, that, even when it fails, the car is referred to as 'little': 'for the first time since I had begun my journey the little car refused to act' (Muir 1996: 190). The use of this diminutive also points to the anthropomorphism associated with car ownership in the early years of the twentieth-century, parodied in stories such as Nigel Balchin's 'The Enthusiast' (Balchin 1959) in which the protagonist, Fergus Drake, is so 'in love' with his elderly but distinguished pre-First World War vehicle that he forsakes wife and home in order to keep 'her' even when he can no longer afford the petrol to go anywhere. While neither Muir nor Morton care about their motors quite this deeply, their accounts sometimes echo these earlier discourses in which the animate being of the car's predecessor, the horse, lives on. The 'little cars' of the 1920s and 1930s were the sort of vehicles that needed to be coaxed not bullied and, even if the aspiration was that cars would ultimately become so functional and reliable that they could be taken for granted, an element of wonder and gratitude still lingered on in the manner of which they are spoken. As is captured in the iconic motoring posters from this period (many sponsored by the oil and tyre companies),[16] the fact that a small metal box on wheels could transport its drivers and passengers to what were, then, perceptibly different worlds was a miracle of sorts.

As seen from the car

Notwithstanding the fact that their cars are mentioned relatively infrequently, both Morton's and Muir's texts abound with vivid descriptions of the world as 'seen from the car' (Kennedy 1919b). Like Bart Kennedy (see Chapter 1), Morton and Muir are writers whose apprehension of the perceptual realm has been demonstrably transformed through their mobilised relationship to it.

One of Morton's most sustained and memorable representations of mobilised perception is the account of his drive through Glenshee in the Grampians. In contrast to those descriptions (discussed below) which are very evidently dependent upon popular discourses and /or a highly conventional visual schema (e.g. 'the picture-postcard Highlands', the 'mythical Borders') – the account of this particular drive is very immediate and, in painterly terms, impressionistic:

> The road runs on between mountains. Rowanberries are reddening, the mountain ash flings out sprays of leaves soon to be the colour of blood, but now just thinly veined with pink. Vast clouds sail overhead sending their shadows racing over the moorlands, and every mile leads into a deeper desolation . . . There is now no sound but the bleating of sheep and the rush

of water down the valley and the tinkle of some small burn falling from the hills. (Morton 2008: 143–4)

What is especially notable here, and what we will see again in Muir's writing, is the way in which the landscape as seen from the car itself becomes mobilised. This is, of course, an accurate impression of exactly what does appear to happen when we move at sufficient speed through a landscape (at least with respect to the views glimpsed from our side windows).[17] As a consequence, every phenomenon as seen from the car is infused with new vitality and captured on paper, by Morton, with a poetic sequence of adjectives : the road 'runs', the rowan tree 'flings' its leaves, the clouds 'sail' and their shadows 'race'. Two sentences later, however, we observe that it is Morton and his car that are really the ones doing the moving: 'but, as the valley narrows to a grim gorge, these are left behind' (p. 143). In singular contrast to Morton's more 'conventional' (in every sense) landscape descriptions, this extract therefore exemplifies how (auto)mobility defamiliarises the landscape (see Chapter 1) and productively 'disturbs' the vision (Mullarkey 1999: 50). Despite the fact that Morton's Bullnose Morris was almost certainly travelling at no more than 30mph, this was still sufficient speed to breathe new life into the gestalt of the 'Scottish Highlands'.

It is striking, perhaps even a little ironic, that Muir's text – which distinguishes itself from Morton's by having no 'tourist guide' pretensions ('I should warn the reader, too, that this is not a survey of Scotland but a bundle of impressions' (Muir 1996: 4)); 'I am not going to describe that beautiful country, so often described already . . .' (Muir 1996: 188) – generally captures the vibrancy of the landscape through which he passes much more effectively. Indeed, from the very first page of *Scottish Journey* we see that this 'search' for a nation and its people – made from the steering wheel of a car – will take the form something more akin to film than literature:

> The first thought of writing this book came to me two years ago, one evening after I had driven through the mining district of Lanarkshire. The journey took me through Hamilton, Airdrie and Motherwell. It was a warm, overcast summer day; groups of idle, sullen-looking young men stood at the street corners; smaller groups were wandering among the blue-black ranges of pit-dumps which in that region are the substitute for nature; the houses looked empty and unemployed like their tenants; and the road along which the car stumbled was pitted and rent, as if it had recently been under shell-fire. Everything had the look of a Sunday that had lasted for many years . . .
> This was the most impressive scene I saw in Scotland . . . (Muir 1996: 1)

What we are offered here, though in poignantly altered form to Morton's, is another landscape mobilised by the car which passes through it. However, in contrast to Morton's living landscape, the people and places seen from Muir's car appear resolutely fixed, lifeless and frozen in time. This does nothing to detract from the filmic nature of the perception, however: for Muir – here, as throughout the text – the subject(s) of his discourse unreel like a canister of documentary film. The things 'seen from the car' are listed in the text, and with an attention that is at once vivid and fleeting.[18] In the short time it takes him to drive through these villages, Muir is able to grasp the nature and extent of the deprivation with great intensity even though 'what' he is seeing is a moving image that, in terms the mechanisms of perception/cognition, owes more to our engagement with a cinema screen than with the material world.

The experience of driving through the Lanarkshire mining villages which inspired Muir's *Scottish Journey* is reproduced and intensified on the tour itself in his drive from Glasgow through to Stirling. One of the many interesting features of this description is that, although it takes in many towns and villages and covers many miles, it clearly coheres in Muir's mind as a single 'driving-event' (see Chapter 1): so much so, indeed, that he struggles to shake it off even once returned to the 'solid, stylish country town air' of Stirling:

> As I neared Stirling I could see on my right a cloud of dense darkness, which showed where Falkirk lay round its furnaces. I decided that I had had enough of this ravaged country, and as I drove into Stirling with its bright, solid, stylish country town air, I felt as if I had been wandering in a strange world and was back in the Scotland I knew . . . From Stirling Castle one can get a more impressive prospect than from any other castle I have seen in Scotland. The Lowlands stretch behind you; the Highlands rise before you . . . The sight almost dazed me after the sights I had seen; and it seemed strange that running streams should be clear and grass green. (Muir 1996: 177–8)

As with his earlier description of the Lanarkshire villages, what strikes the reader here is the way in which Muir's apprehension of the landscape through which he passes is both sharply observed and forensically detached on account of the fact that – from the wheel of his car – he is, in fact, passing over it with all the indifference of a camera lens. His use of the word 'nightmare' in the preceding paragraph ('The towns themselves . . . were like villages on a nightmare scale' (Muir 1996: 168) is especially indicative in this regard; although deployed as an adjective to describe the ugly industrial towns, the concept also captures the quality of his own perception: mobile, panoptic and disturbingly surreal – especially when juxtaposed with the lives of the 'real' men and women who are destined to live all their lives in houses that appear to Muir as little more than ruins (Muir 1996: 169). Parallels with contemporary television footage of devastated war zones spring to mind.

Muir's descriptions of this part of his journey owe their vividness, in part, to their focus not only what he sees, but also what he tastes and smells. As well as being a potent historical reminder of what travelling in an open-topped car would have meant at this time, Muir's attention to these other senses – 'the air itself had a synthetic taste, the taste of a food substitute' (Muir 1996: 168) – exposes an interesting tension between his visual relationship to the landscape and this multi-sensory one. Whereas mobility – Muir's 'rapid' transit through the 'nightmare' towns and villages – may be seen to remove and protect the driver from his visual apprehension of the landscape, the smells *cling* – and function as a reminder that, were he to stop the car and get out, the fleeting image would become an intrusive material reality. Morton, by contrast, uses the multi-sensory experience afforded by his open-topped car not to shock, but to delight, as seen in this account of his passage across the Scottish Border:

> Each footfall crushes from the wet moorland the rich smell of autumn. From the wind, the weather, the peat water, the line of hill against hill, the bleating of sheep, the drone of insects in the heather, the trilling of larks, and the utter solitude of earth and sky is distilled a powerful emotion that soothes while it excites me; for behind this invisible world is a an invisible but immortal host. I have not read my Border balladry in vain. (Morton 2008: 3)

Recognising the power of the senses in bringing this legendary landscape alive for his readers, Morton effects an impromptu halt and wanders a little way onto the heath, before leaping back into the driver's seat and setting forth again (Morton 2008: 6–7), thus evidencing the fully embodied pleasures of early motor touring.

Notwithstanding the grimness of his account of Scotland's Central Belt at the time of the depression – nor his determination (quoted earlier) to eschew 'beautiful descriptions' – Muir's text also features some of the most arresting accounts of Highland scenery from this period that I have encountered. For example:

> The thing that impressed me most in the Highlands on my first day's run . . . was a thing which is common no doubt to all wild and solitary scenery: that is, the added value which every natural object acquires from one's consciousness that it has not been touched by the human will. The larch woods, the streams, all of them active here because of the slant at which they run, the little mounds of turf: all have an exhilarating freshness which is absent from more cultivated places, and seemed to exist completely in themselves, as if for their own end . . . The scent of birch and the light tinkle of streams filled

the air all the forenoon, making it something different from ordinary air, something along with which one inhaled the fine essence of the free things growing round them: there was in it also a tincture of rock. (Muir 1996: 187–8)

The contrast with this glorious mountain 'freshness' and the 'synthetic taste' of the Central Belt could not, of course, be more stark, but what is of particular interest from a phenomenological point of view is the way in which Muir's steady progress through this 'hundred square miles of solitary nature' (Muir 1996: 187) at no more than 30mph causes one sensory horizon to succeed another in rapid succession and to culminate in an improbable mix of birch, ozone and 'a tincture of rock'. Muir's reflection also resonates with the vocabulary of the phenomenologists cited in Chapter 1, not least vis-à-vis the way in which the phenomena he bears witness to appear to impress their 'intentionality' (see Chapter 1 note 24) upon him with an agency that mirrors their natural 'activity'. Also implicit in the analysis is a recognition that the pristine nature of the landscape through which he passes depends, in part, upon the uncontaminated nature of his own perception; in the same way that the plants and animals have freed themselves from 'the human will', so does he find himself in a position to describe the natural world 'exactly in the manner of its appearing' (Moran and Mooney 2002: 2). Further, although no mention is made of the 'little car' in any of this, the implicit reference to his own mobility – through the sequence of phenomena he lists – reminds us that he is not a stationary observer.

Scotland revealed

While both Morton's and Muir's texts feature compelling instances of the driving-event giving rise to fresh and 'unprejudiced' (Moran and Mooney 2002: 2) descriptions of the Scottish landscape, there is a marked – and, indeed, instructive – difference to be drawn between Morton's occasional moments of 'intuition' (Moran and Mooney 2002: 2) and Muir's sustained and self-conscious attention to the world as 'seen from the car' which – especially in the latter part of *Scottish Journey* – give rise to reflections that are implicitly phenomenological in their method. This includes, in the more philosophical reveries, a determination to discover the 'essential structures' of the phenomena and events he encounters, the transcendental (indeed, sometimes overtly mystical) search for which is reminiscent of Husserl's 'reduction' (see note 22 to Chapter 1).

Although working in a very different genre and register to Muir – and

much more obviously bound by discourse and schema – Morton nevertheless expresses awareness of the importance of travelling with open
eyes. In the Preface to *In Search of Scotland*, for example, he observes:
'The *less* a man knows at the start of such a journey as mine the better.
All he needs is restless curiosity' (Morton 2008: xi (my italics)). The
moment his journey begins, however – or, at least, the moment he starts
to record it – Morton demonstrates just how hard it is to hold on to
the principle of the open and enquiring mind. His account of crossing
the border into Scotland (quoted in part above), which groans with
national/cultural stereotypes, is a case in point:

> This is the Border.
> Over it is the loneliness of the sea; the rise and fall of its hills are as the
> sweep of frozen billows, and the eye, like that of the sailor, searches the soli-
> tude for a sign of humanity: a shepherd with his flocks, a farmer in his field,
> or, best of all, a little white house with a curl of smoke from its chimneys
> which suggests the presence of the three advance-guards of civilization: a
> woman, a fire, and children.
> As I go on I feel that every bend will bring me face to face with the prom-
> ised land. A wilderness cannot continue forever . . . So it seems to me as I
> mount hills and descend into valleys, cross streams and skirt the shoulders of
> hills, that I can feel Scotland around the next corner. (Morton 2008: 2)

Mobile as Morton's description manifestly is (the phrase 'as I go on'
reminds us that he is gliding through this rapturous landscape in his
Bullnose Morris), it records perceptions – and even the anticipation of
perceptions – that are taken straight from the pages of guide books,
histories and the poetry of Robert Burns. Doubtless Morton *is* seeing
the billowing hills of heather, but so caught up is he in the history,
mythology and schema of the land through which he passes that he
inadvertently – and, one cannot help but observe, indicatively – 'misses'
both the village of Otterburn and the fact that he has already crossed the
border (Morton 2008: 3–4).

Later chapters, meanwhile, demonstrate a fascinating tension between
Morton's recourse to the generic/schematic and the occasional compulsion to record the 'truth' of what he sees. The record of his visit to
Glencoe is exemplary in this regard, on account of his struggle to recon-
cile what he 'really' sees on this particular visit with what he thinks he
ought to record on account of the burden of history and legend associated with the glen:

> I went into this mountain pass ready, even anxious, to shudder at it. But, alas,
> the sun was shining! . . . Glencoe in sunlight does not make a man shudder
> because it is beautiful. It rather encourages him to sit down and look at it for

a long time as you sit down in the sand and look at the Sphinx, wondering what he – for the Sphinx is masculine – can see in the sky. Perhaps it is God. Glencoe has the same expression.

The worst road in Scotland winds its way through the solitude. The iron-grey mountains fret the sky on either hand. Half the pass is in sunlight; half in cold shadow. Tough grass and soggy bogland fill the narrow valley. There is no sound but the running of icy water, brown with peat; no movement but the wind in the long grass and the wheeling of some sinister bird high over the hills.

The volcanic heights are gashed by sharp gullies, broadening as they descend, in which water has in the course of centuries found its way to the valley. In some of these gashes trees try to hide from the wind like men sheltering. Mostly there are great slashes in the rock, as if giants had sharpened their swords on the hills . . .

The sun is covered by a cloud. The light dies in Glencoe as suddenly as a light is switched off in a room. The pass has changed colour. It is grey and hopeless. Now you can see why Macaulay called it the 'Valley of the Shadow'. (Morton 2008: 266–7)

Arriving in Glencoe in bright sunshine, Morton is, at first, stymied by the fact that the landscape fails to glower at him in the proverbial manner. By the early twentieth century the touristic discourses surrounding Glencoe were so entrenched that they defied the visitor – and certainly the professional travel writer – to find anything other than doom and gloom in the village and its environs. Victorian and Edwardian photographs capture the centuries-laden power of these visitor expectations perfectly with captions like 'The Scene of the Massacre' (Hutton 2011: 19) and, whether transported there by stagecoach or motor charabanc (many photographs of both still exist), we catch glimpses of groups of tourists heading off down the village street to the 'Massacre Monument' (see Figure 2.1) as they still do today. As noted above, Morton's readiness to embrace and reproduce this discourse is nevertheless thrown off-guard by the good weather, and we witness the description stutter and digress before – as he begins his drive through the Pass – he discovers geological features 'savage' enough to elicit his duty as a travel writer. My impression, indeed, having read many scores of such accounts of rides and drives through Glencoe, is that a portrait of the glen any less 'savage' than the one that Morton presents us with here would have been unacceptable to his readership.

Elsewhere in the text, however, there are moments when the driving-event delivers spectacles and sensations grand and unexpected enough to completely rip the controlling schema apart. This is especially well-illustrated in Morton's account of his drive to Blairgowrie through Glenshee. Immediately following the extract quoted in the previous section of this chapter, Morton records his experience of encountering a plethora of rainbows, and the sight appears to have induced a moment of true epiphany:

> Sunlight follows rain and I dive into a glen of rainbows. Never have I seen so many rainbows. They arch themselves, as if trying to bridge the glen, they come into frail splendour over the heads of hills and fall, vibrating with brief life, into the distant fields. I see one that ends in a white house! It pours itself over the chimneys is a broad band of purple, yellow, and blue, like watered silk . . .
>
> A rainbow mightier than the rest almost brings me to death at the Devil's Elbow – a hair-raising hairpin of a bend – and now the road shoots up sky-wards, rising as sharply as 1 in 8 and 1 in 12, and I reach the summit of the highest road in Great Britain; and here I draw a breath and stop, 2,199 feet about sea-level . . .
>
> A wild sense of exhilaration comes to me. I feel a violent desire to run, to sing, or – what a queer thought? – I feel that had I a sword I could give a good account of myself up here among these savage peaks. (Morton 2008: 144–5)

How different, I would suggest, is the description of *this* 'white house' to the cartoon-cottages of Morton's imagination as he crosses the Borders; while there he was waiting to discover something that would match his pre-existing schema, here his senses are stunned by the manifestation of something he did not expect. The participating role of the car in all this is, moreover, crucial, since what enables Morton to see 'so many rainbows' is evidently the fact that he is observing *one* from a moving viewpoint. The fact that the 'mightiest of all' nearly brings about his death has great ironic potential in this regard since, had he not been driving his car into the hairpin bend at this moment, the rainbow in question would not have existed. Scientific ignorance aside, this is nevertheless a superb example of how a moving vehicle can produce a 'shock of disturbance' (Mullarkey 1999: 50) powerful enough to make even the most redoubtable old 'hack' see the world with fresh eyes.

Muir's *Scottish Journey* is often talked of as a negative and somewhat depressing book whose most obvious points of literary reference are J. B. Priestley's *English Journey* (1984 [1934]) and George Orwell's *The Road to Wigan Pier* (2002 [1937]). As well as sharing with these texts its 'documentary' approach to the social consequences of the depression, *Scottish Journey* is also remembered as one of the first critiques of Scottish Independence: a movement that was just coming into being at this time and with which Muir was briefly involved as a result of his friendship with Alistair Grieve (Hugh MacDiarmid) (Muir 1996: xxii).[19] However, by engaging with *Scottish Journey* specifically in terms of its representation of the nation as 'seen from a car', I would – in contrast to his editor, Henry Smout (see note 19) – pronounce it a work that is acutely sensitive to the distinctive character of the Scottish landscape and passionately committed to the future of its culture and its people. In particular, I wish to argue that the perceived 'fragmentation' of place and community that undeniably disturbed Muir was a direct consequence of his tour being by motor car. Conceptually astute in other ways, Muir nevertheless failed to grasp that his means of touring the country – not only by car, but also episodically[20] – would inevitably increase his sense of its *dis*unity and cause him to be unduly pessimistic about the extent to which nations can embrace very different types of community and culture. This said, what *I* discover in Muir's text is a Scotland of extraordinary beauty, diversity and hence surprise – the latter being a crucial ingredient in explaining why, as a nation, it continues to demonstrate such an imaginative hold on both residents and visitors alike. It sometimes seems, indeed, as if Scotland's turbulent geological past – creating such an incredible variety of highland, lowland and island terrains – is also emblematic of its social and cultural diversity and the complex relationship of part to whole. This provocative conjunction – between ways of seeing the physical landscape and ways of knowing the political nation – is certainly implicit in several of Muir's own philosophical musings and emerges as an explicit statement as he nears his journey's end.

Before we reach that endpoint, however, it is first necessary that we investigate further Muir's practice of something approaching a 'phenomenological method' and the role his driver's-eye view of the world plays in this. In the earlier discussion of Muir's mobilised perception of the landscape I provided an example of how 'wild nature' impressed itself upon him with great freshness and intensity, but what distinguishes the quality of his later reflections – as noted above – is a fascination with their essential structures. Further, the fact that such moments of revelation are often associated with *specific* driving-events – i.e. a particular stretch of journey – recalls the earlier discussion of Virginia Woolf's 'Evening Over Sussex' (1942) (see Chapter 1) and the consolidating role that a car journey can play in realising and fixing a moment of phenomenological insight. The following extract – from Muir's account of a thunderstorm while journeying from Edinburgh to the Cairngorms – is a powerful illustration of this process:

> When I stepped into my car the sky had darkened again and the air in my face was cool and wet. The mountains had shrunk, and their sides were inky-blue against the greyish-blue of the thunder clouds. Presently large drops began to fall, and I could hear a faint rumble of thunder behind the wall of hills. I drove on for a little, enjoying the rain in my face. Then with a long leap the thunder jumped the hills and seemed to be all around me. The rain beat down

as if shot from the clouds in liquid bullets which fell with such force that they rebounded several inches from the road. I stopped the car, got out, and hurriedly pushed forward and secured the hood . . . During my short stop a score of cars seemed to have passed me, racing at top speed to get out of the thunder zone. I had not noticed more than three or four on the whole route up to then; but now the road seemed to be alive, and the black glistening shapes rushing past one after another reminded me of a furious host of cockroaches scuttling away from some disturbance . . . Suddenly the storm was over and I was standing in a thin gentle rain, which did not seem so much to fall as to settle in small feathery drops. The air was saturated with odours that rose all around in such a thick cloud that I felt I could almost touch it. The car stood contentedly by the side of the road. I got in, somewhat drenched, and pressed the self-starter. The engine responded at once. (Muir 1996: 189–91)

As well as begging comparison with Morton's 'rainbow' epiphany, the Muir extract also brings to mind Morton's own account of a thunder-storm on his drive across Rannoch Moor. Like Muir, Morton presents himself as being rocked to the core by the violence of the unexpected occurrence and he responds with similar exhilaration and awe (Morton 2008: 274). Apart from the somewhat 'staged' quality of Morton's nar-rative, what Muir's description features that is lacking in Morton's is, first, a detailed account of the role the car plays in the episode (as expos-ing, sheltering, failing and ultimately rescuing its driver) and, second, a profound sensitivity to the ways in which the storm has altered both his perception of the phenomena he beholds and *their* 'intentionality' (see note 24, Chapter 1). Both here and in the passage detailing the aftermath of the storm (pp. 90–1), Muir records his fascination with the way in which distant mountains shape, shift and reshape themselves as the rain moves in and then clears; as well as changing colour, they first 'shrink' and then 'sink' before re-emerging 'soft and distinct' (Muir 1996: 191). The fact that 'they' rather than 'he' are presented as the agents of this change, meanwhile, may be seen as exemplary of a phenomenologi-cal method which insists that we attend patiently to the way in which phenomena *reveal themselves* – and their essence – to us. Indeed, the passage quoted presents us with a portrait of Muir as a traveller who is, quite literally, as prepared to expose himself to the phenomenologi-cal world as to the elements in order that he understand it on its own terms. As may be seen, all his senses are fully engaged in this process to the point of synaesthesia – 'The air was saturated with odours that rose all round in such a thick cloud that I felt I could almost touch it' – and his 'poetic imagination' (Bachelard 1971)[21] activated in order to capture and make sense of the unfamiliar images that present themselves to him, such as the passing cars whose 'black glistening shapes' rush past him like 'a furious host of cockroaches'.

Here, as elsewhere, the attention with which Muir details and reflects upon his driving-event grants it a significance that is not only philosophical but also spiritually cathartic: after fear, thrill and a radical defamiliarisation of the phenomenological world, Muir – notably by means of his car – is restored to the benevolent protection of the fir woods which 'enclose [him] on both sides' (Muir 1996: 191). This is a driving-event, then, which has offered a glimpse into the 'essential structures' (see note 22 to Chapter 1) of the phenomenological world so extraordinary that, during its course, the driver, too, has been 'shrunk' like the mountains, 'stretched' like the road and finally, if temporarily, 'stilled' like the forest.

It is, however, during the last few days of his tour of Scotland that we see Muir begin to take stock of his journey as a whole as well as its constituent driving-events. Because of this supreme effort to pull together his impressions of Scotland (a combination of perceptions, reflections and philosophical and political analysis) at the journey's end, it may indeed be argued that *Scottish Journey* has more in common with the road trip genre than the travelogue it is sometimes mistaken for (see discussion in Chapter 3). At the same time, this move towards an integrated vision of his travels may be seen to sit uncomfortably with the 'phenomenological method' practised in the earlier chapters of the book. Rather than wait patiently for the desolate fastness of Sutherland to reveal itself to him in all its unique splendour, Muir – for the first time – appears to grow impatient (in his desire to get to Orkney, in his quest to finish the book) and allows his publisher's brief to overshadow (at times, quite literally) his perception of the people and places he encounters:

> I started next morning quite early, for I had made up my mind to be at Scrabster next day in time to catch the boat to Orkney . . . For most of the forenoon I found to my surprise that the going was not very difficult; cool, misty weather had set in, and the engine did not get so hot as usual; the road, having mounted steadily for a while, wound in and out around little broken hills among which were scattered a confusion of small lochs, all black and somewhat sinister-looking; there was no sign of a dwelling, nor of life of any kind, during all this stretch . . . I let the car roll of itself down the long descent, giving it a needed rest, and at the foot, in a desolation of sand-dunes, perceived a large, white and polished hotel a little distance from the road. It seemed to have no right to be there . . . (Muir 1996: 216–17)

Muir's *unheimlich* response not only to the landscape, but also the dwellings and communities of the Far North, is a measure of the extent to which this landscape disturbs him, both cognitively and affectively. As all those who have driven through these vast barren and watery lands will be aware, the sense of human insignificance *is* humbling (even, and perhaps especially, when encountering attempts at settlement – be this a crofter's ruin or a 'white and polished hotel'), and the mention of Muir's car suggests that it has become important company during the long stretches of 'nothing else'. However, instead of 'travelling in tandem with the phenomenon' (Marion 2002, cited in Chapter 1) until he properly understands it, Muir appears to let his impatience get the better of him, and this unsettling and dispiriting final driving-event casts its shadow over his journey as a whole. That his retrospective consolidating vision is thus one of *dis*unity – Scotland is perceived to be a nation of irreconcilable differences – is therefore not surprising.

It is in the penultimate chapter of *Scottish Journey* – during the account of his first sight of Orkney – that Muir first begins to set out this pessimistic political conclusion. Significantly, he turns to the incongruities of visual perspective – symbolised by the fact that he does not, at first, recognise Hoy – to argue for the seemingly irreconcilable social and cultural differences within his nation, and the fact that no one person can occupy two places, or lifestyles, at once:

> As I left Durness I saw a round hill rising out of the sea to the far north-east, whose shape seemed somehow familiar to me . . . and because I knew the Orkneys, having lived in them during my childhood, I had a sense stronger than ever before of the double aspect of everything, and realised that if it had been possible for me to live in two places at once, in Durness, say, and my father's farm in Orkney, my life there would have seemed to one part of me merely a dream in the shadow of that round hill rising from the sea. This thought disturbed me, for it seemed to point to a sort of ultimate isolation of every human being, an isolation produced by the mere workings of time and space, which therefore no ideal state or Utopia could ever reform away. (Muir 1996: 217–18)

What Muir's account of this epiphany fails to bring to consciousness, however, is the role of the car in this process of revelation. If we pause to consider the logistics of the event, it becomes clear that Hoy – rather like Morton's rainbow – is rendered unfamiliar partly because it comes into view from a *moving* vehicle. As most of us are aware, driving around any large fixed point, such as a mountain, will cause it to assume radically different shapes and forms in the course of our circumnavigation. Thus, although Muir's subsequent meditation focuses on Hoy as a fixed point in the landscape, it was undoubtedly his own mobile viewpoint that added to its perceived strangeness and stimulated his ensuing cognitive and affective discomfort.

As pre-empted by the concluding sentence of the previous extract, such thinking leads Muir to the conviction that Scotland and its people can never be thought of as a meaningful unity:

From this indistinct and yet vivid image I tried to extract a picture of Scotland as an entity, but I did not succeed: I could envisage the world in these terms, though I had seen very little of it; I could see people everywhere, in the plains of China, the jungles of India, the villages of England . . . following out the law of their being and of being itself, in isolation from the rest of their fellow-men and in inner-harmony with them; but I could not think of any modification of the law of being that fitted Scotland and Scotland alone, any Scottish way of life that would embrace all the ways of life that I had observed from the time I had left Edinburgh for the Borders, the Borders for Glasgow, and Glasgow for the Highlands. (Muir 1996: 224–5)

My personal response to the philosophical and political defeatism of this conclusion is that Muir has 'got it wrong', in part because he has failed to recognise the extent to which his means of travel – the car – has contributed to his impression of Scotland as a disunited nation. Although he acknowledges that it was the car's ability to cover large distances in the course of a single day that has caused him to be 'pleasantly confused' by the (im)possibility of existing in two places at the same time ('this double sensation of time was confusing yet pleasant, and evoked in my imagination an unusually vivid sense of the simultaneity of the many lives and towns and landscapes scattered over the world . . .' (Muir 1996: 224), he nevertheless fails to recognise the way which driving *as an event* – and, in the case of a long journey, *as a sequence of discrete events* – will have had on his overall impression of Scotland when it comes, as here, to the 'summing up'. Had Muir, instead, attempted a 'flying tour' of Scotland in a single day (in the manner of Alec Maclehouse's (1930) drive from London to Edinburgh), his apprehension would arguably have been more inclined to a vision of national unity. Instead, Muir undertook his journey in several stages over a period of several months (see note 20). As a consequence, it is unsurprising that Muir was left with a fragmented sense of the landscapes and communities through which he had driven and failed to secure a positive, consolidating image at the journey's end that would have enabled him to grasp the totality of his nation's parts notwithstanding the rich variety of its differences. Further, and as discussed previously, the rush to this expressly political conclusion is manifestly at odds with what I have presented as his 'phenomenological method' in the earlier chapters; during the final two days of his tour (admittedly in a badly ailing car), Muir was no longer seeing Scotland in all its 'givenness'[22] but as a metaphor for the thesis slowly taking shape in his mind.

Taken together, Morton and Muir's richly insightful journeys 'in search of Scotland' during the period when motor touring was in its heyday provide us with an invaluable glimpse into how, by the 1930s, driving had the potential to transform the way in which we apprehend and make sense of the phenomenological world. In particular, they are texts which capture the tension that existed then, as now, between 'seeing freshly' and through pre-existing schema and discourses, and which recognise the role of the car in facilitating the former even if such moments of newness and clarity are difficult to sustain.

Conclusion

While the days of 'crawling' through the country lanes of England or chugging one's way up a Scottish mountainside in order to stop and admire the view are recreational pursuits that we now largely associate with our twentieth-century past, the purpose of this chapter has been to reconnect us with these early benefits, and pleasures of automobility and to propose that – were they better understood and valued today – motoring (and indeed car design) might be returned to something more sustainable.

Advocates of this sort of alternative future for automobility do, of course, exist – most notably among EV (electric vehicle) enthusiasts (see Kirsch 2000; Mom 2004; Katz and Mom 2014) and academics whose work on the history of cycling (Pooley 2010; Horton et al. 2007) includes an interest in the many and wonderful early twentieth-century inventions that might well have taken personal mobility in a very different direction had not the motor/oil industry (Urry 2013) monopolised the transport system so comprehensively. Since the late 1990s, meanwhile, when both fuel inefficiency (symbolised in the West by the public's love-affair with the 'Urban 4x4') and traffic congestion peaked, ongoing attempts have been made by campaign groups, international government treaties[23] and, to be fair, motor manufacturers themselves to wean the public off their 'gas-guzzling'/'high-performance' vehicles and to champion the virtues of what, in the early days of motoring, was known generically as the 'light car'.[24] In the UK and Western Europe, the best-known exponent of this principle has been the 'Smart Car' (now available in several different engine and body types, including electric)[25] and more recently, and perhaps more radically, through the manufacture of stripped-down vehicles like the Renault Twizy.

The reason the Twizy is of particular interest to me in the context of this chapter is that – unlike the Smart Cars and, indeed, the many other electric and hybrid cars now making a meaningful impression on consumer choice – the Twizy (see Figure 2.4) is a mode of personal transport that *does* compromise many of the comforts and expectations we have come to expect from motoring and returns us to a vehicle that

Figure 2.4 Renault Twizy electric car. Photo by author.

offers a driving experience that is presumably not dissimilar to Edwin Muir's Standard 12.

Notably, and perhaps unexpectedly, this return to the (absolute) 'basics' of motorised transport has been a hit with car enthusiasts. Steve Cropley, the editor of *Autocar*, described the Twizy as 'part car, part scooter, and completely zero emissions at the tail-pipe', and declared that as well as being 'exactly the kind of car' that will 'populate our burgeoning cities in years to come' it was 'fun to drive'.[26] It seems that, for Cropley, the fact that the Twizy has 'no windows, no heater' and a top speed of 50mph (with a battery range of 50mph to match) are positive features inasmuch as they help distinguish it from more conventional electric cars (Renault's own 'Leaf', for instance). My own interest would be in discovering the use and potential of such vehicles beyond commuting and shopping and, in particular, whether the modest speed/distance of the vehicles, alongside their proximity to the world as 'seen from the car', make them especially well-suited to the 'driving-as-searching' that this chapter has been investigating. The fact that, in 2012, the Eco Tourist Network introduced a scheme in the Brecon Beacons (Wales, UK) which enabled visitors to travel between B&B establishments (kitted out with charging equipment) using a Twizy, suggests a potential market.[27] However, for this sort of eco-touring to become anything more than a minority recreation, both drivers and manufacturers arguably need to reconnect with the 'lost' pleasures and privileges of automobility that this chapter has sought to recover. My own speculation on the subject has long been that, were a ban on the manufacture and use of the petrol/diesel-fuelled car to be declared overnight and the motoring public presented with no option other than a vehicle as rudimentary as the Twizy, they would – after their initial outrage – flock to the dealerships and subsequently (re) learn all that is most valuable about motorised transport. This would include being reminded of what it means to be transported 50 miles in (relative) comfort and ease rather than to walk or cycle it, and – equally importantly – a new appreciation of all that the car (however modest) enables us to see as well as the distinctive nature of that seeing.

On this point, it is heartening to observe that pleasure in 'driving-as-searching' has not entirely disappeared. To illustrate this point, I turn – by way of conclusion – to Chris ('Wolfie') Cooper's impressive 'then and now' history of 'The Great North Road' (Cooper 2013). Cooper, a long-distance lorry driver with his own wagon, has used his years of travelling up and down the Great North Road to research and record the changes in this most historic of roadscapes. His meticulous research of every stretch of this old coaching route – including many sections which have all but disappeared from view – is remarkable in its extent, while his 'then' and 'now' photographs and commentaries echo my own fascination with the photograph of Glencoe Village at the start of this chapter. In the preface to his book, Cooper writes movingly about what inspired him to undertake his project:

> It was sometimes a surprising journey, and at times for me rather sad, as parts of the road I knew as a child are now just a memory and even stretches I remembered as an adult lorry driver have now gone . . . I think the biggest surprise was how something could be so thoroughly changed that not even a trace remains.
>
> We take some things for granted: our house, our town, our village is 'just there'. It has been there forever and never changes, and we think that other things made of steel and stone, are the same. Of course this isn't true; towns do change; a building disappears; a housing estate appears, but it is gradual and people don't notice. But the next time an old factory is knocked down and the site built on, wait a few months then go and see if you can remember exactly where it stood. (Cooper 2013: 7)

In the context of this chapter, the similarities between Cooper's archaeo-logical quest and the 'phenomenological method' that I discovered in Edwin Muir's *Scottish Journey*, in particular, should be obvious. What unites Cooper and Muir – as well as my own encounter with the Glencoe photograph – is a fascination with the world as 'seen from the car' that grasps its changing detail in all its particularity precisely on account of the fact that it, like we, are forever on the move. Such a venture echoes, once again, Jean-Luc Marion's observation – quoted in Chapter 1 – that phenomenology is a way of seeing the world that '[travels] *with* the phenomenon, as if protecting it and clearing a path for it by eliminating roadblocks' (Trigg 2012: 23 (my italics)) and, while the movement back and forth between 'then' and 'now' also echoes Gombrich's model of 'schema and correction' (see Chapter 1), its primary objective remains a simple yet passionate desire to observe and record that which presents itself to consciousness as vividly as possible.

Notes

1. One of the early twentieth-century inventions that Peter Cox has written on (Horton et al. 2007) is the 'velomobile': velomobiles, sometimes known as 'bicycle-cars,' have been manufactured (in diverse forms) since the first decade of the twentieth century.
2. As Hutton (2011: 28) himself observes: 'The picture encapsulates 1930s motoring, with petrol pumps and a garage at the gushet and, on the right, an Automobile Association (AA) box which housed a telephone that members could use in an emergency.'
3. The 'new road' (visible in the distance in Figure 2.2) across Rannoch Moor and through Glencoe was constructed because of problems with flooding near Loch Tulla. It was a greatly admired feat of engineering and aesthetics (Wilenski 1930).
4. Many photographs and postcards from this period feature horse-drawn charabanc tours of the Glen (see Hutton 2011) and, from the mid-nineteenth century, circular tours of Oban–Loch Etive–Glencoe – involving transfer by train, steamer and coach (first horse, then motor) – were extremely popular (Cook's Tours 1861).
5. The editorials of motoring periodicals such as *Autocar*, *The Car Illustrated* and *S.M.T.* (*Scottish Motor Traction*) register the extent to which motor touring became increasingly adventurous in the first three decades of the twentieth century. See *S.M.T.*, vol. 5, no. 2 (August 1930), p. 190.
6. Gombrich draws upon John Constable's painting, *Wivenhoe Park*, repeatedly (1980: 29–34, 247–50) in order to illustrate how Constable eschewed convention and achieved freshness of vision in his landscape paintings.
7. The infamous 'Massacre of Glencoe', in which Robert Campbell and his men turned upon their hosts, Clan MacDonald, took place on 13 February 1692; the memorial cairn was erected in 1883 and has been a popular tourist destination ever since. See http://www.visitscotland.com/about/history/jacobite/battles/massacre-of-glencoe (last accessed 27 September 2015).
8. Claude Friese-Green's film, *The Open Road* (BFI 2007 [1925]), offers a spell-binding glimpse of recreational activity – including motoring – in Britain in the second-decade of the twentieth century.

9. Rannoch Moor is one of Scotland's most celebrated tracts of wilderness, extending for 50 square miles to the west of Loch Rannoch and into Perth and Kinross, Lochaber and Argyll in the east. It features in most of the published accounts of tours in Scotland made in the eighteenth and nineteenth centuries as a wild, dangerous and inhospitable environment. See, for example, Dorothy Wordsworth (1981 [1803]: 175–82).

10. See Keir and Morgan (1955) on the origin and development of the Automobile Association (AA) and the work of its patrol men ('On Patrol': 98–123). AA patrol men on motorbikes travelled the highways and byways of Britain looking out for motorists in trouble from 1909 through to the 1960s and always saluted vehicles bearing the AA badge.

11. Histories of electric vehicles constitute an important corrective to the myth that EVs have been compromised by their restricted range (see especially Kirsch 2000; Mom 2004). There has, however, been a significant breakthrough in the battery life of electric cars since the millennium with the latest Tesla cars claiming a range of *c*.300 miles.

12. The mountainous landscape of Highland Scotland, especially, has meant that new roads have been built alongside or on top of old roads and the principal routes – now the trunk roads – are largely unchanged.

13. 'Golden age of motoring': this phrase recurs in many popular histories of British motoring (e.g. Demaus 2006) and typically indexes qualities such as freedom, adventure, empty roads, comfortable vehicles and widening participation. See also the editorials of the motoring periodicals cited in note 4.

14. As Jeremiah (2007: 165–6) observes, the austerity of the immediate postwar period impacted on motoring as a recreational pastime even though the motoring periodicals and petrol companies (e.g. Shell) did their best to put touring and sight-seeing back on the agenda. During the 1950s, the quality and purpose of motoring in Britain compared with the US – not to mention car design (Jeremiah 2007: 190) – became increasingly polarised.

15. Andrew Marr's series, 'Great Scots: The Writers Who Shaped a Nation' was broadcast on BBC2 in August/September 2014. See the following link for clips from the series: http://www.bbc.co.uk/programmes/b04fh0yd (last accessed 23 September 2015).

16. See *The Shell Poster Book* (1998) which includes images from 1920 through to the 1950s. It is notable that the motor car itself disappears from the designs quite early on with the focus, instead, on where the car can take you.

17. The extent to which writers from this early period were familiar with the concept of the 'motion parallax' (whereby near objects are perceived to be moving faster than those in the distance) is hard to determine; however, we may assume that motor tourists like Morton and Muir, travelling at speeds of 20–30mph, would have taken in their side-views more often than today's motorists.

18. The grammatical style – i.e. periodic sentences with multiple subclauses – that Muir adopts to capture what he sees on this drive may be compared with Edith Wharton's descriptions of the French landscape in *A Motor-Flight* (2008) as well as Virginia Woolf's 'Evening Over Sussex' (1942) discussed in Chapter 1.

19. The Scottish National Party (SNP) emerged out of the amalgamation of two previous parties: the National Party of Scotland (formed 1928) and the Scottish Party (formed 1932). The merger was at the expense of left-wing radicals like C. M. Grieve (Hugh MacDiarmid) who was a close friend of Muir's until a falling-out in 1936. See T. C. Smout's Preface to the 1979 edition, reproduced in *Scottish Journey* (1996).

20. Both the editorial to *A Scottish Journey* (1996) and Marr's television programme (see note 15) refer to the fact that Muir completed his journey in several stages rather than the 'one-off' trip it is presented as in the book.

21. For Gaston Bachelard, the practice of phenomenology and the function of poetry are closely entwined (1971 [1960]: 25). See Chapter 5 for further discussion.

22. 'Givenness': According to Moran and Mooney (2002: 7), 'Givenness and intuition are correlative terms; the character of the intuiting corresponds to the character of the givenness or manifestation . . . Phenomenology does not speculate about essences or make inferences, it is supposed to grasp them directly in immediate "intuition".'

23. International treatises: most notably the Kyoto Protocol, adopted by 192 parties, came into force in 2005: See https://en.wikipedia.org/wiki/Kyoto_Protocol (last accessed 28 September 2015).

24. A 'light car' was typically single-cylinder with an engine capacity of no more than 1500cc /30bhp. See http://www.vscc.co.uk/page/vscc-light-car (last accessed: 28 September 2015). Early 'light-cars' – many of them popular with women drivers (see Levitt 1909) – included the De Dion Bouton (both tricycles and four-wheelers).

25. For a history of the 'Smart Car' see https://en.wikipedia.org/wiki/Smart_%28automobile%29 (last accessed 28 September 2015).

26. See *Autocar*'s review of the Renault Twizy: http://www.autocar.co.uk/car-review/renault/twizy (last accessed: 28 September 2015).

27. For information on tourist use of the Renault Twizy in Wales see http://www.ecotravelnetwork.co.uk (last accessed 28 September 2015); see also https://ecofunkytravelling.files.wordpress.com/2015/01/eigg-trial-report.pdf (last accessed 28 September 2015) for a report on a recent 'Twizy Trial' on the Isle of Eigg (Scotland) which proved generally very successful.

Chapter 3

Fleeing

> Triumph of forgetting over memory, an uncultivated, amnesiac intoxication
> ... Driving like this produces a kind of invisibility, transparency, or trans-
> versality in things, simply by emptying them out. It is a sort of slow-motion
> suicide, death by an extenuation of forms – the delectable form of their
> disappearance ... There is no seduction here, for seduction requires a secret.
> Speed is simply the rite that initiates us into emptiness: a nostalgic desire for
> forms to revert to immobility, concealed beneath the very intensification of
> their mobility. (Baudrillard 2010 [1986]: 6–7)

Nothing, it would seem, could be further from H. V. Morton's early
morning crawl out of London or Edwin Muir's stuttering progress
through Scotland's 'Far North' than the vision of automobility – a streak
through America's hot and featureless deserts – laid out here in Jean
Baudrillard's iconic essay on 'astral America'.[1] More often cited as a
signal point of reference for what postmodern America has become and
how it is known to us, Baudrillard's text – like Paul Virilio's *Negative
Horizon* (2008 [1984]) – also endures as a provocative statement about
what the act of driving has become or, more precisely, is in the act of
becoming. Speaking directly to my own project, both Baudrillard and
Virilio contend that the 'denaturing' of perception consequent upon
travelling at speed (the 'invisibility, transparency, or transversality of
things') not only renders the world outside the car 'spectral' (Baudrillard
2010: 9) but also evacuates the mind of the driver. 'Intoxication' is
a key (and repeated) term here (see also Virilio 2008: 94), leading to
what amounts to a loss of consciousness. Driving at speed ultimately
suspends cognition and blanks out memory: a condition that Baudrillard
describes as a 'spectacular form of amnesia' in which 'everything is to
be discovered, everything to be obliterated' (Baudrillard 2010: 9) and
Virilio as a metaphysical 'flight' from 'the matter of the body':

> As Heidegger declared in paraphrasing Plato: 'All grandeur is in the attack',
> but it is a question here of intoxication, an intoxication comparable to that of

the depths, the intoxication of a grandeur that tells the metaphysician that it is necessary for us to flee from here below up to the heights as quickly as possible, for the 'here' is now composed of the matter of the body (animal, social, territorial) cast in the form of a flight that is to be likened to a generalized repulsion, to the point that the aesthetic of disappearance passes abruptly into the disappearance of the aesthetic. (Virilio 2008: 93–4)

For both these philosophers, then, late twentieth-century driving at sufficient and significant speed has the potential to *stop us thinking*. The automobile is, if you will, not only a practical means of escape from difficult and oppressive social and material circumstances, but also one that has the potential to deliver a transcendental separation of the mind from the body: the existential 'flight from the self, as well as from the residential suburbs where s/he has been imprisoned.

So pervasive is this discourse or mythology that I am obliged, in this chapter, to see it to the end of its own particular road. The two texts that comprise my case study – Patricia Highsmith's *Carol* (1990 [1952]) and Jack Kerouac's *On the Road* (2000 [1957]) – feature fictional episodes that appear to corroborate the speculations of Baudrillard and Virilio on the form and future of automotive consciousness, hence enabling us to explore and interrogate those claims further. At the same time, my close study of these texts in the context of the wider preoccupations of this book – namely the inter-animation of perception, cognition and memory in the subject's experience of the driving-event and the ways in which driving facilitates phenomenological insight – means that my discussion also challenges and refutes the implication that it is speed alone that renders an automobile journey a 'flight', or that the experience necessarily numbs, obliterates or otherwise suspends our cognitive faculties. In other words, although there are episodes in both texts which support Virilio's view, there are others which show the fictional characters seeing, thinking, feeling, remembering and philosophising while driving (or passengering) at speed; further, there is widespread textual evidence that it is what the characters *bring* to their road trips in terms of pre-existing objectives and/or psychological mindsets that renders them 'flights'. This, indeed, echoes the philosopher Ernst Bloch's (1986 [1959]: 370) observations on journeys in general, namely that 'the first feeling in the car or the train, when it departs, is crucial for what is coming'.[2] Allowing for the fact that these are fictional texts, such qualifications productively complicate and challenge the spectre of the 'amnesiac' or 'zombified' driver that Baudrillard's and Virilio's theories respectively conjure up and enable me to propose that although driving at speed (especially when other aspects of the road conditions prove testing) *may* result in the suspension of notionally superfluous cognitive activity, this is not necessarily the case, and that here – as with all the other modes of driving explored in this book – the subject's state of mind (i.e. what s/he is thinking or feeling) when they get into the car or commence the trip is – as Bloch observes – crucial in determining what follows. For while, as we saw in my explication of the driving-event in Chapter 1, things seen and encountered on a journey do have the capacity to direct and occasionally transform our thoughts, automotive consciousness does not present itself to the driver at the start of his or her journey as a carte blanche and – as is all too evident from the failure of many road trips to deliver their travellers a 'new beginning' – is rarely wiped clean in the process.

Driving to or for 'oblivion' is not, of course, exclusive to America or the genre (literature and film) of the road trip and, in acknowledgement of this, I begin this chapter with a section which briefly surveys the history and culture of motoring *as sport* at the beginning of the twentieth century. Reflecting on the motivations for these early motoring challenges (hill trials, endurance trials, land-speed records, 'against-the-clock' commutes and transcontinental tours), as well as the lack of attention to either the driving experience or the landscapes the vehicles pass through, we glimpse an 'attitude' to driving that has persisted ever since and which is neatly summed up in the title of one of the articles upon which I draw: 'motoring for motoring's sake'. An element of this attitude is present in most road-trip literature as well, with Kerouac's *On the Road* featuring several episodes in which the challenge of motoring, without stops, from one American city to another as quickly as possible is the ostensible purpose of the journey. In his representation of these hair-raising driving-events, Kerouac captures how little the world as 'seen from the car' (Kennedy 1919b) can on some, though by no means all, occasions signify, and likewise how drivers and passengers can appear to lose consciousness of their immediate environment.

In his illuminating chapter on driving in the United States, Rudy Koshar (2008) identifies this type of attitude to driving – and, indeed, to 'the road' – as 'oppositional'. In contrast to the other modes of driving he investigates – 'pioneering' (early twentieth-century transcontinental quests) and 'democratic' (i.e. the use of the car for domestic and social purposes) – Koshar characterises 'oppositional' driving as a hard-nosed, American version of 'motoring for motoring's sake':

> If democratic driving practices leant themselves to living within the car, the oppositional mode returned the driver to living in the road . . . In the oppositional mode, the road spoke to the driver, who interpreted its language

through feedback gained from the engine, steering wheel, suspension system, and sound of the tires. Had Jack Kerouac's *On the Road* not been suffused with the dissoluteness of 'beat' culture, it would have been the perfect anthem for proponents of oppositional driving, who valued the 'romance' of roads and the traffic they enabled. (Koshar 2008: 32–3)

Characterised thus, oppositional driving may be understood as a type of thrill-seeking[3] whose pleasures are delivered somatically (the 'feel' and 'sound' of the road) rather than intellectually. This is in significant and revealing contrast to the mode of driving dealt with in the next chapter – cruising – which (in certain guises at least) is undertaken for the express purpose of stimulating and liberating the mind rather than evacuating it. The crucial point that emerges in light of this contrast is, as we will see, that speed per se is not a determining factor in whether we 'think' when we are driving or not. While drivers can, on occasion, undertake a high-speed 'motor-flight' in order to escape from their thoughts as well as their material circumstances, other journeys – including road trips – undertaken at similar speeds lend themselves to meditation, self-reflection and philosophical insight.

Having qualified the credentials of the US road trip for exploring driving as a mode and means of escape, this nevertheless presented itself as the chapter where this most charismatic of motoring phenomena was best located. Clearly it had to go somewhere since, for many people, a book 'on driving' equates to a book on the road trip, even if it is a genre (especially in its filmic variant) that is often only minimally concerned with the experience of driving.[4] Historical research on the US road-trip phenomenon, meanwhile, reveals that transnational motor tours became a popular *family* vacation almost as soon as the Second World War ended and that the hardship, adventure and focus on 'endurance' that is so much a feature of Kerouac's text was arguably a residual ('pioneer') discourse by this time. As Cotten Seiler observes, the comfort and reliability of the modern car paradoxically threatened to undermine the status of the road trip as a salutary 'trial' and rite of passage for the young white male (Seiler 2008: 82):

[T]he controlled environments of modern highways, sumptuous, air-conditioned vehicle interiors, and plentiful roadside amenities made the vision of journey-as-trial increasingly difficult to sustain. There was no question that contemporary vehicles were faster; but even speed, which once had promised 'bigger living: quickened senses, aroused faculties, expanded powers of vision; acts of heroism, improvisation and innovation; spectacular crashes and catastrophes; eruptions of laughter and glee' [Schnapp 1999] had been 'routinized'. (Seiler 2008: 87)

Driving had been 'routinized', then, at precisely the moment in American history when individuals (notably men) needed to identify and assert the national values and characteristics of 'newness, self-reliance, innocence, mobility, idealism, authenticity, pragmatism, renewal, dynamism, and modernity' (Seiler 2008: 7), and the occupation that most quintessentially delivered the opportunity to perform/assert such personal qualities – conquering the continent in the footsteps of one's pioneering forefathers – had become something to which anyone – including women like Carol and Therese (Highsmith 1990) – could aspire. Contextualised thus, the mythology created by Kerouac's text may be seen to be strikingly important in cultural terms. By the late-1940s, traversing America by automobile was no longer a big deal; *On the Road* made it one, and the mass-mediatisation of the text has ensured that the challenge has retained its aura and status ever since.[5]

Meanwhile, as any Internet search makes clear, the road connoted by the American road trip is always the *same* road (see Figure 3.1). Often, as here, the equally iconic rock formations of Monument Valley punctuate the middle distance, but the crucial and unerring signifiers are the long, straight road, the distant vanishing point and the vast expanse of nothingness in which it sits; in almost every case, too, the image is shot as if from the driver's seat (see also the frontispiece to Baudrillard's *America* (Baudrillard 2010: x)). Schematised thus, the 'road trip road'

Figure 3.1 'Monument Valley, USA', Lloyd Duffield © Fotolibra (FOT615537).

is the quintessential road 'to' and 'from' nowhere; lacking any visible markers of either destination or point of origin, it is also free of distracting roadside objects. A handful of sculptured rock formations are permissible; equally, a lonely string of telegraph wires. Yet never is the world as 'seen from the car' allowed to distract from the road itself. In the discussion of *Carol* and *On the* Road that follows, we will encounter American roadscapes that both evoke and deviate from this schema, on which point it is also important to observe that Highsmith's and Kerouac's fictional characters traversed America several years before the building of the interstates, although 'motorways' in the form of national parkways, toll-roads and transcontinental routes (6, 11 and the iconic Route 66) were already well established.[6]

In the course of these discussions I pay particular attention to the qualitative difference in what may be thought of as 'flights to' and 'flights from' and, by extension, the objective of the journey in question. Notwithstanding the limitations travelling at speed supposedly puts upon our perception, I draw upon the two novels to enquire what form the world as 'seen from the car' takes during such flights and what conditions (e.g. slowing down, a notable change in landscape type) are necessary to bring it into view. In line with my theory of the driving-event as outlined in Chapter 1, I also return to the significance of the stop or 'rest-break' in consolidating and hence defining the driving experience and I focus, too, on the car as a site of intimacy – in particular, as the locus of intimate conversation (including testimony/confession) between driver and passengers – which serves as an important corrective to what may be perceived as this volume's tendency to focus on the experiences of solo drivers. As ever, the fictional texts which enable the exploration of these themes cannot be presented as sociological or historical evidence for all that characterises this mode of driving, but they do help us to interrogate the neo-Futurist[7] prognoses of Baudrillard and Virilio and bring new complexity to bear upon the figure of 'voyeur-voyager' (Virilio 2008: 101) whom, I would contend, is not quite as 'unthinking' as has been supposed.

Motoring for motoring's sake

In the course of my research for this book I have encountered a great many texts – especially among the legions of motoring periodicals and pre-Second World War fiction – which register little interest in the cognitive dimension of driving/passengering and yet provide us with a fascinating window onto its practice. From a methodological perspective, this means that the texts in question have a similar status to representations of driving in film; the reader is provided with little, if any, information about what these drivers and passengers think or feel as they pursue their adventures and yet the vivid and detailed portraits of the driving-events in question allow us to conjecture what their motivations, thrills and satisfactions were. In terms of building a complete picture of the many different modes driving has assumed in the course of the twentieth century, it is also important to register that this one – 'motoring for motoring's sake' – has coexisted with other modes of car use from the automobile's earliest days and persists today. Even while H. V. Morton and Edwin Muir were happy to chunter along in their 'little cars' at a speed that enabled them to experience the places and people that glided along beside them, other drivers were embarking on motor tours for different purposes entirely. The pleasure in knowing how to handle a car well and to maximise its performance was reason enough to embark upon a journey from Land's End to John O'Groats for such enthusiasts, even as others gave themselves up to the thrill of endurance trials and land speed records or the (often deadly) competition of the race tracks (Jeremiah 2007: 19).

Two early endurance challenges – undertaken in order to prove the speed and reliability of the cars in question – serve to illustrate the passion that existed for this manner of driving: J. W. Stocks's timed run from Land's End to John O'Groat's in 1902 and Dorothy Levitt's bid to get from London to Liverpool and back in two days in 1905 (see note 42 to Chapter 1). This was, of course, the first decade of serious motoring and the fact that both adventurers achieved their feats in modest 8hp De Dion 'light cars' (see note 25 to Chapter 2) is a testament to how quickly these simple vehicles proved to be reliable. Both runs were timed to the second and details of all stops minutely recorded. The accounts of the trials – Stocks's in *The Car* (1902) and Levitt's in *Autocar* (1905), provide us with invaluable historical information on the state of England's roads at that time and, in Stocks' case, a glimpse of what he saw as he 'tore' through the countryside at 20mph:

We went to bed about 9 p.m. and rose at two on Sunday morning, and found hot coffee, boiled eggs, etc. on the table at 2.30 a.m. Being ready at 2.55 a.m. we started away in the dark, the roads being clear and no traffic about (as a matter of fact, the first vehicles we saw were two mail carts in Bodmin, 58 miles from Land's End, at 6 a.m.). Although very hilly in Cornwall and Devonshire, we gradually, shall I say 'crept' in ahead of our timetable, and at Exeter (120 miles) we were 45 minutes to the good. This was our first stop of any description, where we halted to send off a telegram, and then proceeded to Bridgwater (165 miles), our first place for feeding and filling up our tanks.

> We left at 11.55 a.m., and some eight miles south of Bristol we encountered the steepest hill, known as Red Hill, from Land's End. This, however, was negotiated without any difficulty, and we proceeded north, sometimes on fine, smooth, flat stretches of road, with beautiful scenery; and at others, between Bridgnorth and Wellington, through hilly, dirty, black country, where the dust rose from the roads in black clouds. (Stocks 1902: 367)

Driving to a pre-calculated 'timetable' based on the car's capacity and what were considered unavoidable delays ('stops', 'slows', tyre repairs, etc.), Stocks and his co-driver reached John O'Groat's in 2 days 14 hours and 25 minutes which (excluding stops) amounted to a 'nett running time' of 48 hours and 30 minutes (Stocks 1902: 389). Similar calculations embellish Dean Moriarty's mad dashes across the North American continent in *On the Road* (see, for example, the 'final word' on his 1,180-mile, 17-hour streak from Denver to Chicago (Kerouac 2000: 216)), hence demonstrating the genealogical roots of the road trip in motor sport. The fact that Dorothy Levitt, an early twentieth-century female driver, if an iconic one, attempts – and achieves – something similar in her 'jaunt' from London to Liverpool and back also complicates the gender politics of these early trials. For while the heroic and 'manly' nature of Stocks' enterprise is implicit in virtually every word of his retrospective (from the military precision of his calculations to the physical endurance required to motor for such long hours), the record of Levitt's achievement is in line with discourses surrounding the early women transcontinental motorists of America and Australia who, according to Georgine Clarsen (2008: 139), served to bolster nationalistic pride in progress and innovation:

> With the idea of proving that the modern motor car can be driven long distances with the certainty of a railway train, an 8 h.p. De Dion car was started from London on Wednesday last week for a run to Liverpool – distance 204 and three quarters of a mile – returning to London the next day. Miss Dorothy Levitt drove the car throughout the long journey, and the run was timed by Mr. C. J. L. Clark ... Miss Levitt is, perhaps justly, proud of her success in undertaking and completing the longest run accomplished by a lady driver. (J. L. C. 1905: 290)

Although the tone of the report risks patronising a woman who was one of the first people in Britain to set a land-speed record of over 100mph (see note 42 to Chapter 1 and Figure 3.2), the willingness to promote the skills of women drivers during the first decades of the twentieth century is in welcome and significant contrast to the machismo associated with motor sport after the two world wars (Jeremiah 2007; Clarsen 2008). Certainly the women in Kerouac's *On the Road* take a noticeably 'back-seat' role.[8]

Figure 3.2 'Miss Dorothy Levitt in a 26hp Napier, Brooklands, 1908'. Courtesy of the Motoring Picture Library.

Meanwhile, two motoring periodical articles from a little later in the century (dated 1929 and 1930), demonstrate the changing significance of speed for this type of motor sport; rather than demonstrating the merits of the car in question, speed is now one of the recognised thrills of driving, and the ability to cover large distances 'at speed' speaks to the 'nerve' and skill of the driver. Foreshadowing, once again, the feats of Dean Moriarty, S. C. D. Davis and his 'crew'[9] exemplify this manner of 'motor-flight' in their delivery of a two-litre Lagonda to London from Glasgow in less than 12 hours. By 1929, however, driving from Scotland to London in a single day was no longer seen as remarkable and Davis's run is made into an adventure largely on account of the extreme weather (the report in *Autocar* (1929) is subtitled: 'A rapid trip from Glasgow to London in the teeth of a great gale'):

> No less than the difficulty of holding the car against the gusts, it was the howling of the wind, the sight of the trees bending and swaying, the sudden hail of small twigs and little branches, which gave zest to the journey. Not a soul was in sight, not a sheep, nor a man, nor a car was seen until we reached Lockerbie on the southward run. In the wild expanses there came the desire to sing, to shout aloud, to challenge and defy the elements, and to drive faster, ever faster. (Davis 1929: 650)

While other sections of the article are lyrical about the wonderful power and comfort of the Lagonda, it will be seen that equal credit is given to Davis and his crew for being 'man enough' to withstand the violence of the storm. Not only do these drivers demonstrate the physical strength needed to 'hold the car against the gusts', but also the psychological resilience that enables them to plough on when other cars and drivers have given up and pulled off the road. No doubt this particular journey – a verifiable historical event – was a testing one, but its further significance here is the discourse it gives rise to. Written twenty years before Kerouac wrote the 'road trip' into literary history, the seeds of Dean Moriarty's exploits were already being sown.

My second text from this period, and contributing to the same emerging discourse of 'motoring for motoring's sake', is Alec Maclehouse's 'A highway of romance: through Merrie England to the North' (1930), which details another London–Scotland one-day streak, this time in the other direction. This compelling article, which I have written about elsewhere (Pearce 2017), is a different order of text to Davis's in that it does include some reflexive commentary on the driver's thoughts and feelings as he undertakes his mission. Indeed, it is a text in which you can arguably find elements of both Morton and Kerouac: like Morton, Maclehouse is a devotee of his native Scotland, but like Kerouac's protagonists, Maclehouse and his travelling companion have clearly undertaken to make this particular journey in a single day for 'kicks'. Indeed, the spirit of the enterprise is candidly and self-consciously declared in the opening paragraph in which Maclehouse perceptively distinguishes between a motor tour and what he deems 'stern travel':

> I have made the journey often in two, and sometimes in three, days: and once I have done it in a single day. I found that to do it in one day changes its character entirely; it ceases to be a tour from one cathedral in England to another, and becomes stern travel. The experience is rounded and complete, and the emotional pitch, in consequence, greatly heightened. Scotland, as you see it from Carter Fell, looks at you with different eyes when you have come to it hotfoot that very day from London. Some of the amenities of the journey are lost. You are so concentrated on speed that you have no time to turn aside, and little enough even to notice the country you pass through: and by stopping less often, and for shorter intervals, curtail the 'incidents' of the journey. (Maclehouse 1930: 59)

Endorsing my speculation on the crucial role of retrospective consolidation in determining the character of each and every driving-event (see Chapter 1), Maclehouse nevertheless observes how completing a long journey like this in a single streak makes it much easier to apprehend as a satisfying whole. A little later he writes:

> My journey to Scotland in one day was, for various reasons, a journey I shall always remember: it remains in my memory, like the outline of a single majes-

tic mountain against the sky. For enjoyment in a less exalted sense, and for the purpose of sight-seeing, the journey is better done in two, or even three, days. (Maclehouse 1930: 59)

Significant, too, is the fact that although the speed of travel is seen to inhibit the motorists' apprehension of the world as 'seen from the car', the heightened state of consciousness brought about by the speed sharpens the perception and appreciation of the destination when it finally appears:

It is all so perfectly contrived. You have the three hundred miles of steady travelling, never letting the speed drop below forty miles per hour. Your spirits all day have been tempered and moderate: they rise only when you reach Northumberland, and the air blowing about these green hills has a tang of the Border in it. As the road begins its long pull up Redesdale to the top of Carter, your spirits lift in a crescendo with it, until the banks on either side suddenly fall away, and there, before you, is Scotland . . . It was coming on cold when we came to the top. All the hills and valleys were clear in the evening light: I let out the howl of joy which this view always extorts from me, and then my friend said quietly, pointing to Scotland, 'Doesn't it suggest infinite possibilities?' I left the car, and roamed on the heath like a captive who has found freedom . . . (Maclehouse 1930: 65)

Thus while, for Virilio, the contemporary motorist's obsession with his or her 'destination' completely overdetermines and degrades modern travel ('with the speed of the continuum it is the goal [*objectif*] of the voyage that destroys the road' (Virilio 2008: 105)), for Maclehouse and his companion, the race from London to Scotland enables them to see their destination, in all its romantic glory, more intensely. As with the motor touring literature which this description echoes, there is clearly a strong element of 'schema' in the travellers' reported response, but the effect of uninterrupted travel on the moment and manner of the perception would seem to be authentic and (for the travellers concerned) thought-provoking.

As already noted, historians now interpret the post-Second World War American road trip as an ideological response to 'an alleged crisis of the individual . . . which was also a crisis of patriarchy' (Seiler 2008: 15) consequent upon the changes wrought by the nation's 'transition to corporate capitalism' (Seiler 2008:13). Both individuals and families sought to recreate the pioneering exploits of their ancestors which dated back to 1899 (when John D. Davis and his wife made the first attempt to cross the continent and got as far as Chicago) and 1903 (when Dr H. Johnson and Sewall K. Crocker finally succeeded by way of a journey from San Francisco to New York) (Koshar 2008:18). In a continent where the road system was patchy or non-existent – and, for the most part, poorly surfaced – the extent of these achievements cannot be underestimated (Koshar 2008:18). Meanwhile, like Europe and Australasia, America also had its fair share of pioneering female drivers. The first woman to cross the United States by automobile was Alice Ramsay (Ruben 2009). Ramsay and her two sisters-in-law made the crossing from New York to San Francisco in fifty-nine days, and has since acquired the status of a feminist hero, despite the fact that, at the time, the press struggled to make sense of the nature of the achievement: 'Pretty women motorists arrive after trip across the continent' (*San Francisco Chronicle*) (Ruben 2009). There is in this case, however, well-documented evidence of the challenges and privations these women put themselves through in order to complete the trip (unmapped/non-existent roads, atrocious weather, dangerous river crossings and mechanical failure: Ruben 2009) which, if nothing else, confirms the significance of their transcontinental journey in the annals of motor sport.

For Georgine Clarsen, meanwhile, what distinguished subsequent all-women transcontinental tours of North America was their explicit link to the women's suffrage movement in the US, beginning with the 4,000-mile transcontinental crossing made by the Congressional Union in 1915 where relays of feminist activists used the journey to carry the suffragist campaign from West to East (Clarsen 2008: 101). The explicit political objectives of these pioneering women motorists arguably extends their intrepid journey out of the realm of 'sport', but provides a further layer of historical context for the 1950s road trips to which I now turn. Indeed, what this section as a whole has, I hope, revealed is the extent to which the discourse of 'motoring for motoring's sake' – although dominant in the annals of early motoring – was nevertheless annexed for other ideological purposes from the moment of its inception. Even as an 'attitude', then, the practice of mindless and/or uncompromised flight has proven hard to protect and sustain.

Highsmith and Kerouac 'on the road'

In this comparative examination of two North American road-trip novels from the 1950s – one (Kerouac 2000 [1957]) an iconic best-seller, the other (Highsmith 1990 [1952]), a text that began life as a lesbian cult classic before being remarketed for a wider audience in the 1990s[10] – I attend both to the conditions and qualities that render driving a means of escape and the way in which this manner of driving (and, indeed, passengering) impacts upon the perceptual, cognitive and affective dimensions of automotive consciousness as theorised in Chapter 1. My thesis, as presented in the introduction to this chapter, is that speed alone cannot be seen to determine and characterise this mode of driving; it is rather the spirit in which this (and any) driving-event is undertaken, together with the psychological preoccupations of the drivers and/or passengers, that will ultimately render a journey a 'flight' or something else entirely. Here, as in every chapter of this book, it is also important to register that no literary fiction may be seen as a window onto lived experience, no matter how authentic its descriptions and dramatisations appear. This is especially true of road-trip fiction where the central motif is widely understood by both author and reader to be a metaphor of something else ('life's journey' at the very least) before the first page is even turned. These are fictional eyes through which we track the highways and cities of 1950s America – New York, Chicago, Des Moines, Denver, San Francisco – but we can assume that they capture something of the way the world appeared to the mobile subject at this time if not necessarily the phenomenological world itself.

Objectif

For Virilio (2008 [1984]), the 'motor-flight' (see note 33 to Chapter 1) has *no* objective other than its destination:

> On the screen of the automobile trip, the precipitation of images amounts to an evident telluric movement where the epicentre is situated at the blind spot of the arrival ... With the speed of the continuum it is the goal [*objectif*] of the voyage that destroys the road, it is the target of the projectile-projector (of the automobile) that seems to trigger the ruin of the interval, it is the fleeting desire to go right to the end as fast as possible that produces in the opening out [*écartement*] of the travelling, the tearing apart [*écartèlement*] of the landscape. (Virilio 2008: 105)

Indeed, what this statement would seem to imply is that even if the 'driver-prospector' (Virilio 2008: 107) had other objectives (other thoughts, other feelings, other preoccupations) when s/he set out, they are lost in and to the speeding vehicle ('the projectile-projector') which permits no 'place' to be seen or to 'mean' other than the one at the end of the journey ('the blind spot of arrival'). By virtue of this 'cultural revolution of transportation' (p. 105), even a journey not intended as an 'escape' becomes one, and the driver fixated on the 'distant/future' at the expense of his/her immediate surroundings in the perceptual realm and the world left behind:

In the driver's seat, the immediate proximity matters little, the only important thing is that which is held at a distance; in the continuum of the trip, what is ahead governs the progress, the speed of propulsion produces its own horizon: the *greater* the speed, the more *distant* the horizon. The philosophy of the windshield demands a prevision far more than simple vision since the latter is distorted by the advancing movement, it is the future that decides the present of the course. In the accelerated itinerary the past is passed over, the landmarks are in essence those of the future. Thus the dromovisual apparatus ... only transmits what is to come, in the unidirectionality of the trip, what abides has already long ago disappeared in the archaeology of the departure. For the driver-prospector of the trip, the driver's seat is a *seat of prevision*, a control tower of the future of the trajectory. (Virilio 2008: 106–7 (italics in the original))

Although Virilio's folding together of 'speed' and 'destination' – so that one becomes an effect of the other – is certainly not the only way in which speed may be thought about in relation to driving (see Chapter 5), their imbrication does speak to those literary texts where the destination becomes the *pretext* for the (motor-)flight. In such instances, speed itself – and the states of consciousness to which it gives rise – is, indeed, the *objectif* in contrast to Virilio's formulation where it ostensibly functions as a means to an end (i.e. the 'destination'). Both scenarios, however, may be seen to deliver the same transcendental benefits to the driver, namely a steer towards the future and a concomitant pleasure/relief in leaving the past behind. This said, and as will emerge in the analyses following, there are plenty of instances in which a road novel is better understood as a 'flight from' rather than a 'telluric' (ibid.) surge towards.

Since the early days of motoring (see, for example, Ehrenburg's 'Charles Bernard' (1999 [1929])), the anaesthetising effect of motoring at speed has been a widely adopted convention in the literature(s) of escape. A frequently quoted contemporary example of this is Paul Auster's, *The Music of Chance* (2006 [1990]), in which the central protagonist, Jim Nashe, is pleasantly numbed by his tour of the North American interstates:

The car became a sanctum of invulnerability, a refuge in which nothing could hurt him anymore. As long as he was driving, he carried no burdens, was unencumbered by even the slightest particle of his former life. That is not to say that memories did not rise up in him, but they no longer seemed to bring any of the old anguish ... After three or four months, he had only to enter the car to feel that he was coming loose from his body, that once he put his foot down on the gas and started driving, the music would carry him into a realm of weightlessness. (Auster 2006: 10–11)

What is especially interesting about this account of Nashe's experience is the way in which what begins as a 'flight from' is transformed, through the very act of non-stop driving, into a 'flight towards'. Although Nashe himself recognises the destinations on his road map as no more than 'pretexts' (Auster 2006: 12) for his predilection to keep driving, they ultimately become a more meaningful *raison d'être* than the one that sent him 'on the road' in the first instance (an unexpected inheritance from his late father). In this regard, this is a story that notionally bears out Virilio's observations on our compulsive fascination with the *objectif*; without the *raison d'être* represented by the 'next town on the horizon' Nashe's life certainly falls spectacularly apart.

The use of destination-as-pretext is also a feature of the first road trip undertaken in Kerouac's *On the Road*. Notwithstanding the higher purpose implicit in Sal's famous declaration – 'we were . . . performing our one noble function of the time, move' (Kerouac 2000: 121)[11] – there is a very banal reason why he and Dean Moriarty (along with Dean's girlfriend, Marylou, and Ed Dunkel) make their trip from New York to Virginia and back, and that is to deliver Sal's brother's furniture. The very functionality of this objective – not unlike Davis's 'commission' to deliver his Lagonda to London by tea-time (see the previous section) – may be seen, paradoxically, to liberate this particular trip from existential considerations and hence protect its status as a latter-day example of 'motoring for motoring's sake':

> We packed my brother's furniture in the back of the car and took off at dark, promising to be there in thirty hours – thirty hours for a thousand miles north and south. But that's the way Dean wanted it. It was a tough trip, and none of us noticed it; the heater was not working and consequently the windshield developed fog and ice; Dean kept reaching out while driving seventy to wipe it with a rag and make a hole to see the road. 'Ah, holy hole!' . . . And Dean talked, no one else talked. He gestured furiously, he leaned as far as me sometimes to make a point, sometimes he had no hands on the wheel and yet the car went straight as an arrow, not for once deviating from the white line in the centre of the road that unwound, kissing our left front tire. (Kerouac 2000: 104–5)

Indeed, I would suggest that none of the subsequent trips ever manages to capture the innocence or *purposelessness* of this first wild night of furniture delivery. Even by the time of their second trip (from Rocky Mountain, North Carolina to San Francisco via New Orleans),[12] the sexual tensions within the group are already running so high that this, alone, may be seen to pitch the company into a 'flight from' their collective selves. Therefore, although the mood in the car is exultant, Dean's command – 'we must all admit that everything is fine and that there is no need in the world to worry' (Kerouac 2000: 121) – arguably casts the first shadow of doubt over the purity of their objective, if not the 'purity of the road' itself:

We flashed past the mysterious white signs in the night somewhere in New Jersey that say SOUTH (with an arrow) and WEST (with an arrow) and took the south one. New Orleans! It burned in our brains . . . Dean suddenly became tender. 'Now dammit, look here, all of you, we all must admit that everything is fine and there's no need in the world to worry, and in fact we should realize what it would mean to us to UNDERSTAND that we're not REALLY worried about ANYTHING. Am I right?' . . .

We all jumped to the music and agreed. The purity of the road. The white line in the middle of the highway unrolled and hugged our left front tire as if glued to our groove. Dean hunched his muscular neck, T-shirted in the winter night, and blasted the car along. (Kerouac 2000: 121)

Quite apart from their more immediate personal issues (symbolised by Dean's insistence on keeping different girlfriends on either side of the continent), the weight of memory and personal loss quietly weaves itself into the fabric of Kerouac's text even if it is regularly drowned out by the raucous 'high life' that is simultaneously being enjoyed. This is certainly true of the reception of Dean's non-stop monologues on his colourful past, often prompted by the places and people he (re)encounters along the road (see, for example, the drive through Houston (Kerouac: 2000: 144)). Even as Sal's narration provides the reader with no more than snatches of this material, so, too, do we imagine Marylou and Ed – as back-seat passengers – tuning 'out' as much as 'in'; and yet Dean's rumbling back-story represents an ever-present question mark as to whether there can really be such thing as 'unidirectional' flight (Virilio 2008: 107) if we allow for the automotive consciousness of the driver (and his 'crew').

Centred on the love story of two women – the married socialite, Carol Aird, and the nineteen-year old apprentice theatre designer, Therese Belivet – who pursue, and consummate, their relationship on a road trip West (New York to Colorado), Patricia Highsmith's *Carol* is an unequivocal 'flight from'. While barely necessary in the context of a plot that, in most regards, follows the simple lines of a formula romance,[13] the text dutifully includes some early dramatisation of its protagonists' *objectif*: Carol is in the process of divorcing her husband, Harge, as the result of an unfulfilling marriage (Highsmith 1990: 113) while Therese, though barely old enough to understand what it means, voices her own sense of 'imprisonment' when trying to 'explain' Carol to her boyfriend, Richard (Highsmith 1990: 137). An additional edge is, nevertheless, added to their subsequent elopement through the historical context in which the story is set. Speaking of her own entrapment, Carol reflects cynically on Harge's 'acquisitiveness' and 'inability to love' as symptomatic of 'the times' (Highsmith 1990: 113), which Therese (ventriloquising Richard) translates as 'war and big business and Congressional witch-hunts' (p. 114). While rarely made the subject of explicit discussion, the dark underbelly of 1950s American culture means that this road trip was always going to be defined by something more than a flight from the protagonists' personal circumstances.

In line with my earlier hypothesis *Carol* also helps us to recognise the extent to which driving-as-escape need not necessarily involve speed. In contrast to Kerouac's text – where the break-neck speeds at which Dean invariably drives has made it all too easy to confuse the two – *Carol* shows how it is possible for the driver's/passenger's consciousness to be consumed with a desire for escape without travelling very fast at all. Moreover, instead of the *objectif* of their trip being focused on a predetermined destination (Virilio's 'blind-spot of arrival' (Virilio 2008: 105)), Carol and Therese are happy to make their way across the continent steadily, if determinedly, choosing their route on a day-to-day basis:

> Therese sat on her bed in a robe, looking at a road map, spanning it with her hand. A span and a half was about a day's driving, though they probably would not do it. 'We might get all the way across Ohio today,' Therese said.
> 'Ohio. Noted for rivers, rubber, and certain railroads. On our left the famous Chillicothe drawbridge, where twenty-eight Hurons once massacred a hundred – morons.'
> Therese laughed. (Highsmith 1990: 159)

Therefore, although the logistics involved renders this transcontinental adventure 'stern travel' (Maclehouse 1930) rather than a mere sightseeing tour, the women are relaxed about their route and unconcerned about the time they make. Sometimes they achieve their notional destination, sometimes they exceed it; but very often they fail and end up staying somewhere completely different.

Subjective as the nature of this flight unquestionably is for both women, its objective nevertheless acquires a new material and dramatic expression when they realise that they are being pursued by a private detective (commissioned by Carol's husband to procure evidence of their 'sexual relations'). For the first time on the trip, speed suddenly *does* matter:

> They hadn't had lunch yet, and it was after three. They had talked about this stretch last night, the straight road west from Salt Lake City across the Great Salt Lake Desert. They had plenty of gas, Therese noticed, and probably the country wasn't entirely deserted, but Carol was tired. They had been driving since six that morning. Carol drove fast. Now and then she pressed the pedal down to the floor and held it there a long while before letting up.

> Therese glanced at her apprehensively. She felt they were running away from something.
>   'Anything behind us?' Carol asked. (Highsmith 1990: 182)

While the high drama of this and the ensuing car chase – which leads to the text's narrative climax and temporary separation of the lovers – is clearly a literary device in the first instance, it does also serve to dramatise the difference between the 'flight to' and the 'flight from' and the extent to which both driving-events are determined by the personal and psychological circumstances in which they are undertaken. In other circumstances, Carol and Therese would have looked forward to this run across the Great Salt Lake Desert as one of the highlights of their trip (see Figure 3.1) and – in all probability – driven it just as fast. With the paranoid suspicion of their being followed (and 'found out') uppermost in their minds, however, Carol's flooring of the accelerator translates into one thing only: escape. The fact that such extreme qualitative differences are nevertheless invisible to the eye of the impartial observer is something to which I return at the beginning of the next chapter; however, in the context of my discussion here, the episode is a welcome, even cathartic, expression of what we know so much high-speed driving to be about. For while few of us will, I trust, have had the experience of being tailed by a private detective, we will almost certainly have encountered situations in which we or other drivers have sought to escape our 'inner demons' by pressing the accelerator pedal a little harder and using the journey in question to give physical expression and psychological relief to any number of memories, anxieties and material circumstances that we are desperate to leave behind.

As 'seen from the car'

The fact that Carol and Therese are embarked upon a serious transcontinental road trip rather than casual 'touring' is confirmed by their lack of interest in sightseeing. Indeed, Carol's ironic (and, to the contemporary ear, embarrassingly racist) assessment of Ohio – 'Ohio . . . On our left the famous Chillicothe drawbridge, where twenty-eight Hurons once massacred a hundred – morons' (Highsmith 1990: 159) – exposes the extent to which, by the late-1940s, the North American road trip had already been reduced to a schema. Therefore, when Carol upbraids Therese on her 'second-hand' apprehension of the world on the first day of the trip – '"I wonder if you'll really enjoy this trip", Carol said. "You so prefer things reflected in a glass, don't you? . . . I wonder if you'll even like seeing real mountains and real people"' (Highsmith 1990:

156) – the dramatic irony is resounding. Already it is crystal clear that Carol – whose personal tourist objective seems to centre on where she can get her next drink and packet of cigarettes – is no more interested in the world as 'seen from the car' (Kennedy 1919b) than Therese. Like many others in the genre (see note 4), this is a journey that focuses on what the travellers discover about themselves and each other rather than anything or anyone they encounter on the road itself. For the automotive historian this is, admittedly, disappointing given that their journey takes them all the way from New York to Denver and Colorado Springs at the pivotal moment in US history (1952) when the shadow of postwar austerity was just beginning to shade into boom-time prosperity.

The one striking exception to the text's general disregard for location is this picturesque snapshot of Minnesota, focalised through Therese:

> They went on westward, through Sleepy Eye, Tracy and Pipestone, sometimes taking an indirect highway on a whim. The West unfolded like a magic carpet, dotted with the neat, tight units of farmhouse, barn and silo that they could see for half an hour before they came abreast of them. They stopped once at a farmhouse to ask if they could buy enough gas to get to the next station. The house smelled like fresh cold cheese. Their steps sounded hollow and lonely on the solid brown planks of the floor, and Therese thought in a fervid burst of patriotism – *America*. There was a picture of a rooster on a wall, made of coloured patches of cloth sewn on a black ground, beautiful enough to hang in a museum. The farmer warned them about ice on the road directly west, so they took another highway going south. (Highsmith 1990: 177–8)

Even here, however, the narration makes clear that we are seeing the landscape not for what it is but as the backdrop to Therese's ecstatic pleasure in travelling through it with Carol. This is the day immediately following the consummation their relationship (in Waterloo, Iowa) and Therese's euphoria spills over into a barely sublimated 'burst of patriotism' (for 'America' read 'Carol'). The visit to the farmhouse, too, would seem to echo Carol's earlier jibe that Therese would only ever see the world second-hand; although the pair have made a conscious effort to stop the car and engage with the world beyond the windshield, there is still no sense that they are seeing it with anything resembling 'fresh eyes'. Not only might the patchwork on the farmer's wall be hanging in a museum, but virtually everything they have seen.

Long before Baudrillard's (1994 [1981]) theorisation of the simulacra, then, it appears that Highsmith grasped that the extent to which contemporary America was in the process of being schematised and thematised. Indeed, there is little suggestion in this text that any journey made by car will necessarily sharpen or interrogate our perception of the phenomenological world. Thus, although the lovers' adrenalin-fuelled flight from Harge's detective does appear to bring the 'reflected world' (Highsmith 1990 [1952]: 156) somewhat closer to Therese, everything she sees is still translated into something else – now on account of her fear and superstition:

> Because they went a little slower now, Therese had a panicky feeling of not moving at all, as if the earth drifted under them and they stood still. She watched the road behind them for another patrol car, for the detective's car, and for the nameless, shapeless thing she felt pursuing them from Colorado Springs. She watched the land and the sky for the meaningless events that her mind had insisted on attaching significance to, the buzzard that banked slowly in the sky, the direction of a tangle of weeds that bounced over a rutted field before the wind, and whether a chimney had smoke or not. (Highsmith 1990: 198)

Such inability to engage with the roadscapes through which they pass in and of themselves does not, however, diminish the significance of the car in Highsmith's road trip. As we will see in the next section, Carol's car is a distinctive – and instrumental – space in the deepening of their relationship and the trip itself a prototype for subsequent 'love-on-the-run' narratives, most notably Vladimir Nabokov's *Lolita* (2000 [1955]).[14]

For all its ostensible celebration of what Baudrillard and Virilio condemned as the 'de-realising' effects of driving – including, most notably, the impossibility of seeing anything from the 'projective-projector [i.e. the car]' (Virilio 2008: 105) on account of its speed and intent – *On the Road* features considerably more descriptions of the world as 'seen from the car' than *Carol*. The first of these are the passenger-eye views of Sal Paradise on his first trip West in 1947, first from the window of a Greyhound Bus (Kerouac 2000: 12–13), and then the various cars and trucks he hitches a ride with (p. 15). Although these accounts are memorable largely on account of their ability to capture the joyous enthusiasm of a young man making his first trip alone, they also evoke what was to become a highly conventionalised (and, indeed, *valued*) way of looking at America's heartland through the windscreen of a moving vehicle (see Cross (2002) discussed in Chapter 4): whether a feature of the desert (Baudrillard 2010) or the Prairies, it is the huge flat expanses of America that give the road, and the road trip, its unique properties and promote a uniquely *panoptic* vision that – as here – can rip through whole states while searching out its destination. The sensation of omnipotence associated with such a prospectus – in camera terms, the combination of a massive zoom with an extreme wide-angle facility – may, indeed, be seen to determine the thrill of this category of driving-event as much as speed. On Sal's first trip West, moreover, this mode of seeing – whether from car, truck or bus – is integral to the characterisation of his journey as an unequivocal 'flight towards':

> But they were tremendous drivers. How that truck disposed of the Nebraska nub – the nub that sticks out over Colorado! And soon I realized I was actually at last over Colorado, though not officially in it, but looking southwest toward Denver itself a few hundred miles away. I yelled for joy. We passed the bottle. The great blazing stars came out, the far-receding sand hills got dim. I felt like an arrow that could shoot out all the way. (Kerouac 2000: 25)

If point of view and perspective are the crucial factors in convincing Sal that he is on the proverbial 'road to freedom' on this occasion, we must nevertheless allow that speed *is* the means by which driving-events become flights (both 'to', and 'from') elsewhere in the text. This is also to acknowledge that there are episodes in Kerouac's text where the account of driving – both its practice and its purpose – do, indeed, resonate with the analyses (and rhetoric) of Baudrillard and Virilio and, of course, the origins of both in the discourses of Futurism (see note 7). Probably the most memorable and defining of these episodes centres on the trip that Dean and Sal make from Denver to Chicago to deliver a 1947 Cadillac in a 'record-breaking' seventeen hours (Kerouac 2000: 209–16). Focalised through Sal, this is, however, a drive that yields very few glimpses of the world as 'seen from the car' on account of the fact that Sal is so traumatised by Dean's risk-taking that he cannot bear to look out of the windows and, instead, curls up on the floor in the back of the car:

> 'Don't worry, man. I know what I'm doing.' I began to flinch. Dean came up on lines of cars like the Angel of Terror ... then the huge car leaped to his touch and passed, and always by a hair we made it back to our side as other lines filed by in the opposite direction and I shuddered. I couldn't take it anymore ... I saw flashing by outside several scenes that I remembered from 1947 – a long stretch where Eddie and I had been stranded two hours. All that old road of the past unreeling dizzily as if the cup had been overturned and everything gone mad. My eyes ached in nightmare day.
> 'Ah, hell, Dean, I'm going in the back seat, I can't stand it any more, I can't look.' ...
> Great horrors that we were going to crash this very morning took hold of me and I got down on the floor and closed my eyes and tried to go to sleep ... now I could feel the road some twenty inches beneath me, unfurling and flying and hissing at incredible speeds across the groaning continent with that mad Ahab at the wheel. When I closed my eyes all I could see was the road unwinding into me. When I opened them I saw flashing shadows of trees

vibrating on the floor of the car. There was no escaping it. I resigned myself to it all. And still Dean drove, he had no thought of sleeping till we got to Chicago. (Kerouac 2000: 212–13)

This is a driving-event I return to in Chapter 5, but in the context of this chapter it may be seen to provide a vivid account of the way in which the senses work together in their apprehension of the car's – and its passengers' – flight. Even with his eyes closed, Sal continues to see the road unreel itself before him and to glimpse the landscape in the 'flashing shadows of trees vibrating on the floor of the car'. Vis-à-vis the tendency (discussed in Chapter 1) for theoretical accounts of driving practice to polarise around (visual) perception on the one hand (notably the psychologists from Gibson (1938) through to Groeger (2000)) and embodiment on the other (more recent mobilities scholars such as Dant (2004), Sheller (2004) and Merriman (2012) as well as Modernist literary critics like Danius (2002) and Kore-Schröder (2007)), Sal's multi-sensory response to his distress may be read as a productive complication to the binary. For although the account very obviously confirms the extent to which (auto)mobility is apprehended – and interpreted – by the *whole* body in ways that echo Merleau-Ponty's (2002 [1945]) theories of embodied knowledge, it also foregrounds the proactive role of the intellect – in particular memory – in recording and analysing the visual components of the process. With echoes of Bergson's account of how memory may be seen to 'shadow' perception in the present (2000 [1908]), this description of how the road 'unwinds' itself in Sal's consciousness thus raises fascinating questions about what we are actually 'seeing' when we look out of a car window/windscreen when travelling at (sufficient) speed. Do we see what is passing by *now*, or – given the continuity of the moving picture – a composite of 'frames' snatched seconds previously? Such questions – which also return us to Husserl's agonising attempts to distinguish between past, present and future through the example of a note of music (2002 [1964]) – clearly cannot be answered by means of this short extract from a literary classic, yet the very fact that they are raised is a tribute to Kerouac's insight into the complex ocularity of automotive consciousness.

Elsewhere, the text delivers a rather simpler analysis of the 'blinding' properties of speed. The vast state of Texas is disposed of in a single 500-mile run (Kerouac 2000: 146) and Nebraska unrolls itself as a single reel (with clear echoes of Kerouac's 'scroll'):[15] 'I saw the entire state of Nebraska unroll before my eyes. A hundred and ten miles an hour straight through, an arrow road, sleeping towns, no traffic and the Union Pacific streamliner falling behind us in the moonlight' (209).

Dean's obsession with achieving the fastest times available leads Sal to conclude: 'With frantic Dean I was rushing through the world without a chance to see it' (Kerouac 2000: 187). Implicit in this remark is, of course, recognition of the difference of embarking upon a transcontinental drive purely as sport (wherein driver and passenger may simply seek to 'lose' themselves in the speed) and a dedicated road trip, undertaken to order to deliver not only sensation but insight. The fact that Sal chooses the word 'see' to denote this failure of moral and intellectual engagement may be seen as a measure of the extent to which, apropos Baudrillard and Virilio, Kerouac, too, understood the distorting or 'extenuating' (Baudrillard 2010: 7) effect of driving at speed in specifically visual terms. Certainly, it is a text which – for long stretches of the road it follows – seems to confirm Virilio's indictment of what automobility and the postmodern culture(s) that it represents threaten to become: a mode of transport (and being) that is fixated *only* on the 'blind spot' of arrival (Virilio 2005: 105).

In this last regard, Part IV of the *On the Road*, which focuses on the final road trip of the 'crew' to Mexico, may be seen as an important corrective. Reduced to travelling in an old 'jalopy' purchased by Dean with the little money he now has left, the journey is undertaken at the *maximum* speed of 45mph, and this constraint – combined with Dean's overwhelming sense of having 'arrived' as soon as he crosses the Mexican border ('It's the world!' (Kerouac 2000: 252)) – facilitates a very different order of perception. Finally, it seems, Dean and his companions are apprehending the world as 'seen from the car' with something resembling fresh eyes:

> We arrived at Sabinas Hidalgo, across the desert, at about seven o'clock in the morning. We slowed down completely to see this. We woke up Stan in the back seat. We sat up straight to dig . . .
> 'Yes,' said Dean and drove right on at five miles an hour. He was knocked out, he didn't have to do the usual things he would have done in America . . . 'Sal, I am digging the interiors of these homes as we pass them – these gone doorways and you look inside and see beds of straw and little brown kids sleeping and stirring to wake, their thoughts congealing from the empty mind of sleep, their selves rising, and the mothers cooking up breakfast in iron pots, and dig them shutters they have for windows and the old men, the *old men* are so cool and grand and not bothered by anything' . . . Schooled in the raw road night, Dean was come into the world to see it. He bent over the wheel and looked both ways and rolled along slowly. (Kerouac 2000: 252–3 (italics in the original))

Finally, then, the immediacy of the phenomenological world crowds out all other thought, and instead of responding to the places through which they pass as prompts for stories of his own past life, Dean Moriarty really *does* 'dig' the scenes outside his car window in a 'fresh' and 'unprejudiced' way (Moran and Mooney 2002: 2). True, the car has to be slowed – then slowed again, almost to walking pace – for these wonders to be fully comprehended, but in the process this road-trip is improbably transformed from a flight into something more akin to H. V. Morton's 'searching'.

Intimacy on the road

As readers will be aware, almost all road-trip films explore – to a greater or lesser extent – the evolving relationship between two or more travellers even if the narrative is focalised through just one of them (see Borden 2013: 99) for an especially interesting discussion of the 'outlaw' variant of this). There are some notable and memorable exceptions – such as Chris Petit's *Radio On* (2008 [1979])[16] – but they demonstrate the challenge of representing the interiority of a solo driver's consciousness in terms *other* than detachment or alienation given that few drivers communicate their thoughts and feelings when driving alone except when moved to 'rage' (Katz 1999). By contrast, texts representing two or more characters have the benefit of conversation as a means of representing interiority – even if, as recent psychological and sociological research on driving and cognition attests, the accompanied driver's thoughts are determined by the conversation – and/or the other's presence – rather than what he or she would have been thinking when alone (Laurier and Dant 2011). Given that this book's focus, thus far, has been on texts which communicate the experiences of the solo driver, the shift of attention in this chapter to the thought processes that drivers and passengers are engaged in when travelling in couples or groups will, I hope, add a further layer of complexity to the discussions.

In Highsmith's *Carol*, the car functions as a closed and private space that separates Therese and Carol from the rest of the world and, to an extent, protects them. Indeed, once the detective is on their tail, it is the *only* place in which they are free from his surveillance (given that their motel rooms have been bugged). As we have already seen, the world as 'seen from the car' has little bearing upon the way in which this fictional relationship evolves or is presented to the reader, but the lovers' in-car 'dwelling' (Urry 2007) most certainly does. In line with recent automobilities theory which has emphasised the somatic and sensual pleasures of driving (Sheller 2004), *Carol*'s car 'embodies' the women's relationship in the most literal of ways; indeed, it is arguable that Therese 'gives' herself to Carol on their very first drive together – a night-time tour of

Manhattan Island – by physically and emotionally surrendering herself to Carol's skilful driving and the acceleration of the speeding car:[17]

> They drove uptown. It was like riding inside a rolling mountain that could sweep anything before it, yet it was absolutely obedient to Carol.
> 'Do you like driving?' Carol asked without looking at her. She had a cigarette in her mouth. She drove with her hands resting lightly on the wheel, as if it were nothing to her, as if she sat relaxed in a chair somewhere, smoking. 'Why're you so quiet?'
> They roared into the Lincoln Tunnel. A wild, inexplicable excitement mounted in Therese as she stared through the windshield. She wished the tunnel might cave in and kill them both, that their bodies might be dragged out together. She felt Carol glancing at her from time to time. (Highsmith 1990: 48)

Read thus, the consummation of the relationship, completed some weeks later in Waterloo, begins here (for Therese at least). The enclosed intimacy of the car, symbolically reinforced by the further layer of womb/vaginal-like protection provided by the tunnel, initiates an involuntary abandonment in the younger woman that finds its resolution in Waterloo:

> While a thousand memories and moments, words, the first darling, the second time Carole had met her at the store, a thousand memories of Carol's face, her voice, moments of anger and laughter flashed like the tail of a comet across her brain. And now it was pale blue distance and space, an expanding space in which she took flight suddenly like a long arrow. The arrow seemed to cross an impossibly wide abyss with ease, seemed to arc on and on in space, and not quite to stop. Then she realized that she still clung to Carol, that she trembled violently, and the arrow was herself. (Highsmith 1990: 1678)

Notable here is the way in which the sexual climax is, itself, likened to moving objects (comets, arrows, the cosmos itself), all of which evoke the flight of the car in which her arousal began.[18]

In the same way that the soothing movement of a car may be seen to symbolise and facilitate emotional and erotic abandonment for motoring couples, the occasions when it stops – either voluntarily or as the result of a jam, mechanical breakdown or wrong turning – can seriously disrupt the fantasies of one or both of its passengers and force uncomfortable differences into the open. This is certainly the case in *Carol*, where – early on in the trip – rest-stops are often uncomfortable interludes in which Carol interrogates Therese on what she's been thinking or why she's kept so silent. As theorised in Chapter 1, such breaks slice any long journey into a number of discrete driving-events, and – in Highsmith's novel – each stage is characterised by another turbulent emotion for the impressionable Therese. As the journey and relationship progresses such stops also tend to be the occasions when Therese blurts out her feelings for Carol ('I was so excited about you' (Highsmith 1990: 155)) or asks her about her past (including, most notably, her previous lesbian relationship with a woman called Abby (Highsmith 1990: 172)).

Yet if most of the (verbal) heart-to-hearts in *Carol* occur when the car is stationary (in contrast to the many moments of silent physical intimacy when they are driving (e.g. 'Carol held Therese's hand and drove with her left hand' (Highsmith 1990: 201)), it is notable that, in *On the Road*, the reverse is the case. Although it is true that Dean talks incessantly both inside and outside his cars (significantly, his all-night 'philosophy' sessions with Carlo Marx are likened, by Sal, to (another) 'machine' that cannot be stopped (2000: 243–4)), it is his wild disquisitions while *on* the road that distinguish Kerouac's text from others in the genre. Part running commentary, part personal confession, Dean both performs and mediates the driving-event in question for his fellow passengers: often to the extent that their own thoughts and impressions are crowded out.

Nowhere is Dean's role as a conduit and medium for his fellow travellers more extravagant than on the final trip to Mexico. As we have already observed, Mexico effects a qualitative change in Dean's mode of driving as 'flight' gives way to something more akin to 'probing' (see Chapter 1), but this change of gear does not signal a change of practice as far as his relentless explication is concerned (see extract quoted earlier). Indeed, he subsequently reflects upon his role as witness to the journey as if it was a special gift – and duty – ('[w] hile you've been sleeping I've been digging this road and this country, and if I could only tell you all the thoughts I've had, man!' (Kerouac 2000: 254–5)), but is altogether oblivious of the role played by his companions in the inspiration and actualisation of these thoughts. Mikhail Bakhtin's theories on the crucial role of the 'interlocutory other'[19] in the production of thought are helpful here, not only in exposing Dean's egocentric blind spot, but also in causing us to reflect upon the way in which car drivers and passengers help shape one another's thoughts more generally. Although such dynamics apply to all conversations, both the intimacy of the car setting, and the fact that this is a mode of transport that allows one to travel for long stretches *without* speaking – or, indeed, without driver and passenger(s) having to look at one another (Laurier and Dant 2011) – invites similarities with both the psychiatrist's couch and the church confessional. Alongside the practice of everyday conversation, Kerouac's text thus points to a range of cognitive roles that the cohabitants of a car may perform for one another. Like Dean, our travelling companions may signal and/or interpret something seen through the windscreen that we would otherwise have missed; equally, they may help us define and articulate a problem that has occurred to us during the drive; further, and without saying a word, they may induce and bear silent witness to something that presents itself to our consciousness in the course of our journey. As we will see in Chapter 4, one certainly does not need to be driving alone in order to meditate.

Conversation is also the means *to* intimate relationships in Kerouac's novel. In contrast to *Carol*, the male protagonists of Kerouac's text forge their relationships through their convoluted, quasi-intellectual exchanges while on the road, none more significant than the conversation Sal and Dean participate in on their return trip to Denver from San Francisco in 1949:

> Then I began talking; I never talked so much in all my life. I told Dean that when I was a kid and rode in cars I used to imagine I held a big scythe in my hand and cut down all the trees and posts and even sliced every hill that zoomed past the window. 'Yes! Yes!' yelled Dean. 'I used to do it too only different scythe . . .'
>
> We were telling these things and both sweating. We had completely forgotten the people up front who had begun to wonder what was going on in the back seat. At one point the driver said, 'For God's sake, you're rocking the boat back there.' Actually we were; the car was swaying as Dean and I both swayed to the rhythm and the IT of our final excited joy in talking and living to the blank tranced end all innumerable riotous angelic particulars that had been lurking in our souls all our lives. (Kerouac 2000: 188–9)

This exchange marks a significant deepening in the two men's relationship, with the symbolic passing backwards and forth of shared (driving) fantasies echoing both the intimate physical exchanges (food, hot drinks, cigarettes) and verbal sparring in *Carol*. Also comparable to Highsmith's text is, of course, the implication that the intense kinaesthetic environment of the car initiates a sexual dimension in the relationship. On one of the rare occasions when Dean is figured as passenger rather than driver, he (albeit briefly) abandons himself to an experience that he shares rather than directs.

That Dean ultimately regains his authority over his friend – notwithstanding a emotionally charged spat between the two when they finally arrive in Denver[20] – is evident in the dynamics of their next trip together, the 1,180-mile streak to Chicago to deliver the 1947 Cadillac, discussed earlier. We have already seen how, on this occasion, Sal is so terrified by Dean's driving that he curls up on the floor of the car and wills unconsciousness, only to find the image of the road still burning upon his retina and 'unwinding' itself into him (Kerouac 2000: 213), but it may equally be read as a further comment on the erotically charged power struggle between the two men. Rather than simply a means of fleeing some past oppression, actual or psychological, the Cadillac, driven by Dean (recast, by Sal, as the 'Angel of Terror'), becomes an instrument of punishment that demands Sal's absolute submission to his friend's will.

Read through the lens of psychoanalysis, the innuendoes here are all too obvious; from an automobilities perspective, however, the episode serves as an instructive reminder of the power dynamics that inscribe automotive consciousness (the passenger's as well as the driver's) when two or more travellers share a car. Sal's humiliation may be an extreme example, but how many of us have been passengers in cars driven too quickly or recklessly for our comfort and had our wishes challenged and undermined by those means? Flight and fright: Sal's experience reminds us that Baudrillard's 'death by an extenuation of forms' (Baudrillard 2010: 7) is something that can be done *to* us, as well as a thrill we seek for ourselves.

Conclusion

The figuration of the car as both the means and the symbol of escape has become an enduring mythology. This association – between one of the most revolutionary technologies of the twentieth century and one of its most pervasive compulsions – may thus be seen to demonstrate the ways in which driving is expressive of the distinctive culture(s) of that now fast-receding century as well as the individuals who drove the cars. Escape is still a meaningful need and compulsion in the twenty-first century, of course – as graphically expressed by the current international refugee crisis – but what the 1950s case study featured in this chapter reveals is the way which the urge extends into the aftermath of periods of social and economic turmoil. In the shadow of the Second World War, and all the privations, opportunities and social change that this threw up, what we discover – in the literary and other texts from the period – is a generation of American citizens demanding their rights to what would, today, be spoken of as 'lifestyle choices': recreational pursuits, freedom of expression, sexual liberation and – underlying all the others – personal mobility. Whatever the gripe, taking to the road became one of the most definitive ways of asserting these rights and symbolically rejecting the world (albeit temporarily) left behind.

The historical specificity of what we understand by 'the need for escape' is well-illustrated by the changing nature of the 'motor-flight' across the twentieth century. In the first decade, as already discussed, 'motor-flight' was the term elected by Edith Wharton and others to describe their genteel tours of America and Europe, while in the 1920s and 1930s the 'out-of-control car' became a synonym for 'madness' (sometimes treated with sensitivity, sometimes with mawkish humour). During the interwar years, meanwhile, the speeding car features prominently in middle-brow romances (see Chapter 5), where they become the locus of secret liaisons and dramatic crises, as well as becoming a staple of the crime genre (both fiction and film: see Borden 2013: 40–9). Therefore, although one speeding car may look very much like another, the reasons for the escape in question will vary not only in accordance with the circumstances pertaining to each driver/passenger but also the social and cultural context that informs or fuels their desire.

In the course of the chapter, I have sought repeatedly to test out my thesis that speed alone is not sufficient to characterise a driving-event a 'flight' and, along with that, to challenge the view – implicit in both Baudrillard and Virilio's essays from the 1980s – that automotive speed is indicative of a profound denaturing of perception, cognition, memory and our temporal orientation in the world. While there are, as my analysis has shown, episodes in Kerouac's *On the Road* that may appear to enact escape purely through driving from one location to another as fast as possible for no apparent reason other than the thrill of it, there is little way of evidencing – in either fiction or real life – if the drive truly did figure as an escape in the consciousness of the driver. Dean's commentaries at speeds in excess of 100mph suggest that *his* mind, at least, does not 'switch off' easily. Meanwhile, other moments – such as the Denver–Chicago Cadillac run – serve as a useful critique of Virilio by demonstrating just how much drivers and passengers continue to see, sense and interpret at speed. Indeed, the account of Sal Paradise's experience in the back of the Cadillac suggests that, even *in extremis*, the cognitive faculty is *not* 'turned off', with (short-term) memory playing a crucial role in analysing and consolidating the data that flashes before our eyes.

Stepping back from the lure of explaining automotive flight in purely existential terms, my textual analysis here appears to have validated my opening hypothesis that driving becomes 'fleeing' only when the driver/ passenger concerned brings this need and expectation to bear upon the journey. Apart from their attempt to escape Harge's detective towards the end of the narrative, there are no descriptions of driving at undue speed in Highsmith's *Carol*, and yet this road trip is unequivocally undertaken in the spirit of escape. By the same token, and picking up the previous discussion, driving more slowly does not, of itself, cause drivers and passengers – fictional or otherwise – to observe the world as 'seen from the car' in a fresh and 'unprejudiced' way (Moran and Mooney 2002: 2). While it is true that there is a qualitative change in Dean Moriarty's perception consequent upon his arrival in Mexico, Carol and Therese never seem to get beyond the schema of the 'American Road Trip' no matter how slowly they motor or how often they stop.

The importance of conversation – and the role of interlocutors in the production of automotive consciousness more generally – is the final conclusion to be drawn from this chapter. As the texts I have explored here make very clear, our fellow travellers can have a profound impact on the nature and direction of our thoughts in the course of a journey and not merely through conversational exchange. The mere presence of another person positions them as a silent witness or interlocutory other (sympathetic and/or critical) to our thoughts. Similarly, the power dynamic inherent in driver–passenger roles – not least the tendency of the driver to exercise his/her authority over the passenger through the act of driving (as demonstrated by both Dean and Carol) – may structure not only the passenger's thoughts (both intellectual and emotional), but also the relationship itself, in a very explicit way.

With so many provisos brought to bear upon it, the vision of the open road with its promise of mindless flight with which this chapter opened has been purposefully compromised. This is not, however, to deny that the practice of driving *as flight* – however fuelled – remains a singular pleasure or that the altered states of consciousness to which speed gives rise may deliver significant cognitive insight. These are matters to which I return and explore through a different lens in Chapter 5.

Notes

1. 'Astral America': this concept – a translation of Baudrillard's own 'l'Amérique sidéral' – is used in the text to signify the 'postmodern' surfaces of contemporary America (desert highways, motels, films, television, highway signs and speed itself) as opposed to the 'deep America of mores and mentalities' (Baudrillard 2010: 5).
2. Ernst Bloch (see Chapter 5) further distinguishes between journeys which are undertaken in a state of 'expectant emotion' and those undertaken in a state of boredom (Bloch 1986: 370). I would suggest that this rationale may also be employed to contrast journeys undertaken for the purposes of escape, as here, and those undertaken for the purpose of mental stimulation and/or problem-solving as is the case with 'cruising' (as in Chapter 4).
3. Michael Balint's *Thrills and Regressions* (1959) was one of the first studies to identify a thrill-seeking personality (the 'philobat') who is contrasted with

the 'oncophile' (who is 'inhibited by the trauma brought about by unusually intense movement') (reproduced in Wollen and Kerr 2002: 14–16).

4. Borden (2013) observes that very little of the academic literature on road movies deals specifically with the representation/experience of driving (p. 15) and focuses himself on this genre in the section of his book on the 'existential self' (pp. 85–117).

5. An Internet search of 'Kerouac road trip' reveals thousands of images associated with *On the Road*, including a large number of 'word and image' collages created by fans. See https://www.google.co.uk/search?q=kerouac+road-trip&tbm=isch&tbo=u&source=univ&sa=X&ved=0CEQQsARqFQoTCIbkgpGUnMgCFUdcFAodoY8OJw&biw=1280&bih=699 (last accessed 29 September 2015).

6. Many phases of American road-building preceded the building and completion of the 'interstates' (1956–73). The protagonists of Highsmith's and Kerouac's novels (both set in the late 1940s/early 1950s) use the numbered 'highways' (introduced in 1925) rather than the interstates. The road used most frequently in *On the Road* is the old Route 6 (see Davis 2008).

7. Both men draw upon the discourse and vocabulary of Futurism while supposedly standing Marinetti's 'celebration' of speed and 'mindless' pleasure/sexual gratification on its head (see Marinetti, quoted in Humphreys 1999: 11).

8. Deborah Clarke's *Driving Women* (2007: 116–17) contrasts Kerouac's representation of his male and female drivers/passengers and also shows how American women writers, like Barbara Kingsolver and Bobbie Ann Mason, have styled alternative female 'getaway' drivers.

9. Davis uses the term 'crew' to refer to the passengers who accompany him on his journey (presumably as co-drivers, navigators and mechanics). The term survives in Formula One racing today, as in 'the pit[-stop] crew'.

10. Highsmith's *Carol* was first published as *The Price of Salt* under the pseudonym Claire Morgan; it was republished as a Bantam paperback and immediately sold several millions of copies. It was then republished (under Highsmith's own name) by Bloomsbury Press in 1990 and has recently been made into a feature film by Todd Haynes (2015). See http://www.theguardian.com/books/2015/may/13/patricia-highsmith-film-adaptation-carol-only-openly-lesbian-novel-cannes-cate-blanchett (last accessed 3 October 2015).

11. *On the Road* has taken its place in literary history as the defining text of the 'Beat' movement, a concept that Kerouac struggled to explain to the general public (Holmes 1952) but which is typically understood as a willingness to open oneself fully to the experience of being alive, often by means of also taking oneself to the limits (of speed, travel, exhaustion, drug-use, etc.).

12. Dan Mansker's fascinating interactive maps of all the different trips featured in *On the Road* can be found at: http://www.dennismansker.com/ontheroad.htm/ (last accessed 3 October 2015).

13. Terry Castle (2006) observes how the formulaic romance plot that underpins Highsmith's novel is given a menacing edge by the historical moment in which the action is set. See http://www.slate.com/articles/news_and_politics/pulp_fiction/2006/05/pulp_valentine_4.html (last accessed 3 October 2015).

14. Castle (note 13) also points out that Highsmith's text pre-dates Nabokov's *Lolita* (2000 [1995]): 'I've often thought that Nabokov must have stolen the cross-country car trip in *Lolita* . . . from Highsmith's novel.'
15. The first draft of *On the Road* was written over a period of three weeks in 1951 using a typewriter and rolls of paper that were taped together into a long scroll so that Kerouac's 'creative flow' was uninterrupted. See http://www.telegraph.co.uk/culture/books/booknews/9557844/Original-manuscript-of-Jack-Kerouacs-On-the-Road-to-be-exhibited-in-London.html (last accessed 3 October 2015).
16. Chris Petit's *Radio On* (2008 [1979]) is often cited by automobilities scholars as a 'rare example' of a British road movie. The BFI DVD includes a booklet with several excellent essays and commentaries on the film.
17. Therese's 'death-wish' in the Lincoln Tunnel recalls other literature and film that has centred on the car crash as an erotic site – most notably J. G. Ballard's novel (2008 [1973]) and David Cronenberg's (1996) film adaptation – although Borden's discussion of the phenomenon (2013: 199–225) attests to its pervasiveness as a motif in contemporary film. Another intertext – probably more in tune with Therese's state of mind – is The Smiths' song 'There is a light that will never go out' (1986).
18. 'Becoming-arrow': this is the very same image that Kerouac uses to describe Sal Paradise's moment of ecstasy when he first catches sight of Denver (Kerouac 2000: 25). Highsmith's novel was published five years previously.
19. Mikhail Bakhtin's dialogic theory foregrounds the role of the interlocutor/addressee in the production of meaning both at the level of discourse and the individual word of speech. See Pearce (1994: 50–1).
20. Dean teases Sal about getting old when they are urinating together in a public toilet (Kerouac 2000: 193–4); Sal gets mad and lashes out, causing Dean to cry. Reference to a 'fag' they have recently travelled with and the fact that the altercation takes place in a public toilet lends the episode both erotic and homophobic overtones.

Chapter 4

Cruising

Walk across any motorway bridge (see Figure 4.1) in the UK or else-where – as most of us have done at some point in our lives – pausing briefly to wonder at the colourful pulse of cars and wagons that rumble beneath you, and it soon becomes clear that neither the type of road nor the speed at which individual vehicles travel along it tells us what sort of journeys or driving-events the travellers in those vehicles are engaged in. For while motorways and their variants – freeways, autobahns, autostradas, etc. – are the class of road most typically associated with the manner of driving that is the subject of this chapter – i.e. cruising – a

Figure 4.1 View of M62 from motorway bridge (2009). Photo by Viv Tabner.

moment's reflection reminds us that this is a practice which may equally well be enjoyed on A-roads, minor roads and the roads of history. From the bird's-eye perspective of the motorway bridge, meanwhile, there is absolutely no way of telling which of the vehicles that whizzes by at a typical speed of 70–80mph is engaged in an act of cruising (as defined below) and which, by contrast, is, for example, fleeing. By placing the driver's automotive consciousness at the centre of each driving-event rather than functionalities that pertain to the car-as-transportation (road-type, journey-type) we can begin to grasp the true diversity of the 'travel' being undertaken on any given stretch of road (Dant and Martin 2001: 151; Edensor 2003: 161; Merriman 2012: 217–18) and, I would suggest, marvel at the way in which the driver in Car A travelling at 80mph is engaged in such a qualitatively different motoring experience to the driver in Car B travelling at an identical speed (Pearce 2012). Paused thus on a bridge not only over a hypothetical motorway but also between this chapter and the last, I wish to propose that the cognitive/ affective distance between fleeing and cruising can be both miniscule and substantive. For the most part, this chapter will focus on the latter since – as will be seen from my attempt at a definition below – the manner of driving most typically evoked by the term cruising is also the one that, if conditions are favourable, facilitates the type of thinking that may be associated with personal reflection, problem-solving, meditation or the practice of mindfulness;[1] in other words, a mode of automotive consciousness which, in the manner of cruising itself, is open yet pur- poseful, and – in its ostensible steadiness – in significant contrast both to the mind-numbing properties of the motor-flight, as explored in the previous chapter, and the 'altered' states of consciousness that are the subject of Chapter 5. Given the extent to which motoring literature – from the earliest periodicals and early twentieth-century fiction through to postmodern theorists like Baudrillard (2010 [1986]) and Virilio (2008 [1984]) – has focused on the more extreme psychological states that driving can give rise to, the stereotypically laid-back figure of the cruising-driver is not only a necessary corrective to a taken-for-granted discourse but also one that exemplifies what I shall be presenting here as quintessential 'drivetime'.

Cruising, even within the confines of motoring discourse, can connote many things. Indeed, it is possible that the most popular gloss on the term today is sexual: that is, a mobile practice (walking as well as driving) with the specific intention of picking up a (casual) sexual partner (*OED* online). It was, of course, the youth and car culture of 1950s America that leant a certain glamour – even, paradoxically, an innocence – to this inflection: a seemingly light-hearted courtship ritual in which boys and cars performed a hyperbolic version of masculinity (soundtracked by the rock and roll music of the era) in order to feel good about themselves – and, of course, attract the girls. Further, as Jack Windmer reflects in his essay on this unique moment in twentieth-century popular culture: 'driving – or, more specifically, cruising and playing the radio – is so pleasant in and of itself that destinations have become superfluous' (Windmer 2002: 72). That this version of 'cruising' is something other than 'driving' per se also points to its fascinating ambiguity as a type of mobility: movement *is* a factor (it is part of the performance), but it is not an objective.

Dictionary definitions of cruising are useful here, not least as a marker of the contradictions inherent in the term's usage. Originating in a generalised concept of mobility sourced to the Dutch verb *kruisen* – 'to cross' – twentieth-century applications include purposeful travel on the one hand – e.g. 'to take a holiday on a ship or boat following a prede-termined course' or 'to travel or move around a place slowly, typically in search of something' – and, on the other, excursions defined by their very aimlessness, e.g. 'to sail about in an area *without* a precise destina-tion' (*OED* online (my emphasis)). Meanwhile, although automobiles are secondary to ships and boats in terms of the transportation most typically associated with cruising, it is significant that the connotations of relaxed and temperate mobility are exemplified not by boats but by cars and aircraft, hence: '(of a motor vehicle or aircraft) *to travel smoothly at a moderate or economical speed*, e.g. "we sit in a jet, cruis-ing at 30,000 ft"' (*OED* online (my italics)).

The contradictions manifest in these definitions – purpose/aimless-ness, speed/slowness, effort/ease – thus characterise a mode or manner of moving around the world that is ambiguous in both expression and intent. For American musician, Neil Young, for example, a determined *lack* of destination or purpose is the (paradoxical) objective of 'serious' cruising. Although his autobiography, *Special Deluxe* (2014), includes many instances of driving that bear all the hallmarks of cruising even though he is on tour or making his way to the studio, there are notable occasions when he and his companions embark on an outing where '[the lack of] a precise destination' (*OED* online) is its *raison d'être*:

This particular [DeSoto] Suburban was really fun to cruise in, so we would generally fire up a joint or take some blow with us when we took off on a mission exploring local habitats like bars and restaurants, leaving Tunitas Ranch in the late afternoon for points unknown, or at least undecided . . . There was a willingness to engage in anything that came along, to meet anyone, to go anywhere that seemed interesting. Failure was not in my expe-rience. These, then, were the best of times . . . (Young 2014: 268)

Associated with a purpose-built car – the DeSoto Suburban 1950 – Young's memory vividly embeds cruising, thus defined, in a particular historical and cultural moment (California in the late 1960s/early 1970s). It is, nevertheless, a use of (and attitude towards) the car that extends beyond nation and culture (as will be seen in the following section) and one that is, I feel, crucial to our understanding of the full spectrum of automotive consciousness. Cruising is, one might argue, the unremarkable and hence undervalued 'middle-ground' of driving; in terms of automotive consciousness, it represents the occasions when driving at a comfortable speed and (as the dictionary suggests) with 'ease' permits drivers[2] to pursue all manner of thoughts in a relaxed, contemplative manner. To maximise this sort of 'drivetime' it would seem that the vehicle needs to be moving at sufficient yet moderate speed: drive too fast and/or in difficult road conditions and the brain's 'central executive' (Groeger 2000: 57–60) will kick in (see discussion in Chapter 1); drive too slowly and our thinking is prone to become distracted and fragmented (sometimes by things outside the car, sometimes by small anxieties) and altogether too pressed upon by more immediate concerns to achieve the detachment necessary for successful meditative practice.

A writer/artist who has explored the pleasures of cruising in some depth and appreciated the significance of this 'intermediate' speed, is Andrew Cross.[3] In his essay, 'Driving the American landscape' (2002), Cross identifies the special factors involved in American cruising thus:

> Except for a few concentrated urban areas, the cultural manner of driving in America is quantifiably different from that in Europe. Traffic is significantly less dense, and the pace is seemingly more leisurely – most people drive at fairly similar and consistent speeds averaging 60 mph ... The relatively stress-free driving conditions are, however, only part of the attraction. It is the whole dreamscape of America that will condition your anticipation and satisfy your every need when you are on the road. It is where the expansive existential abstracts can be encapsulated by a mug of coffee set on a formica counter. These are the scenes set in wayside diners and motel nowherevilles that provide the indelible romantic tone to the American road that is so singularly lacking on the European motorway. (Cross 2002: 249–50)

Along with the romantic/kitsch paraphernalia that constructs and sharpens the pleasure of cruising along an American highway for many a European driver, Cross draws our attention to the qualitative difference of cruising at 60–70mph in a 'relatively stress-free environment' to what might pass as cruising (at 80–90mph) on a British motorway. A fascinating implication here is that American drivers on these types of roads (i.e. the open highways) do not appear to feel the need to travel as fast as drivers on British/European motorways. While some of my North American friends have disputed the truth of this impression, even *as* an impression it is instructive since it surmises a bilateral link between automotive consciousness and speed. A hypothetical cycle would seem to present itself whereby drivers, joining a phalanx of other motorists moving at sufficient yet comfortable speed, are themselves lulled into a state of relaxed reverie/contemplation and hence disinclined to speed or otherwise drive aggressively. Cross continues:

> As the ideal province of cruise control, interstates possess their own person-alities, which range from the exhilarating to the stupefyingly dull. As you glide at a steady 65 or 75 mph across the continent, interstates will fly you over houses and train yards in suburban Chicago or Houston, grace you with wide, immaculately manicured verges and meridian as you gently roll through rural Indiana or Pennsylvania; or offer spectacular views as you sharply descend off an escarpment on a desert plain – as the 15 does near the Utah/Nevada border. (Cross 2002: 252)

While this statement acknowledges that the roadscape, itself, may be 'stupefyingly dull', the *moderately* fast cruising speed of 65–75mph (the very speed, indeed, that most of us associate with the automated 'cruise-control' facility on contemporary cars) is sufficient to induce sensations of 'gliding' and 'flying': sensations which, although presented here as bodily, are very clearly indicative, also, of the driver's psycho-logical state. It is not only the car but its driver who 'looks down' on all s/he surveys. This is not to imply, however, that the driver has stopped *thinking*; as this chapter aims to demonstrate, the state of driver-reverie that Cross's extract describes is typically the gateway to all manner of cogitation.

Contentious as this national stereotyping might be, Cross is not alone in drawing comparisons between British and American drivers when it comes to our capacity to adopt a 'cruising' mentality. Ian Parker also remarks on the way in which the 'average' American inhabits their auto-mobile differently and, although mobile, never appears to be in a hurry:

> Seen at the wheel of his or her car, a typical American has an air of someone with various projects underway, just one of which happens to be driving a car. He or she will also be involved in the solemn business of, say, sitting com-fortably. A London driver – even a London driver on the telephone – always looks more fully consumed by the act of driving, and rarely achieves a state of blissful, armchair disengagement allowed by automatic gears and carefully engineered holders for cans of soft drinks. (Parker 2002 [1999]: 306)

Implicit here is the assumption, shared by other commentators, that the car itself plays a crucial role in inculcating ease and reverie. In material terms, what this would seem to translate into – though it is rarely expressed directly – is the fact that certain cars have been manufactured for driving experiences other than speed.[4] Both Cross and Parker comment, wistfully, on interior features that signify domestic comfort, luxury and relaxation (armchair seats, holders for drinks, state-of-the art radios (Cross 2002: 253)), the consequence of which is that drivers will enjoy taking their time to get from A to B.

On this point it is worth pausing to remind ourselves how contrary this mode of motoring is to the 'motoring for motoring's sake' discussed at the beginning of the previous chapter. Between the challenge of using an automobile to get from one place to another in the quickest time possible and the cruising ethos that we have discovered here, there is a qualitative difference of such enormity that it calls into question many of the generalisations that have been made about motoring. For example, most of the post-millennial explorations of driver-car 'hybridity' (see the following discussion) incline towards the view that high-tech, in-car technology has caused drivers and passengers to become less in touch with the world outside the car and, following Virilio (2008), focused only their destination, whereas these evocations of the 'American cruiser' would suggest a very different scenario. These are drivers who enjoy their in-car comfort and technology, for sure, but in order to enhance their leisurely progress rather than as a distraction to make the time pass more quickly.

So far, then, we have established that cruising, in a motoring context, is a manner of driving that (following the contradictions identified in its dictionary definitions) frequently combines a sense of purpose (however trivial) with the practice of spontaneity (i.e. there is no 'precise destination'), and wherein the essential quality of 'ease' is closely linked to speed, though in complex ways. In the accounts of American cruising (notably from a British perspective) we have also witnessed passing reference to both the role played by certain types of road (notably the interstates) in facilitating this type of driving, as well as comfortable and luxurious car interiors (Parker 2000: 306). I return to the first of these in some detail in the first subsection of this chapter which looks, expressly, at the way in which highways, freeways and motorways have given rise to driving-as-cruising and the distinctive brand of automotive consciousness that accompanies it, but conclude this introduction with a brief consideration of the latter vis-à-vis recent automobilities theorising of driver-car 'hybridity' and the consequences of the rise of the 'intelligent car' (Dennis and Urry 2009; Laurier and Dant 2011).

Although Nigel Thrift's article, 'Driving in the City' (2008 [2004]) is often cited as a landmark publication in this regard, his conceptualisation of the car and its driver as a 'hybrid' mechanism has its origins in Jack Katz's research on 'road rage' in Los Angeles which forms a chapter of his book *How Emotions Work* (1999). Thrift cites Katz in his own exploration of the form that driving now takes:

> [We need to] understand driving (and passengering) as both profoundly embodied and sensuous experiences, though of a particular kind, which 'requires and occasions a metaphysical merger, the intertwining of the identities of the driver and the car that generates a distinctive ontology in the form of a person-thing, a humanized car, or, alternatively, an automobilized person' (Katz 2000). (Thrift 2008: 80)

I return to Katz's work in my discussion of 'road rage' in Chapter 5, but his identification of the twentieth-century car as a 'person-thing'/'humanized car' also requires consideration in the context of cruising. While, as already noted, I do not subscribe to the over-generalised assumption that the highly technological or 'intelligent' car necessarily prohibits or destroys the type of driving pleasures and/or thrills explored in the previous two chapters – i.e. we can still drive in search of things, we can still open the windows and/or roof and expose ourselves to the smells of the road and the countryside if we wish, we can still enjoy the thrills of 'motoring for motoring's sake' provided we find a suitably challenging stretch of road – I do, nevertheless, acknowledge that the hermetically sealed late twentieth-century car has brought a new 'interiority' to the practice and experience of driving on certain classes of road (typically highways and motorways) which has had consequences not only for how we experience the world as 'seen from the car' (Kennedy 1919b) but also how we think while we are in it. In other words, I recognise that advances in car design and technology have facilitated the brand of automotive consciousness associated with cruising, even though technology, alone, does not produce this mindset.

Tim Dant's (2004: 62) critique of the concept of 'hybridity' to characterise the contemporary 'driver-car' is instructive here, and his alternative formulation – i.e. the driver-car *assemblage* – supports my own view, expressed above, that drivers can *dis*aggregate themselves from a car's technology by something as simple as opening a window and switching off their phone and/or satellite systems if they choose. This qualification noted and the more sinister overtones of human mechanisation put to one side, most of us will nevertheless recognise and concur with the sort of observations that John Urry (2007: 130) and Andrew Cross (below) have made about the ways in which the modern car cocoons us from the 'outside world' and seemingly erects a screen between the driver/passenger and his or her apprehension of it:

Today, there is no landscape if it is not seen through the windscreen, only a series of places, postcard snapshots separated by time and space. It is only within the frame of the windscreen that places co-exist, that they become animated along the continuous narrative of the landscape through which you drive. (Cross 2002: 255)

For these commentators, as for Baudrillard (2010) and Virilio (2008) cited in the previous chapter, it is the fact that the modern, sealed car (in contrast to the open-tops of the early days of motoring (Urry 2007: 125–6)) presents the world to the driver through *glass* that is of particular significance; from the days of St Augustine,[5] glass has, of course, figured in Western culture as a potent symbol of distorted and/or '*dis*reality' and, during the twentieth century, has gathered additional resonance on account of the multiple and various 'screens' which are perceived to mediate our sense of being and belonging in the world (Urry 2007: 130). In the specific context of the role of the windows/windscreens of automobiles, however, I would suggest that it is a symbolism that has oversimplified our understanding of the driver/passenger's automotive experience, both with regard to their perception of the landscape through which they travel and how this impacts upon their thought processes. For while it is easy to assume that motoring along a country lane at twenty or thirty miles an hour in an open-topped car – or, alternatively, with all the windows down – will deliver a more immediate and 'authentic' engagement with the landscape through which we pass and thus enable us to apprehend it more freshly and immediately, historians of motoring repeatedly remind us of how uncomfortable open-top driving can be: often, indeed, to the extent that drivers and passengers are more preoccupied with the total sensation of the event (Merriman 2012: 2) than with registering or otherwise attending to the world as seen from the car. The windscreen, then, may perhaps cause us to 'see the world darkly' (see note 5), but at least we *do* see it.

The conception of the contemporary driver (or, at least, the driver of the 'sealed car') as an automaton who has morphed into his or her machine and, through a sinister alliance of speed and technology, become both unseeing and unthinking, therefore stands to be corrected; while it has, perhaps, suited scholars, environmentalists and artists opposed to automobility to caricature this driver as a robot, many contemporary drivers are acutely attentive to what presents itself to them through their windscreens when cruising at comfortable speeds. Evidence of this is, I hope, to be found in my own 'Interlude' and also Tim Edensor's auto-ethnographic article, 'M6: Junction 19–16' (2003), discussed below. The late twentieth-century cruiser in his or her 'cyber-car' (Sheller and Urry 2000) may not 'know' the world through their cars in the same way as early motorists and/or walkers and cyclists, but they most certainly *do* see, think and feel in the course of their journeys. Nigel Thrift, of course, recognised this by arguing that driving facilitates and delivers its own phenomenology (Thrift 2008: 75) and in the case study that follows I include examples of how the practice of cruising affords drivers and passengers an opportunity to process, often in an explicitly phenomenological manner, 'scenes' and scenarios from their own lives.

The cruising road

> Whether on interstates or older highways, a lot of time is spent travelling on roads that change only imperceptibly. Yet these sometimes tiresomely long bouts of driving are somehow effortless. *And it is while floating through the slow vastness of the landscape that you can exercise your deepest thoughts and most wondrous adventures* . . . (Cross 2002: 252–3 (my italics))

Having previously argued that cruising, when figured as a state of automotive consciousness as well as a manner of driving, does not necessarily require a long straight road for its practice, in this section I have nevertheless elected to explore – and acknowledge – the role of the multi-carriage highway – the motorway, the freeway, the autobahn – in the production of 'cruiser-consciousness': that unique cognitive pleasure that Cross (above) poetically likens to 'floating'.

For many of the scholars and commentators who have traced the evolving cultural significance of driving across the twentieth century, the relationship between the road infrastructure and the practice/experience of travelling on it has been a key consideration. Indeed, Iain Borden's book, *Drive* (2013), which works with film texts in order to explore the ways in which we inhabit and encounter a mobilised world, is organised around this principle with chapters on city driving, journeys (including the road trip) and motorways. It is the last of these – entitled 'Motopia' – that speaks most directly to my own concerns in this chapter and, in particular, his view – shared with Edensor (2003), Merriman (2007) and myself – that motorways (and their international variants) are not inherently 'boring'. In response to Chris Petit's film, *London Orbital* (2002), based on Iain Sinclair's book (2003 [2002]) of the same name, he observes that it is the seemingly 'endless time' of motorway driving ('a world where the past has departed, where the future is visible but never reached' (Borden 2013: 153)) that constitutes its special freedoms in terms of thought: 'Even more significantly, freeway driving is a space and time for contemplation – where the very neutral and supposedly boring experience of driving is reinvigorated by thoughts, memories, ideas and inspirations of all kinds' (Borden 2013: 153).

As noted in the previous section, this is a view with which Tim Edensor – as someone who came to love his daily commutes up and down the M6 in the 1990s – is completely in agreement:

> Assertions that the world is apprehended via a 'two-dimensional view through the car windscreen' resonate with other accounts about the dominance of the visual, virtuality and mediatisation of the world . . . Such versions suggest that levels of detachment from immediate surroundings preclude irruptions of fantasy and reveries, and they ignore the connections between immediate surroundings and a host of intertextual and interpractical spaces, places, eras, and occasions. In the case of driving, they neglect the ways in which individuals enfold elsewheres, pasts, and futures during their journeys, concoct and rehearse narratives; and sensually apprehend the world in ways additional to the visual. (Edensor 2003: 163)

There is, however, a small but significant difference in the ways in which these two scholars account for the 'drivetime' afforded by the motorway. While Borden focuses on the mental liberation afforded by 'relatively *constant views* [my italics], road conditions and speed' (Borden 2013: 154) – Edensor's auto-ethnography details and reflects upon the rapid succession of visual/cognitive *prompts* (see the discussion in Chapter 1) which are notably proactive in stimulating and directing the driver's thoughts and memories even – indeed especially – on a familiar stretch of motorway:

> But when you get to know a journey, familiar sights crowd each mile, are reassuring signs of continuity and subjects for speculation, becoming axes of orientation after a period of immersion in sound or reverie . . . The linearity of the road also dissolves as monuments, signs and surprises form a skein of successive and overlapping features, enveloping the motorway in a web of association. This is a topography of possible sights and destinations that reference other spaces and times because motorways are spaces of material, imaginative, and social flows. (Edensor 2003: 156)

For Edensor, as for myself (see Interlude), then, the motorway is anything but the empty, featureless space of 'Kraftwerk' mythology[6] or Marc Augé's 'non-places' (1995) (see the discussion in Chapter 1) if it is at all familiar to the driver/passenger. Although sporting an aesthetic that has become an all too convenient cliché for alienation, the British motorway is, to quote Merriman, a surprisingly 'meaningful place' (Merriman 2007: 2017–18) for all those of us who regularly incorporate it into the narratives of our unfolding and often fast-receding lives.

It is, nevertheless, important that we recognise that such expressions of affection for the British motorway network go against the grain of the history that is often told of it (see especially Moran 2009: 101–11). For Richard J. Williams (2002), for example, this is in large part due to the 'spirit' in which the British motorway system was conceived and executed: that is, no-nonsense utility rather than an expression of the new 'freedom' (national and individual) that one might have expected to characterise the mood of postwar Europe. With reference to the oft-quoted speeches of Transport Minister Ernest Marples made before and immediately after the opening of England's 'first' motorway,[7] Williams reflects on the way in which the minister's authoritarian and sobering advice to drivers (i.e. 'If in doubt, don't') has cast its shadow over British motorways ever since ((Williams 2002: 281). This is a view echoed by Peter Merriman in his much-lauded 'cultural-historical geography' of the M1, *Driving Spaces* (2007). Merriman observes that 'in the weeks and months following the opening of the M1, there were many commentaries published on the qualitative difference of this sort of driving'(Merriman 2007: 163). Some of these were positive, such as the *Birmingham Mail*'s observation that '"the absence of villages, sharp bends, crossroads, roundabouts, speed limits and traffic lights leads to a curious elation"'(Merriman 2007: 163), but the general cultural reception was negative and was seized upon by the writers and artists of the day as a signifier of angst, alienation and emptiness. (He cites David Turner's 1962 play, *Semi-Detached*, and the motorway paintings of Julian Opie (see note 35 to Chapter 1) as particular examples.) Merriman's own research into the material circumstances of driving on the M1 at this time, drawing on contemporary newspaper and other reports has, however, shown how far this mythology differed from the visceral, lived experience of the majority of motorists, even if the power of the hostile discourse has left its mark on the popular imagination (Bracewell 2002).

The discourse which stands in signal opposition to that associated with the beleaguered British motorway is, of course, the unequivocal celebration of the American 'freeway'.[8] However, before we proceed to a consideration of the freeway phenomenon in advance of this chapter's case study, it is important to register that *pre*-Second World War Britain shared a more idealised vision of high-speed cruising roads with its European and international neighbours. In his evocative chapter, 'Roads today – highways for tomorrow', historian David Jeremiah (2007) draws upon a fascinating range of texts – including several memorable visual impressions of Britain's 'highways of the future' – to demonstrate the ways in which both the public and the planning authorities embraced, yet feared, fast roads. Jeremiah's analysis also offers a credible sociological explanation for the negative discourses that subsequently attached themselves to the British motorway system, namely a small island's environmental concerns and historical attachments. Significantly, many of the drawings/designs which attempt to envisage a solution to the 'traffic problem' do so by separating out the different types of road-user in such a way that the vestiges of rural life (the horse and cart, the country lane) are accommodated and preserved. Guy Lipscombe's 'Utopian: "A thoroughfare of the future"' (1908) is a case in point (Jeremiah 2007: 129), as is the extraordinary 'Proposed motor track, carried over an existing road' published in *Car Illustrated* on 25 October 1905 (Jeremiah 2007: 61). The fact that groups like the Council for the Preservation of Rural England and the motor trade struggled to relinquish their nostalgia for the 'early years of motoring and distaste for new arterial roads' (Jeremiah 2007: 73–85, 135) well into the 1930s and 1940s, helps explain why not only motorways but highways in general have been greeted with such ambiguity in Britain. The inference is clear that while the prospect of fast, uncongested cruising roads was appealing, this could not be at the expense of the sort of motoring pleasures discussed in Chapter 2 which favoured 'byways' over 'highways'.

What the tensions in these historical debates about road type and road use return us to, of course, are further – though largely unvoiced – questions about the different sorts of *driving* British motorists recognise and prefer; whether, for example, the sort of 'searching' and touring activity explored in Chapter 2 has retained such a residual hold on the imagination of British drivers that the that motorway/freeway concept would always have struggled to establish itself in the UK. What is perhaps most remarkable in this regard is the extent to which, a century later, Britain has preserved its vast hinterland of minor roads and lanes, many of them dating back to the era of horse-drawn transport. In 2013 this amounted to 214.4 thousand miles of byways (or 'minor roads'), in comparison to its 2.3 thousand miles of motorways,[9] reminding us that that highway cruising must still be an occasional practice for many drivers and passengers even if, for others, it has become the norm. The residues of the British driver's preference for the country lane over the six-lane highway is also demonstrated by those who purposefully avoid motorways and make their journeys – sometimes long ones – on 'A' and 'B' roads. While a proportion of these will be nervous and/or elderly drivers, the fact that this option remains a possibility in the motoring imagination is, I would suggest, significant. It is, at very least, in marked contrast to Reyner Banham's impression of the drivers of Los Angeles in the 1960s, of whom he writes 'the freeway is where . . . [they] live a large part of their lives' (Banham 1973 [1971]: 214).

Reyner Banham's *Los Angeles: The Architecture of Four Ecologies* (1973) is one of the three texts, all centred on California in the 1970s, that comprise this chapter's case study. In advance of that discussion, Banham's essay also constitutes a suitable end point to this section inasmuch as it has become *the* text that automobilities scholars cite when differentiating between British and American road systems and British and American driving practices (e.g. Williams 2002: 284; Merriman 2007: 208; Moran 2009: 105–7; Borden 2013: 141–2). At the time of its publication, Banham's book – and, in particular, its 'fourth ecology', 'Autopia' – attracted the interest of reviewers the world over on account of the way in which its celebration of the LA Freeways (see Figure 4.2) revealed the extent to which auto/mobility was in the process of radically reshaping the twentieth-century subject's relationship to his or her world. In this regard, it is, of course, a text that anticipates much of the social geography introduced in Chapter 1 (Doel 1996; Thrift 2008; Merriman 2012). That it took an architect like Banham to grasp the extent to which our mobilisation as subjects has also mobilised the (perceptual) landscape is often remarked upon, and the fact that others like Mitchell Schwarzer (2004) and Iain Borden (2013) continue his project is an indication of how far-reaching his revisioning of the built environment was.

Figure 4.2 'California CA, Los Angeles', Jeff Greenberg © Fotolibra (FOT1174667).

As well as recognising the extent to which the 'Angelenos' took to their freeways ('everyday commuting tends less and less to move by the classic systole and diastole in and out of downtown, more and more to move by an almost Brownian motion over the whole area' (Banham 1973: 36), Banham's essay also captured the special kinaesthetic thrills of 'riding' them. While, as we will see, this is – at his own admission – cruising of a very different order to that practised on British motorways, the 'redistribution' (Edensor 2003: 159) of the senses and the cognitive processes the practice opens up are, to a degree, comparable. Indeed, it is clear that, in a remarkably short space of time (1950s–1970s), Angelenos came to love the experience of driving the freeways, and the practice quickly became as much of a defining characteristic of Californian culture as chuntering along 'byways' are to Britain.

'Drivetime': California cruising with Neil Young and Joan Didion

So immersive is the experience of driving or riding the Los Angles freeways that it demands active participation to be properly understood and appreciated. It was this realisation – way back in the late 1960s – that prompted Reyner Banham to learn to drive and put in hundreds of miles cruising the freeways, 'in order to read Los Angeles in the original' (Banham 1973: 23). Given that this remains a driving experience that the majority of us, myself included, can only engage with second-hand, photographs (see Figures 4.2 above and 4.3 below), film[10] and 'YouTube' videos perform a crucial role in helping us apprehend the intricate and, indeed, mesmerising challenge of weaving one's vehicle through multiple strands of traffic at variable speed. Fascinated by the special skills required to achieve these manoeuvres safely, Banham famously observed:

> Furthermore, the actual experience of driving on the freeways prints itself deeply on the conscious mind and unthinking reflexes. As you acquire the special skills involved, the Los Angeles freeways become a special way of being alive, which can be duplicated, in part, on other systems (England would be a much safer place if those skills could be inculcated on our motorways) but not with this totality and extremity. If motorway driving anywhere calls for a high level of attentiveness, the extreme concentration required in Los Angeles seems to bring on a state of heightened awareness that some locals find mystical. (Banham 1973: 214–15)

For the purposes of the of this book's focus on the mechanisms of automotive consciousness, Banham's passing recognition that these skills depend upon 'the conscious mind' as well as the 'unthinking reflexes' present themselves as especially insightful, even though different schools of psychology will explain the binary rather differently (see the discussion in Chapter 1). Even more crucial for the exploration and definition of cruising that I am attempting here is his further insight that the *outcome* of this 'extreme concentration' is not simply a matter of a safe and successful manoeuvre, but rather a 'state of heightened awareness'. In other words, it is the cognitive *effort* required to drive these roads that otherwise liberates the mind and facilitates a state of enlightenment.

A sense of the driving conditions that engender the rhythm of concentration/relaxation associated with these skilled driving-events may be gleaned by sampling some of the plentiful YouTube footage available of the LA freeways. Two recent home videos (Koocamorph1 2010 and Kurmann 2010) provide a useful comparison of the experience for 'mainstream' and 'car-pool' drivers,[11] the latter having access to a designated lane (similar to a British bus lane) which allows them to stream through and across the different highways at a consistent (though not excessive) speed, while the rest of the traffic is consigned to an elaborate dance of stop-start progress and restless lane-hopping. While the car-pool motorists (in this case two European men) appear to be practising the sort of driving/passengering that is more commonly associated with highway cruising, the voiceover to the other video (Koocamorph1) – which features exchanges between a man and woman – also demonstrates a familiarity with the driving conditions relaxed enough for the car's occupants to think and converse between the tricky manoeuvres. This car is also host to a GPS navigator which periodically reassures the driver that she is still following the best (i.e. quickest) route, as well as providing instructions on when to switch lanes. Each of the five lanes of traffic acquires its own internal rhythm, alternating between a decent cruising speed and a crawl, the latter typically brought about by another driver changing lanes. It is noticeable, even on this short film, that the driver and passenger become more relaxed and talkative when the car accelerates to cruising speed and fall silent (with the driver sometimes sighing) when they brake and slow down. This, of course, suggests a measure of frustration with the stop-start progress,[12] but – some forty years after the first publication of Banham's essay – there is the impression that these twenty-first-century 'Angelenos' are still subscribing to the 'mystique' of their freeway system (Banham 1973: 221) and finding the experience of driving it surprisingly 'calming', even in heavy traffic (Banham 1973: 222).

The film produced by the car-pool drivers, meanwhile, captures something of the sense of what it means to soar through and across this amazing feat of road architecture at a speed sufficient to register the magnificent sweep of the ramps (see Figure 4.2 above), the downward plunge of the underpasses and the sound of the tyres 'singing' on the anti-skid concrete road surface (an unfamiliar and distinctive sound to the British motorist's ear) as celebrated in Banham's text:

> But psychologically shocked [about the pollution affecting downtown LA in the 1970s] or no, most Angeleno freeway-pilots are neither retching with smog nor stuck in a jam; their white-wall tyres are singing over the diamond-cut anti-skid grooves in the concrete road surface, the selector-levers of their automatic gearboxes are firmly in *Drive*, and the radio is on. And more important than any of this, they are acting out one of the most spectacular paradoxes in the great debate between private freedom and public discipline that pervades every affluent, mechanized urban society. (Banham 1973: 216)

I return to the significance of 'discipline' in the challenge of driving the LA freeways in the discussion of Didion's novel below. Here, however, it is their distinctive sensory pleasures that I am seeking to capture with the help of film/video texts that simulate the experience for those of us who lack the first-hand knowledge. A further piece of footage posted on YouTube that offers a rare and fascinating insight of what it would have been like to drive these roads at the time Banham was writing is an 8mm film, 'Los Angeles Area Freeways 1975' (2008). This silent (and grainy) home-movie takes the viewer on a journey from 'the 405 at 605, the 405 at 55, the 101 to 5, the 1011 into downtown, the Pasadena Freeway Tunnels, and the 405 through Long Beach'. The film provides a vivid portrait of the way in which the different highways fly over and under one another and, although the traffic appears lighter than in the videos from 2010, the multiple-lane highway and its 'exits' has already initiated the demanding lane-changing skills featured in Didion's novel. The fact that the roads are quieter and the traffic is moving more quickly makes these manoeuvres very noticeably *more* of a challenge than in today's congestion and this period footage – unlike the 2010 videos – helps us visualise protagonist Maria Wyeth's four-lane crossing at speed (Didion 2011: 16). This 1970s film also captures, incidentally, the haze of fog over downtown LA to which Banham refers: in 1975, both the benefits and the environmental cost of building a city around the car were visible for all to see.[13]

Having made a case for why the technical skills and intense concentration needed to negotiate the LA freeways may nevertheless be seen to induce its own special brand of reverie and 'heightened awareness' (Banham 1973: 215), it is nevertheless important to remind ourselves that the state of automotive consciousness typically associated with cruising is significantly more chilled. This will be amply demonstrated in my discussion of Neil Young's *Special Deluxe* (2014) to which I now turn and which, when placed alongside Didion's novel, helps capture the full spectrum of driving experience that the Californian highways offered drivers in the early 1970s. As well as the home of one of the world's most iconic urban freeway systems, California also possesses many thousands of miles of equally spectacular non-urban freeway, a good deal of it flowing through mountains and desert or hugging the Pacific coastline.[14] In the popular imagination these, and not the LA freeways, are probably still regarded as America's most iconic roads (National Geographic 2010: 71–4): roads designed, as self-confessed 'pothead' Young evocatively puts it, for 'cruising around' and 'trippin' along' (Young 2014: 272).

The cruising car

It will be remembered that a section of Chapter 2 was dedicated to the 'little cars' of H. V. Morton and Edwin Muir. As well as being undeniably small – and light – by contemporary standards, these cars were also distinguished by their functionality: the purpose – and, indeed, wonder – of this still relatively new invention was that it could transport driver and passengers to new and previously out-of-bounds destinations with *relative* ease and comfort. The cars both men used were open-top convertibles, though it will also be remembered that operating the top was something of a challenge in Muir's case and led to his getting very wet on one occasion (Muir 1996: 189–91). Following Urry's distinction between cars built for the 'paved road' and the postwar period during which motorists came to 'dwell' within their increasingly 'sealed vehicles' (Urry 2007: 126), the assumption – as previously noted – is that cruising, as it is now popularly understood, only became possible once drivers could travel comfortably in an environment which placed the 'outside world' at a distance through the cage of steel and glass the car had now become. However, when we move towards an understanding of cruising which replaces external factors (road type, road conditions, speed) with a focus on the driver's automotive consciousness so, too, do we interpret the all-important criterion of 'ease' rather differently. As I have already proposed, cognitive ease or relaxation may be seen to be expressly linked the driver's concentration (rather than his or her lack of it), thereby suggesting that factors other than our in-car comforts are key to the sort of reverie we have come to associate with cruising. This is not to suggest that the comfort or 'feel' of the car does not contribute to this special zone of consciousness, but that a complex interchange of cognitive *effort* (however minimal) and bodily sensation conspire to take us there. Therefore, although the driving space in which most of us enjoy this combination of factors today is a sealed car on the motorway, it is arguable that Morton, Muir and the other drivers from the 1920s and 1930s that this book features experienced, on occasion, something similar; chugging along at a steady 30mph, with the top down, on a favourable day, is also cruising – providing the driver is content to give him or herself up to contemplation rather than ticking off the 'sights' with the eye of the tourist. Regarded thus, any car is potentially a 'cruising car' even though, as Young's memoir reveals, in the United States whole generations of them were built expressly for that purpose.

Reminding us of another crucial factor that has long-distinguished British and American motoring – i.e. the weather – it is notable, but not surprising, that several of Young's favourite cruising cars were open-top convertibles. This included his 1959 Cadillac Eldorado Biarritz (Young 2014: 214), his 1959 Lincoln Continental Mark V Convertible (Young 2014: 288), his 1978 Cadillac Eldorado Biarritz (Young 2014: 302) and the car that became the flagship of his environmental bio-fuel mission, his 1959 Lincoln Continental.[15] For Young, all this 'stable' of cars – dating from the era of maximum extravagance and luxury in US car design – share particular qualities which may be enumerated as beauty, power and history. His eulogy to the 1959 Lincoln Continental Mark V is typical:

> Cars always tell a story and, as you will see, this one had a lot to do with women. As I walked around the great Continental's stylish form, I could feel its history . . . All in all, it was an astounding vehicle in every respect – magnificent power, unique styling, groundbreaking mechanical design in the convertible top mechanism, and a luxuriously spacious interior . . .
>
> It was a true survivor. I took the keys, put the keys in the ignition, and started the engine. The Continental's monster V8, 463 cubic inches of very powerful iron, roared to life and rumbled toughly as if it anticipated a long trip, perhaps an escape.
>
> I purchased the car right there and drove it to its new home. It was perhaps the most remarkable car I had ever seen, and it would play a huge part in my life. I had absolutely no idea of what I was in for with that car or what a catalyst for change it would be. (Young 2014: 291–2)

As Blake Morrison (2014) observes, Young's cars are also 'all too predictably' feminine, but this gendering may be seen as a measure of the sense of maternal protection/well-being associated with the type of ride the cars provided as well as their sexualised glamour. Even without a roof, these deep-seated cars are redolent of the womb and/or the mother's embrace. Of the 1959 Cadillac Eldorado Biarritz, for example, Young writes:

> Crazy Horse returned to LA as Ben and I drove the metallic-blue 1959 Cadillac Eldorado Biarritz convertible south down the highway, relaxing in a pair of bucket seats as the world flew by, south to Nashville and the rest of my new life . . . [here the memoir interpolates the lyric to Young's 'Changing Highways'] . . . This was the car I had dreamed of owning ever since high school in Winnipeg, since the Flamingo Club, since forever. When we arrived at Nashville, we went right into the studio and started recording. (Young 2014: 217)

While symbolic of (adult) 'freedom', these cars of Young's childhood dreams also enfold their drivers and passengers in the warm glow of the recent past and hence facilitate new dreams and fantasies in a manner that chimes with Gaston Bachelard's theories in *The Poetics of Reverie* (1971 [1960]) (see further discussion of this in Chapter 5).

The conceit of the cruising car as a womb is also a core trope in Didion's *Play It As It Lays*. Deborah Clarke describes the wider narrative context for this thus:

> Maria drives to cope with the breakup of her marriage and the removal of her daughter . . . Driving gives shape, meaning and safety to her days, staving off 'unspeakable peril'. We do not see her become one with the car so much as we see her look to the car for a sense of who she is. Rather than incorporating her into family life, the automobile serves almost as a retreat where she can recoup and regain her position as a mother. She needs to reassure herself of her competence as a driver in order to perceive herself as a mother; successfully negotiating the roads serves as a necessary prerequisite to regaining custody of her daughter. (Clarke 2007: 93–4)

With reference to Maria's persistent need to cruise the LA freeways, Clarke indexes the car both as a figure of womb-like protection/'retreat' and a space in which Maria can practise and perform her identity as a mother. The womb analogy becomes explicit later in the text when Maria, having endured an abortion and incessant psychological abuse from her husband, Carter, undertakes a course of hypnosis. During a session in which the hypnotist attempts to take her back to the womb, she resists and substitutes the environment of the womb with the 'dwelling' (Urry 2007: 124) of her car:

> 'You're lying in water,' the hypnotist said. 'You're lying in water and it's warm and you hear your mother's voice' . . .
> 'I'm driving over here,' Maria said. 'I'm driving Sunset and I'm staying in the left lane because I can see the New Havana Ballroom and I'm going to

turn left at the New Havana Ballroom. That's what I'm doing'. (Didion 2011: 124)

What is especially significant about this wonderfully ironic observation on the significance of the car in modern life for my own purposes is the fact that it substitutes an inactive state of 'being' (lying in water) with the active state of 'becoming' through the practice of driving. The most secure and plenitudinous state that Maria's ego can re-enter is one which grants her the agency and control that comes with driving. Therefore, although the shell of the car does function for Maria as a womb of sorts (she retreats there on one of the occasions she is humiliated and, indeed, cries 'for her mother' (Didion 2011: 141)), it is also arguably a phallus: a connotation which becomes most explicit when Maria, towards the end of the novel, drives off into the desert with a gun and shoots at road signs (Didion 2011: 192).[16] This episode is, in fact, the last time Maria is seen driving a car and may thus be read as the apotheosis of the journey she has been on as a driver: the freeway novice who had to teach herself to 'master' the lane changes is now a 'highway avenger' – even if, as an expression of agency, this fails to resolve the immediate situation she finds herself in.

As will be seen from this first introduction of Didion's novel, *Play It As It Lays* is a text in which cars and driving are put to explicit symbolic use. This said, Didion – in her non-fiction essay, 'Bureaucrats' (2009 [1979]: 79–85) – cites and echoes Reyner Banham's account of what it means to drive the LA freeways[17] and, like Banham, clearly bases her observations on her own experiences as a driver. Although the car Maria Wyeth drives is a sporty Corvette,[18] there is no discussion in the novel that certain makes of car are especially suited to the sort of 'cruising' the protagonist is engaged in. Such is the nature of Maria's need to 'hit the highway' every morning, one suspects that any vehicle, within reason, would have been acceptable. This is in signal contrast to Young, for whom the make, style, performance and vintage of his cars is seen to fully determine the quality of his driving or cruising experience. Allowing for the fact that most of his vehicles are – as he acknowledges himself – 'cruisers', there are some which have the special capacity for projecting their drivers and passengers back into time: both to their personal pasts and to what Young refers to on several occasions as 'the year of the car'. I return to this theme later, but end this subsection with an extract describing what, for Young, constituted the quintessential cruising car: his 1948 Lincoln Continental:

One evening, Abraham was rolling along the Pacific Coast Highway and Stephen and I on our way to a gig at the Earl Warren Showgrounds in Santa

Barbara. It was January 16, 1968, and we had known each other three years. We shared a liking for big American cars and were having a fine time, enjoying the smooth, luxurious ride of the old classic Lincoln Continental. The Pacific Coast was perfect cruising for Abraham, whose big V12 engine, built for the open road, could easily overheat when stuck in slow traffic. (Young 2014: 111)

This car was so heavy and so vast that when Young moved to his ranch at Topango Canyon, he could not get it up the steep drive to his house and had to park it on the road below. On the open highway, however, the 'gas-guzzling twelve cylinder engine' (Young 2014: 112) appears to have delivered the finest of 'drivetimes' for Young and his companions: a rare state of automotive bliss which, in the footsteps of the three-litre 1908 Bentley referenced in note 4, combined the potential to accelerate to speeds far in excess of what any domestic highway would allow with the lulling sensation of not needing to.

Drivetime

In this book, and especially in this chapter, I have repeatedly returned to the concept of reverie to describe the state of automotive consciousness associated with cruising. As rich with connotation as the notion of cruising itself, reverie – as theorised by Gaston Bachelard and Ernst Bloch – will play a central role in Chapter 5 where it is key to my exploration of the altered states of consciousness which driving may give rise to. In this chapter, however, the more banal dictionary definition of the term – 'a state of meditation' or 'being pleasantly lost in one's thoughts' (*OED* online) – serves very well. For while the content and character of our thoughts can vary and, indeed, fluctuate in the course of any driving-event, what cruising – at moderate speed and in manageable (though not necessarily incident-free) traffic conditions – seemingly provides is a cognitive environment of calmness, steadiness and purpose that enables a driver to 'stay' with his or her thoughts in the manner of the phenomenological practices discussed in Chapter 1. Banham, as we have seen, discovered 'calmness', against the odds, in the drivers of the LA freeways – 'for whom the freeway is not a limbo of existential angst, but the place where they spend the two calmest and most rewarding hours of their daily lives' (Banham 1973: 222) – and both Tim Edensor (2003) and myself (see Interlude) identify these special properties of motorway driving as conducive to constructive thought:

Solitarily, a space for contemplation is enabled by an interlude in which no decisions about how to fill in time are required. A relaxed awareness of road conditions cultivates a disposition toward thinking, planning, rehearsing encounters, and fantasizing, which becomes second nature, a part of the motorway driver's habitus. According to recent events, drivetime may become a period in which we can celebrate or grieve. (Edensor 2003: 161)

Edensor's designation of these enjoyable motoring conditions as 'drivetime' is not coincidental to my choice of the term for the title of this book. As noted in the Preface, a long, steady run along a clear stretch of motorway is, for me, one of life's most restorative pleasures and one that I would sorely miss – and struggle to substitute – were it no longer available.

As already observed, Neil Young's text includes many examples of the flamboyant, 'gas-guzzling' vehicles built for cruising the American highways in the 1950s and 1960s. However, it is a more everyday car – the 1950 Plymouth Deluxe Sedan celebrated in his book's title – that is most obviously associated with the sort of 'drivetime' experience I am interested in here. This was a car built not only to drive but to live in, and its familiarity and comfort made it a special sanctuary for Young:

> The Special Deluxe has traveled many more miles with me and it still does, especially at home on the roads of Broken Arrow Ranch. With springs perfectly suited for the rough terrain, the old Plymouth is comfortable on back roads that would challenge any sedan that was not sturdy and well made . . . Up and down the ranch roads for years upon years, vacuum wipers beating away the winter rains, big round tires handling the potholes with ease, and the trusty six-cylinder engine firing up responsively whenever asked. The Plymouth Special Deluxe has persisted. (Young 2014: 253)

The association between this car and the 'redwoods' through which Young and his father used to drive also points to the expressly spiritual role it played in their lives. Later in the book Young writes:

> Sitting inside of my old cars while I was driving on these roads, it was easy to lose track of who I was and what year it was. After driving for a while and not seeing anyone, it became the year of the car. I was generally not in a hurry, especially back in those days, when time was on my side.
> The redwoods are still like church to me, good for the soul, I love driving along surrounded by their grace while the sun streaks through like God-rays. (Young 2014: 161)

Car and forest together, then, would seem to constitute a latter-day 'cathedral' for Young (see note 11 to Chapter 1): a space in which he can enjoy sufficient solitude, privacy and anonymity to engage with the natural world and explore his spirituality.

It would, however, be a mistake to assume that 'drivetime' is always characterised by solitude and quiet. As readers will be aware, the concept was arguably an invention of prime-time radio, and the popular music channels are, for many of us, an aid to – rather than a distraction from – motorway meditation (Pearce 2000: 163; Edensor 2003: 161). Michael Bull's 'Soundscapes in the Car' (2001), based on an ethnographic survey of young British drivers, reveals not only the extent to which music has contributed to the status of the car as a 'dwelling' (Urry 2007), but also the way in which it typically enhances the mood of the drivers/passengers and promotes positive thoughts and/or conversation. For example:

> When I get in my car and I turn on my car radio, I'm at home. I haven't got a journey to make before I get home. I'm already home. I shut my door, turn on my radio and I'm home. I wind down the window so I can hear what's going on and sometimes as the sun's setting and I'm in town and I think. Wow. What a beautiful city that I'm living in, but it's always at the same time when that certain track comes on. It's a boost. (Automobile user) (Bull 2001: 185)

Bull uses his many responses along these lines to counter Theodor Adorno's proposition that recorded sound is the anathema of thought: 'By circling people, by enveloping them . . . It leaves no room for conceptual reflection between itself and the subject' (Adorno 1976; Bull 2001: 190). Like Bull, I profoundly disagree with Adorno's assumption, though I would also suggest that a distinction should probably be drawn between talk-radio (or, indeed, spoken-word CDs) and recorded music, since the 'conversational' engagement that many drivers derive from the former is arguably more likely to interrupt or suspend reflexivity than promote it. Appropriate music, however, as Edensor observes 'potentially transforms or transcends the mundane through conjuring up important occasions or periods of one's life' (Edensor 2003: 161) and can contribute to the channelling of our thoughts in a particular direction.

While Neil Young's memoir does not mention playing music in his cars, we can assume he did and – rather more significantly – we learn that he composed many songs while 'trippin' along'. This synergy between driving and writing is reproduced in the text of *Special Deluxe* by the interpolation of lyrics into the memoir. One example of this, cited above, is the incorporation of the lyrics of 'Changing Highways' into the chapter on the 1959 Cadillac Eldorado Biarritz (Young 2014: 217); another is this account of the time he was working with David Briggs and driving his 1934 Bentley Close-coupled Coupe Mulliner:

> So that was exactly what Briggs and I experienced every night, cruising along the 101 highway, talking about the record, what we would do tomorrow,

what was good, what needed to be done again, everything, all while this spirited Bentley flew down the road, creating its amazing sound, faithfully carrying us to our destination. How throaty it was! What a sensation. Those were some of the best driving moments I can ever remember having in a car. The spirit of the automobile was undeniable ... That Bentley close-coupled Mulliner coupe was an incredible feat of engineering, flying down the road with the engine's throttle wide open.

Soon after we finished our first record ... (Young 2014: 124)

As well as the 'spirit' of the car and the experience of cruising at 'full throttle' being an integral part of the composition process, Young's memories also underline the fact the special thinking time afforded by motorway/highway cruising can be a comradely and interactive process as well as a solitary one. We have already considered the romantic/sexualised form in-car intimacy can take in Chapter 3, but twentieth-century literature also includes numerous examples of married couples (see Struther 1989 [1939]) and friends conversing companionably about whatever is brought within the cognitive orbit of that particular driving-event. Young's reminiscence here certainly conjures up this sort of shared and interactive facility; the two men and their work are united in the protective and evocative shell of their historic car.

As noted above, what he calls 'the year of the car' has special significance for Young, and there are moments in the memoir when his vehicles assume the properties of a 'Tardis',[19] transporting him back to a previous decade as well as putting him in touch with his own personal past. This is especially the case with his beloved 1950 Plymouth Special Deluxe which appears to outlive all the other cars in terms of use. Young remembers 'using it all the time' while recording *American Stars n' Bars* (1976–7) and it is still bumping around the ranch in 2012 (Young 2014: 259). This particular car, then – which is also the home of his old dog, Elvis, until he dies (Young 2014: 254) – becomes a capsule of memories that can be activated simply by climbing into its worn leather seats (Young 2014: 250). Though somewhat less glamorous than many of Young's other cars, the Special Deluxe may thus be seen as an extra-special cruising car: one that not only facilitates contemplation and creativity, but one that conjoins past, present and future in the manner of the Bachelardian reveries I discuss in the next chapter: 'we had a lot of fun reliving our glory days as we cruised south in the Special Deluxe on California Highway 1' (Young 2014: 264). In this case, then, the car's own history, combined with the many decades it has shared with Young and his family, lends a further gloss to the meaning of 'drivetime'. Functioning, on one level, as a simple descriptor of the way in which the activity of driving gives rise to and is bounded by its own unique temporality (which is both the duration of the journey and the hiatus in everyday life it gifts the driver), 'drivetime' – when overlaid with these more complex associations (the memories of journeys made in the car, the memories evoked by the places the car is driven through) – helps explain the deep, psychic hold automotive transport has gained over its users in the course of the twentieth century.

Cruise control

Joan Didion's *Play It As It Lays* is, on first impressions, a text that represents the angst-ridden, shadow-side of cruising: the American equivalent, perhaps, of Chris Petit's, *Radio On* (see note 18 to Chapter 3). As already established, Didion's central protagonist, Maria Wyeth, spends a large part of every day (from 10 a.m. in the morning until mid-afternoon) cruising the LA freeways in order, as Clarke observes, 'to cope with the break-up of her marriage and the removal of her daughter' (Clarke 2007: 94):

> In the first hot month of the fall after the summer she left Carter (the summer Carter left her, the summer Carter stopped living in the house in Beverly Hills), Maria drove the freeway. She dressed every morning with a greater purpose than she had felt in some time, a cotton skirt, a jersey, sandals she could kick off when she wanted to touch the accelerator, and she dressed very fast . . . for it was essential . . . that she be on the freeway by ten o'clock. Not somewhere on Hollywood Boulevard, not on her way to the freeway, but actually on the freeway. If she was not she lost the day's rhythm, its precariously imposed momentum. Once she was on the freeway and had maneuvered [*sic*] her way to a fast lane she turned on the radio at high volume and she drove. She drove the San Diego to the Harbor, the Harbor up to the Hollywood, the Hollywood to the Golden State, the Santa Monica, the Santa Ana, the Pasadena, the Ventura. (Didion 2011: 15–16)

What characterises this as cruising – returning, for a moment, to our opening definitions – is that Maria is very evidently driving the highways 'without a precise destination' even though, as previously discussed, the semblance of a purpose (picking particular routes, identifying particular exits) is part of its complex pleasure. 'Pleasure' and 'ease' are, however, concepts that would seem to sit oddly with a character whose fragile mental state, as established in the opening pages of the novel, is all too easily catalogued as the familiar (proto-feminist) tale of a young, exploited woman 'going mad'.[20] However, my own reading of the driving scenes in this text – following Banham's comments on the calming and liberating benefits of cruising the freeways (Banham 1973: 222) and the evidence provided by the 'YouTube' videos discussed earlier – is that they serve not only to illustrate the 'narcotic' benefits of Maria's obsessive habit,[21] but also the ways in which driving can direct and sustain positive thought sequences.

In its clear-eyed exposition of the protagonist's breakdown, the text makes explicit that Maria is sane while in the car and (increasingly) insane out of it. Cruising does, indeed, equal control. However, in contrast to Clarke who reads Maria's practice of driving as a means of performing her 'identity' ('she needs to reassure herself of her competence as a driver in order to perceive herself as a mother' (Clarke 2007: 94)), I would suggest that it also tells us something about the therapeutic potential driving offers for the correction and redirection of negative thought sequences through mechanisms not dissimilar to those used in cognitive behavioural therapy.[22] Furthermore, the text's association of driving with expressly conscious and/or 'rational' thought may be seen in the way that Maria dresses for the job. Her practical clothing and the scarf she uses to tie back her hair style her as a professional woman rather than an 'actress', while her obsession with timing may be seen to mimic the scientific cast of early motor sport (see Chapter 3). This hypothesis – that, for Maria, driving is a means of controlling and directing conscious thought rather than indulging and/or annihilating her unconscious desires and fears – is subsequently borne out in her encounter with the hypnotist, quoted earlier (see Didion 2011: 124). Instead of reading Maria's substitution of the hypnotist's womb scenario with her memory of driving the freeway as an example of 'the car as mother' (Clarke 2007: 74–94), it may be seen, instead, as evidence of her refusal to surrender her rational, problem-solving faculties, even under hypnosis. Her statement, after all, never mentions the car, but focuses in precise detail on the *driving* manoeuvres she needs to exit the freeway safely ('I'm driving Sunset and I'm staying in the left lane because I can see the New Havana Ballroom and I'm going to turn left at the New Havana Ballroom. That's what I'm doing' (Didion 2011: 124)) (see Figure 4.3). Given that it is the performance of rational thought (i.e. sanity) that will win Maria back her daughter, it is arguably this – and not 'identity' per se – that she is practising (rather like chess or a mathematical puzzle) when she cruises the LA freeways. In the absence of other training, support or therapy, the LA freeway system teaches Maria Wyeth how to 'manage' her thoughts in increasingly desperate times:

> She drove as a riverman runs a river, every day more attuned to its currents, its deceptions, and just as a riverman feels the pull of the rapids in the lull between sleeping and waking, so Maria lay at night in the still of Beverly

Figure 4.3 'Hollywood Freeway', James W. Fowler © Fotolibra (FOT420853).

Hills and saw the great signs soar ahead at seventy miles an hour, *Normandie* ¼ *Vermont* ¾ *Harbor Fwy* 1. Again and again she returned to an intricate stretch just south of the interchange where successful passage from the Hollywood onto the Harbor required a diagonal move across four lanes of traffic. On the afternoon she finally did it without once braking or once losing the beat on the radio she was exhilarated, and that night slept dreamlessly. (Didion 2011: 16)

Meanwhile, the extent to which the practice of driving may be seen to be associated with the control and training of the conscious mind rather than the indulgence of its dark underbelly becomes evident when, for Maria, the driving stops. As well as exhibiting symptoms of severe depression and incipient psychosis when she is back at the house – for example, she takes to sleeping outside by the swimming pool under a towel (Didion 2011:16) – Maria is shown to live in fear of running out of road:

Sleep was essential if she was to be on the freeway by ten o'clock. Sometimes the freeway ran out, in a scrap metal yard in San Pedro or on the main street in Palmdale or out somewhere no place at all where the flawless burning concrete just stopped, turned into common road, abandoned construction sheds rusting beside it. When that happened, she would keep in careful control, portage skilfully back, feel for the first time the heavy weight of the becalmed car beneath her and try to keep her eyes on the mainstream . . . the organism which absorbed all her reflexes, all her attention. (Didion 2011: 17)

Continuing the 'riverman' imagery of the previous extract, the text thus marks the difference between what Maria's car feels like and symbolises when she is cruising and what it becomes when she is 'becalmed' or, worse, stationary: a 'heavy weight', her vehicle is now a canoe to be portaged rather than a car to be driven. This pre-figuration of the danger Maria would find herself in if and when the road ran out is finally realised on the day she inadvertently leaves the freeway and finds herself in the town of Baker:

> On the tenth day of October at quarter past four in the afternoon with a hot dry wind blowing from the passes Maria found herself in Baker. She never meant to go as far as Baker, had started out that day as every day, her only destination the freeway. But she had driven out of the San Bernardino and up the Barstow and instead of turning back at Barstow (she had been out that far before but never that late in the day, it was past time to navigate back, it was far too late, the rhythm was lost) she kept driving. When she turned off at Baker it was 115 degrees and she was picking up Vegas on the radio and she was within sixty miles of where Carter was making the picture. (Didion 2011: 30)

Removed from the thought-controlling environment of the freeway and its 'rhythms', Maria is exposed to a welter of discomforting images and prompts indicative of her unresolved personal circumstances. Although she may have been sorting her way through aspects of these troubles while driving, the unplanned stop throws her off guard and unleashes her bleakest unconscious and existential terrors. This manifests itself in a fantasised telephone conversation with her husband, Carter, in which – in the manner of Mikhail Bakhtin's 'hidden polemic'[23] – her every word invites and is directed towards his hostility and disapproval (Didion 2011: 32).

Such is the trauma occasioned by her unwonted detour that Maria subsequently stops driving the freeways:

> Maria looked at the pay phone for a long while, and then she got out of the car and drank a warm Coke. With the last of the Coke she swallowed two Fiorinal tablets, then closed her eyes against the sun and waited for the Fiorinal to clear her head of Carter and what Carter would say. On the way back into the city the traffic was heavy and the hot wind blew sand through the window and the radio got on her nerves and after that Maria did not go back to the freeways. (Didion 2011: 32–3)

In the context of the reading I am making here, the nemesis represented by Baker may readily be understood, in psychoanalytic terms, as a confrontation with the Lacanian 'Real'.[24] By running out of road, Maria is plunged into her deepest unconscious fears and desires (she clearly wants to 'murder' Carter as much as he wants to 'murder' her) and, as a consequence, is brought face to face with the 'meaninglessness' of existence. While this proverbial existential crisis – which extends beyond Maria and Carter's personal circumstances to all the text's central protagonists – figures as the ostensible subject of Didion's text, in the context of my rather more instrumental reading it provides, I think, a useful corrective to the assumption that the thinking generated by motorway or freeway driving is primarily escapist. For although in the next chapter we will indeed encounter instances where driving at speed gives rise to madness, *Play It As It Lays* speaks to me of the way in which the concentration required to safely handle a multi-lane highways helps to focus and structure drivers' thoughts and develop transferable cognitive-behavioural strategies. As noted above, things fall apart for Maria not when she is driving but when the driving stops.

Conclusion

Readers who have come to this chapter via the previous two may already have observed that it lacks substantive discussion of the world as 'seen from the car' (Kennedy 1919b) featured there. This is not because the cruising-driver is inherently disinterested in the roadscapes s/he passes through; Andrew Cross (2002), Tim Edensor (2003) and myself (Pearce 2000, 2013) all reflect upon the ways in which our apprehension of the phenomena glimpsed through the windscreen are absolutely central to the experience, often serving as prompts to and/or signposts for our meditations. At the same time, the fact that neither Young's memoir nor Didion's novel details the road environment through which their protagonists pass is a useful reminder of the extent to which cruising – especially on a freeway or motorway – may promote an interiority of thought so complete that the details of the world outside the car become secondary.

   One of the reasons I have delayed acknowledging this factor until the conclusion is that, at face value, it feeds into many of the generalised, often prejudicial, characterisations of motorway driving as outlined earlier. As part of a dedicated investigation of automotive consciousness, however – where drivers are understood to enter and leave such zones of intense self-absorption intermittently – this is very evidently a feature of cruising that it is important to acknowledge and, indeed, interrogate. By reading Didion's text somewhat against the grain and presenting Maria's freeway driving as the exercise/practice of alternative cognitive behaviours (the skills needed for safe and effective driving and the skills needed for constructive thought) I have, I hope, pointed to the way in which these driving-events are far more than an occasion for the subject to dive deep into their unconscious; instead, they may be seen to demonstrate the ways in which we can learn to engage pro-actively with our more immediate concerns via a practice that echoes the 'phenomenological method', as discussed in Chapter 1, as well as cognitive behavioural therapy. On this last point it is, indeed, important to remind ourselves that phenomenology is not only concerned with the phenomena of the external world, an error that is easily introduced in more simplistic definitions (Moran and Mooney 2002: 5). In other words, the 'abstract' and/or personally inflected conundrums that present themselves to the motorist's psyche may become the deserving subjects of meaningful phenomenological attention just as much as the objects and scenarios that pass by his or her window. Therefore while, in Chapter 2, our early twentieth-century tourists – H. V. Morton and Edwin Muir – were shown, on occasion, to be practising a phenomenol-ogy of '*the world* as seen from the car', here we have encountered texts that suggest their drivers are 'bearing witness' to phenomena sourced in their memory and/or imagination (see also Bachelard (1971: 4) as discussed in Chapter 5).

While, as we have seen, the role and status of memory within the phenomenological method is a somewhat vexed and complex issue – not least because Edmund Husserl changed his opinions on this matter over time (see Chapter 1) – it is evident from my own personal experience that the recent past, in particular, can preoccupy a driver for a signifi-cant portion of a long journey, expressing itself as both clusters of visual impressions and questions/observations that we are seeking to clarify or resolve. This was, for example, the mental attitude that attended my return journey from Cornwall (as far as Bristol) as described in the Interlude; so preoccupied was I with all the events, concepts and comparisons I had encountered on my visit 'home' that I paid relatively little attention to the road, in signal contrast to the drive south where the latter had commanded all my attention. As will also be recalled, so absorbed was I in this process that I had no interest in listening to music for the whole of this stage of the journey. Therefore, while Didion's text gives little indication of what, in particular, is presenting itself to Maria's consciousness as she cruises the LA freeways, we must assume that it includes the recollection of events recounted, a-chronologically, elsewhere in the novel, and centred on the referral of her daughter to a psychiatric hospital.

'Drivetime', therefore, as I am characterising it here, is not merely – or, at least, not *only* – an opportunity to 'switch off' and stare vacantly from a car window while listening to music or radio, but a time/space in which we can work hard at pinning down, turning over and 'solving' all manner of images and propositions that present themselves to our well-tuned consciousness. As our car glides smoothly on – be this for three hours or fifteen minutes – so, too, do our thoughts. Acknowledging this, it also seems reasonable to speculate that the reason Maria Wyeth is ultimately seen to 'chose life' may, in part, be due to all the hours she puts in 'working' the freeways:

> *I know what nothing means and keep on playing.*
> *Why, BZ would say.*
> *Why not, I say.* (Didion 2011: 214)

Driving, as we see in the next chapter, has long been associated with madness, but it can also be seen to perform a significant role in keeping us sane.

Notes

1. Here it is important to distinguish between largely involuntary thought processes such as daydreaming or reverie and more proactive reflexivity and problem-solving (see Thompson (2015) and further discussion in Chapter 5).
2. Travelling at cruising speed arguably constitutes a very different experience for drivers and passenger(s). While, for the driver, the attention/concentration required to manoeuvre a car safely even at moderate speed mitigates boredom, this is not the case for passengers (especially children) who often become restless on long journeys. The driver's 'contact' with the road via his/her steering wheel, gear stick and other controls means that even long, flat stretches of motorway have a cognitive 'interest' for him/her that is absent in passengers.
3. See Cross's (2004) recreation of J. B. Priestley's *English Journey* (1984 [1934]) in book/DVD format; see also Rosemary Shirley's chapter (2015) which takes Cross's 2004 text as its subject.
4. Jeremiah reproduces an advertisement for a three-litre Bentley which shows how a preference for steady – but *empowered* – driving also established itself in Britain early on: 'Speed in itself is not the great charm of such a car, although speed has its thrills. It is the sense of controlling lightly a vehicle of immense possibility in the way of speed, the feeling that for you – the driver – steep hills are but gentle inclines to be swept, in a flash, beneath your wheels if you so desire' (Jeremiah 2007: 142).
5. Thomas Aquinas (1224–74) adopted Saint Paul's expression – 'for now we see as through a glass darkly, but then we see face to face' (1 Corinthians 13: 12) to distinguish between this life and the next: an indication of how long glass has been seen to signify a barrier to our 'vision'.
6. Kraftwerk's chart-topping album *Autobahn* (1974) has been described

as an 'ode to the motorway' (Bracewell 2002: 289). As well as its distinctive sound, seen to replicate the aural and visceral experience of motorway driving, the album's aesthetic was also encapsulated by its minimalist album-cover design. See http://www.kraftwerk.com/ (last accessed 21 October 2015).

7. Ernest Marples' speeches, which have long been the butt of much humour, are discussed in detail in Moran (2009: 101–11) and Merriman (2007: 152–4). It should also be noted that the M1 was preceded by the Preston bypass, still regarded by many as Britain's 'first' motorway. See video of Marples' speech at: https://www.youtube.com/watch?v=AWymCebAl6g (last accessed 21 October 2015).

8. 'Freeway' is the American term for a controlled-access highway with a divided carriageway and multiple lanes. The first US freeways were the 'parkways' which opened in the New York area in the 1920s. See Davis (2008: 35–58).

9. The RAC Foundation reports that (in 2013) the total road length in Britain was estimated to be 245.7 thousand miles. 'A' roads (including motorways) account for 12.7 per cent of this total road length; 'B', 'C' and 'U' (unclassified) roads for 87.3 per cent. See http://www.racfoundation.org/motoring-faqs/mobility (last accessed 20 October 2015).

10. Films set in Los Angeles include Halicki's *Gone in 60 Seconds* (1974), Polanski's *Chinatown* (1974), Tarantino's *Reservoir Dogs* (1992) and *Pulp Fiction* (1994) and Dayton and Faris's *Little Miss Sunshine* (2006). See Borden (2013: 124–7, 141–6).

11. Didion expressed scepticism about the introduction of the 'car-pool' or 'Diamond Lanes' in 'Bureaucrats' (2009: 80–5).

12. Katz (1999: 33) observes that drivers typically experience this sort of frustration more than passengers.

13. Banham discusses the Los Angeles fog and smog problem in some detail in the essay (1973: 215–16).

14. For example, US 101 runs for 807 miles between downtown Los Angeles to San Francisco and Redwood Country, with 487 of these being classed as 'rural highway'. See http://www.cahighways.org/stats1.html (last accessed 20 October 2015).

15. Young has a website dedicated to his 'Lincvolt' project which involved converting his 1959 Lincoln Continental to run on bio-diesel. See http://www.lincvolt.com/lincvolt_lincvoltgazette (last accessed 20 October 2015).

16. The episode which features Maria Wyeth shooting road signs in the desert is used as the trailer for the film of the book (Perry 1972: unavailable on DVD). See https://www.youtube.com/watch?v=WVUiTmMvV9U (last accessed 20 October 2015).

17. Didion's account of 'driving the freeways' closely echoes Banham's (whom she cites): 'To understand what is going on it is perhaps necessary to have participated in the freeway experience, which is the only secular communion Los Angeles has. Mere driving on the freeway is by no means the same as participating in it ... Actual participation requires a total surrender, a concentration so intense as to seem a kind of narcosis, a rapture-of-the-freeway. The mind goes clean. The rhythm takes over' (Didion 2009: 83).

18. First produced by Chevrolet in 1953, the Corvette (or 'Stingray') is a

sports car (available as both a coupé and a convertible). 'Maria Wyeth' would probably have been driving a Mk 2 (1963–7) or Mk 3. For a photograph of Joan Didion in her Corvette see https://msless.files.wordpress. com/2013/09/didion-car.jpg (last accessed 6 November 2015).

19. 'Tardis': 'the name (said to be an acronym of *time and relative dimensions in space*) of a time machine which had the exterior of a police telephone box in the British TV science fiction series *Doctor Who*' (http://www. oxforddictionaries.com/definition/english/Tardis (last accessed 20 October 2015)).

20. Other classic novels on this theme that have been adopted by the feminist movement even though their authors, like Didion, do/did not necessarily identify as feminist include Kate Chopin's *The Awakening* (1994 [1899]) and Margaret Atwood's *Surfacing* (1997 [1971]).

21. 'Narcotic': see note 17 above and also the discussion of Paul Auster (2006) in Chapter 3.

22. Cognitive behavioural therapy (CBT) focuses on helping patients identify and adapt negative thought patterns. See http://www.rcpsych.ac.uk/ mentalhealthinformation/therapies/cognitivebehaviouraltherapy.aspx (last accessed 21 October 2015).

23. Mikhail Bakhtin (1929) identified 'hidden polemic' as a variety of double-voiced discourse. See Pearce (1994: 53–4) for a full explanation.

24. See the *Stanford Encyclopedia of Philosophy* (http://plato.stanford.edu/ entries/lacan/ (last accessed 21 October 2015)): 'Throughout the 1960s and up through the end of Lacan's teachings, the Real ... comes to be associated with libidinal negativities (*objet petit a, jouissance*) and sexual difference, material meaninglessness both linguistic and non-linguistic, contingent traumatic events, unbearable bodily intensities, anxiety, and death'.

Chapter 5

Flying

And these pictures that flash through your consciousness as this magic of speed is enveloping you! They come from the mind's deepest recesses. They whirl from a darkness and live for an instant before you. Pictures from the past, and pictures from out of the time that is now upon you, and pictures perhaps of things to come.

Speed! Speed! Speed!

The wonder is upon you. It is carrying you into a greater world. You are living as you have never lived before . . . You have never grasped the strangeness of time – you have never pierced its mystery till now. (Kennedy 1919a: 115)

One of the many memorable motoring images in Scott Fitzgerald's *Great Gatsby* is Nick Carraway's account of his drive across the Queensboro Bridge in Gatsby's 'gorgeous car': 'with fenders spread like wings we scattered light through half Astoria' (Fitzgerald 2008 [1925]: 51, 54). The extravagant styling of Gatsby's car – thought by commentators to be modelled on a 1922 Rolls Royce Silver Ghost[1] – reminds us just how quickly early twentieth-century car design and manufacture turned to another mode of transportation – aviation – to symbolise and embody the experience of driving and passengering. As David Jeremiah has observed:

> From the outset, flying along had a strong association with motoring. Austin had the winged wheel as its trademark. Chrysler had a winged helmet; and the Hillman and Aston Martin names were winged. At the same time, the artist-illustrators [most notably, Gordon Crosby – see Figure 5.1][2] worked to give a visual expression to the sensation of cars flying over the crest of a hill, with the driver struggling to retain control and keep the wheels on the ground. (Jeremiah 2007: 113)

Yet, as the texts discussed in this chapter reveal, the reason designers – as well as artists and writers – turned to the metaphor/motif of flying was almost certainly in order to capture the heightened cognitive aware-

Figure 5.1 'Meteors of road and track – 12 cylinder Sunbeam', Gordon Crosby, *Autocar*, 22 February 1929. Courtesy of the National Library of Scotland.

ness that motoring afforded alongside its novel physical sensations (see also Mom 2014: 649–50). 'Flying', in other words, quickly established itself as a suggestive concept with which to figure the so-called 'altered states of consciousness' (see note 12 to Chapter 1) that driving was perceived to give rise to, even though the passenger's experience of aviation per se – typified by the illusion of being stationary and the earth below moving extremely slowly – is notionally at odds with the sort of mental excitation described by Bart Kennedy (see note 15 to Chapter 1) in the epigraph which heads this chapter. However, while excitement, frenzy and a mind leaping incoherently from one subject to the next may be one consequence of motoring at speed, another is the experience of acute mental clarity and empowerment as evidenced in this further extract from Kennedy's extraordinary essay:

Faster! Faster! Faster!

You are passing into a yet higher plane of life intenseness. You are becoming bigger, greater, stronger still. And still you have over yourself control. You are guide of yourself.

And there comes a strange power into your mind. Things that were dim to you in the snail life of the past are now becoming clear. Veils are being swept from before mysteries. You know things now that in the past were beyond your ken.

Your mind has grown. Your imagination is reaching out. You are solving strange problems. Life and the meaning of life is unfolding itself before you. You are high above all things. The world is stretching down beneath you. You see the lands and seas and oceans. To you an all-vision is coming as you are rushing swiftly. (Kennedy 1919a: 115)

As a consequence, driving at speed may also be seen to offer a perspective on the subject's everyday life that may be likened to the transcendent calm – the impression of being 'above and beyond it all' – that we experience from the window of an aeroplane. This sensation evidently impressed Kennedy a great deal since, in another of his essays, he reflects further on the paradox of the 'motion parallax' (see note 17 to Chapter 2) and its consequences not only for perception (i.e. distant objects appearing stationary) but also for cognition:

> Out again on the straight road. Out again, going smoothly and swiftly. So smoothly, and so evenly, does the car go that, at times, it almost seems as if you were not moving at all. It is almost as if you were sitting still whilst all things in the scope of your glance were passing you. As if you were holding some strange review wherein the earth and the things of the earth were going by.
> With you is a sensation of calm power. You sit here easily, passing without effort over your domain. For surely this is your domain! It is yours by the right of conquest. It comes to you as you pass with even swiftness over the road. Over it you exercise a spell. (Kennedy 1919b: 125)

Fashioned thus, motoring *is* like flying in the way it promotes an out-of-body experience that has a notable impact on our thinking as well as our bodily sensations, and one that is experienced in terms of clarity and insight rather than disorder and chaos. The fact that such moments of perceived enlightenment may equally be characterised as delusional (readers will doubtless have noted that Kennedy's epiphany is accompanied by a marked inflation of his ego) is one of the binaries this chapter seeks to probe, but for the moment it simply serves to illustrate why the metaphor/motif of flying is well-chosen and far-reaching when it comes to capturing the cognitive, as well as the sensory, 'benefits' of driving. Other writers to have likened the heightened sense of consciousness brought about by driving to this sort of aerial perspective include Dixon Scott (discussed in Chapter 1) who celebrates the driver's 'god-like detachment' and ability to 'swoop easily from point to point, with the calm surveillance of a bird' (Scott 1917: 47–8) and Elizabeth Bowen, whose *To the North* (2006 [1933]) is one of the texts featured later in this chapter. Bowen's protagonist, Emmeline, also enjoys a moment of panoptic vision as she speeds 'insanely' to her death (Bowen 2006: 304–5),[3] and the fact that the moment mirrors what she saw and felt when crossing the Channel in an aeroplane (Bowen 2006: 171) makes explicit the connection between the two forms of transport:

> Blind with new light she was like someone suddenly not blind, or, after a miracle, somebody moving perplexed by the absence of pain. Like earth shrinking and sinking, irrelevant, under the rising wings of a plane, love with its unseen plan, its constrictions and urgencies, dropped to a depth below Emmeline, who now looked down unmoved at the shadowy map of her pain . . .
> For this levitation a total loss of her faculties, of every sense of his presence, the car and herself driving were very little to pay . . . (Bowen 2006: 304–5)

The fact that Bowen's text presents Emmeline as both 'blind' and 'all-seeing', lost to herself and yet perfectly centred, speaks to the complexity with which the altered states of consciousness associated with driving are dealt with in this and the other 1930s novel featured in this chapter, Rosamund Lehmann's *The Weather in the Streets* (1981 [1936]). Enlightenment and delusion – as psychological states precipitated by the perils of falling in love as well as driving at speed – are never far apart in these texts, in significant contrast to the motoring journalism and more populist fiction from the period which tends to polarise into a celebration of the heightened awareness such automotive 'flight' could bring about (Kennedy 1919a, 1919b; Filson Young 1904; Scott 1917) and satirical disgust (Ehrenburg 1999 [1929]; Balchin 1959 [1954]; Huxley 1959 [1925]). In short, the transcendental states of consciousness that driving (and passengering)[4] were seen to facilitate – and even in those decades when 'speed' was understood as 20 or 30 rather than 60 or 70mph – was regarded both as a blessing and a curse.

The explicitly future-oriented nature of automotive flying, as I have characterised it here (in contrast to the focus on 'fleeing' – as 'escape from' in Chapter 3), leads us directly to the two theorists whose work on reverie and daydream[5] informs this chapter, namely Gaston Bachelard and Ernst Bloch. Bachelard's two books *The Poetics of Space* (2014 [1958]) and *The Poetics of Reverie* (1971 [1960]) and Bloch's *The Principle of Hope* (1986 [1959]) were first published within two years of one another and, despite the absence of cross-referencing, mark an important – if transient – shared moment in the history of Western thought. Working at the interface of Freudian psychology and philosophy/phenomenology, both men identify and seek to redress what they perceive to be the retrogressive thrust of psychoanalysis, in particular the assumption that the unconscious and its attendant mechanisms, such as dreams, function primarily in relation to the past. For Bloch,[6] 'anticipatory consciousness', as discovered in the daydream, is as important to the personal and social lives of human beings as their 'unconscious' processing of the past:

> *The content of the night-dream is concealed and disguised, the content of the day-fantasy is open, fabulously inventive, anticipating, and its latency lies ahead.* It comes itself out of self- and world-extension forwards, it is wanting to have better, often simply wanting to know better. (Bloch 1986: 99 (italics in the original))

As well as delivering personal redemption, the daydream is, by its very nature, 'world-extending'(Bloch 1986: 99) and hence a much needed 'principle of hope' in a beleaguered world.[7] For Bachelard, meanwhile, the daydream is an expression of what he outlines in *The Poetics of Space* as a 'phenomenology of the imagination' (pp. 152–3) which requires that we pay as much attention to the 'new world' that presents itself to our consciousness through our reveries as to our observations of the empirical world (Bachelard 2014: 152–3). For Bachelard, as for Bloch, then, the extraordinary value of the reverie or daydream is that it helps us break free from our personal and collective pasts and fantasise an alternative future for ourselves and others.

For both philosophers, meanwhile, the daydream is positively distinguished from night dreams and the workings of the unconscious more generally by the mechanisms of conscious control through which it operates: 'the daydream projects its images into the future, by no means indiscriminately, but [remains] controllable even given the most impetuous imagination' (Bloch 1986: 99). Such direction is possible because 'the ego in the daydream is nowhere near so weakened as in the night dream' (Bloch 1986: 88) and the fact that reverie itself is characterised by 'a tireless incentive toward the actual attainment of what it visualizes' (Bloch 1986: 87–8). Similarly, in *The Poetics of Reverie* (1971), Bachelard emphasises the agency of what he describes as the 'cogito of the dreamer':

> And here is the radical difference for us between the nocturnal dream (*réve*) and reverie, the radical difference, a difference deriving from phenomenology; while the dreamer of the nocturnal dream is a shadow who has lost himself (*moi*), the dreamer or reverie, if he is a little bit philosophical, can formulate a *cogito* at the centre of his dreaming self (*son moi rêveur*) . . . Even when the reverie gives the impression of flight out of the real, out of time and place, the dreamer of reverie knows that it is he who is absenting himself – he, in flesh and blood, who is becoming a 'spirit,' a phantom of the past or of voyage. (Bachelard 1971: 150)

This incidental allusion to 'flight' (as escape) returns us to the discussion in Chapter 3 of how different *motivations* can shape and determine states of consciousness that, superficially, appear to resemble one another. What both Bachelard and Bloch are at pains to make clear, however, is that daydreaming, as they have conceived it, is a species of '*semi*-conscious' thought, undertaken not for mere escapism and/or the gratification of fantasies, but for the constructive imagining of a better future.

I return to the work of these two theorists in the next section of this chapter which reviews the practice and significance of reverie and daydreaming for drivers. By placing Bachelard's and Bloch's passionate investment in this particular state of consciousness against contemporary psychology's characterisation of it as an unremarkable 'default network activity'[8] and the work of dedicated automotive psychologists like Groeger (2000), Van Lennep (1987), He et al. (2011) and Charlton and Starkey (2011), we begin to see how and why daydreaming is such an important aspect of driving even if, for many of those working in the field of accident prevention (including the psychologists cited above), its pervasiveness is a cause for concern.

As already observed, the writers of the early twentieth century – novelists as well as motoring journalists – quickly picked up on the fine line that separates the sharpening of the cognitive faculties afforded by driving and passengering and the psychoses (from mild delusion to outright 'madness') it may also induce. For the purposes of the discussion that follows, this slippage between enlightenment and delusion becomes one of three binaries I have identified in my textual sources in order to explore the different 'altered' states of consciousness to which driving and/or passengering gives rise to, the others being euphoria/anxiety and utopia/death-drive (see Figure 5.2).

Together, this matrix of cognitive-affective states may be thought of as a double set of traffic lights that drivers encounter differently on each and every driving-event depending upon the personal circumstances they bring to the journey and, of course, the road conditions. On certain days, and in favourable conditions, they may glide through the first set of (metaphorical) lights – moving swiftly from feelings of euphoria, through enlightenment to a glimpse of a personal or 'world-extending' (Bloch 1986: 99) utopia. On other days and in less favourable conditions euphoria may quickly convert to anxiety (including 'road rage', discussed below), enlightenment to delusion, and – in certain circumstances – an earthly despair that finds relief only in *thanatos*: the death-drive. Needless to say, what a close reading of my literary sources reveals is just how volatile, and mutable, these different states of

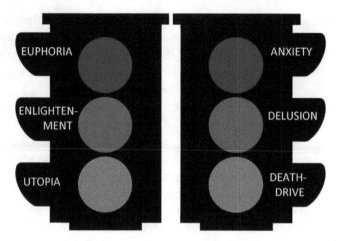

Figure 5.2 Six types of automotive reverie. Drawing by Lee Horsley.

automotive consciousness are, with the consequence that the daydream which forms at the start of a journey may have been replaced by something very different by that journey's end as figured in my concept of the 'driving-event' (see Chapter 1).

Driving and daydreaming

This, of course, is a subtitle that I may live to regret given that for most members of the public – not to mention the police and the motoring organisations – daydreaming is something that 'good' or 'responsible' drivers would never be seen to do. Given the enthusiasm with which I have explored literary and other texts which grant us a window, albeit fictional, on such reveries it could easily be assumed that I am advocating the mind-expanding and/or tranquilising properties of driving in a naive and unproblematic way. This, however, is far from my objective, and I open this subsection with a brief discussion of the work of automotive psychologists who, for some time, have recognised the extent to which we are able to think – and converse – about non-driving-related matters, as well as perform secondary manual tasks, without necessarily compromising our safety.

As noted in the discussion of Tim Dant's conceptualisation of the 'driver-car' (Dant 2004) in Chapter 4, one of the earliest psychologists to investigate the special psychological skills needed to drive a car was J. J. Gibson in the 1930s (Gibson 1982 [1938]). As Dant (2004: 64) reports, Gibson was 'astounded' (1982 [1938]: 130 fn 10) at the amount of information the average driver had to process in order to carry out a routine operation such as overtaking and began to acknowledge an element of embodiment, in addition to the perceptual/cognitive faculty, in order to account for it. Like the psychologists who followed him, J. J. Gibson's research into driver psychology was motivated by a desire to fully understand 'what skills drivers needed to help reduce deaths on the road' (Dant 2004: 64). As David Jeremiah reports, by the late 1930s road traffic accidents had already become an unwelcome phenomenon on British roads (as throughout the world)[9] and there was a growing need to better understand what contributed to them. Not surprisingly, speed, road type and overtaking were identified as the chief culprits, although – as many of the fictional texts discussed later in the chapter attest – the notion that driving (at speed) tipped otherwise sane people into madness was also given serious scientific consideration. In other words, it was widely believed that a chemical reaction took place in the driver's brain when he (or, occasionally, 'she') got behind the wheel of the car that manifested itself as a change of personality; timid men became fearless (see Aldous Huxley's 'Lord Hovenden' (1959), and fearless men became 'gods' (see Kennedy extract above). Iain Borden, whose own book, *Drive* (2013), ends with a chapter called 'Altered States', quotes Lou Marinoff (1941) as an example of these sorts of speculations: 'Once you "turn a ton" you're in a different world . . . The scenery flashes by a lot faster, but everything else decelerates. It becomes strangely still and you feel a floating sensation' (Borden 2013: 174–5). For Marinoff, as for many *fin-de-siècle* medical men (Kern 2000: 125–6) – and, arguably, for Virilio (2008) – the human mind/body is hard-wired to respond to the stimulus of speed in a dramatic way. In contrast to Virilio, however – who, it will be remembered, characterised 'dromoscopy' as a blind, unthinking/unfeeling 'will-to-destination' (see Chapter 3) – Marinoff describes the way in which the driver achieves new 'calmness' and his choice of the word 'floating' is especially interesting since it suggests a dream-like psychological state as well as a bodily sensation. This, I would argue, complicates the simplistic link between flooring the accelerator and losing one's mind, and questions whether it is speed alone that that lifts the driver into an alternative state of consciousness.

A psychologist who has worked extensively in the field of automobility is John Groeger (see note 29 to Chapter 1). Since the 1990s, Groeger and his co-investigators have sought to determine which factors impair driver function through wide-ranging laboratory experiments, and this research has caused him to challenge the assumption (now held by many cognitive psychologists)[10] that driving is, for the most part, an 'automatic' skill (Groeger 2000: 55). Groeger's principal conclusion here – that *some* 'secondary tasks' impact upon driver performance while others do not – nevertheless helps to explain why certain practices, such as engaging in an (amicable) conversation, listening to music or 'thinking about other things', can be pursued by drivers without compromising safety unduly. Such 'distractions' can be accommodated providing the 'supervisory attention system' (Groeger 2000: 57) is ready to 'spring into action' at any given time. The corollary to this, however, is that those tasks which compete for the attention of the brain's 'central executive' most consummately *do* put drivers at risk and, for Groeger and his co-researchers, this includes events that are demanding of 'spatial working memory' (such as 'localising a sound in space', e.g. a siren) and 'attention-demanding' (Groeger 2000: 109, 111) telephone conversations. The implication here, that *some* telephone conversations are likely to be more attention-demanding than others, also points to the important issue of how 'in control' a driver feels about the secondary task in question. My sense is that this variable could equally apply to in-car conversations (with 'difficult' ones obviously demanding more attention), the driver's ability to memorise directions (another key demand on 'spatial working memory') and, indeed, the content – and direction – of one's thoughts more generally (see also Eric Laurier's recent research: Laurier 2011; Laurier and Dant 2011). On this last point, we could, indeed, hypothesise that a depressed/grieving person's obsessive focus on a single matter, or another's 'sustained' daydream, are potentially less in competition with the brain's 'supervisory attention system' than, for example, a scenario in which the driver is processing important new information (e.g. the offer of a job or a house sale) or rehearsing a confrontation with a colleague at work. We have already considered a number of fictional scenarios in which the practice of driving is, itself, seen to help control and direction our thoughts (e.g. the case of Maria Wyeth in Joan Didion's *Play It As It Lays* (2011), but personal experience has taught me that it is our more immediate circumstances (events which have just happened or are about to happen) that are most likely to compete with our decision-making faculties as drivers and lead to accidents.

As well as the signal role played by the brain's 'central executive' in directing a driver's attention back to the road when danger threatens, Groeger and his colleagues follow earlier psychologists like Gibson in acknowledging the role schemata play in enabling a driver to manage the complex demands of driving (Groeger 2000: 57). In other words, our ability to pursue 'secondary tasks' while driving depends, in part, on our pre-existing familiarity with a wide range of road conditions. This perceptual mechanism is described by D. J. Van Lennep, writing in 1987, thus:

> At a single glance he [the driver] must survey what is happening on his left
> and on his right and what is happening in front of him and further ahead. But
> he sees all of this in a determinate structure and what is important and what
> is unimportant is divided according to the meaning which the things have for
> him in his situation and which he gives to them on the basis of his judgement.
> (Van Lennep 1987: 219)

There is a an echo here of Bergson's theorisation of the interanimation
of memory and perception (Bergson 2000: 148) as discussed in Chapter
1, whereby 'everyday' perception is seen to be *strategically* restrictive
and directed towards preservation in the present; in other words, our
minds recall and actualise only what we need to deal with in our present
situation.

Like Gibson before him, however, Van Lennep recognised that the
semblance of automation seen in drivers could not be purely attributed
to cognitive processes and introduced the concept of 'motor-skills' to
help account for the way in which drivers deal with so many simultane-
ous demands on their attention:

> Our motor-reactions not only depend (as we thought formerly) on our
> perception, but our perception, which in practical life is always pragmatic
> perception, depends upon our motor involvement ... Anyone who after
> having been a passenger suddenly takes the wheel knows how the aspect of
> the world changes immediately ... An open spot in the traffic which while we
> were sitting beside the driver we were not or at least only with difficulty able
> to judge as to the possibility or impossibility of our being able to get through,
> we can now, that is now that we are sitting behind the wheel with our foot
> on the pedal, evaluate accurately and without hesitation. (Van Lennep 1987:
> 221–2)

As well as providing a useful account of the differential experiences
of drivers and passengers, Van Lennep's observations also echo Tim
Dant's conclusions in 'The Driver-Car' (2004: 73) (see Chapters 1 and
4), even though Dant is working with very different theoretical models
(e.g. Merleau-Ponty's phenomenology of the body) that dispense with
a mediating 'consciousness' as such. What several decades' worth of
research into the ways in which drivers are able to handle the complex
demands of driving at the same time as conducting secondary tasks
would therefore appear to have revealed is the ontologically dispersed
resources of the human body to meet such demands (see also Laurier
2004; Laurier and Dant 2011).

Contemporary psychology also provides us with another answer to
the question of how drivers can pursue reveries or daydreams while they
are driving, namely that – rather than the fascinating substratum of consciousness that Bachelard (2014, 1971) and Bloch (1986) perceive them

to be – they are simply an expression of the brain's 'default network' (see note 8). In other words, daydreaming is a *habitual* practice that we all revert to as soon as the brain is otherwise 'off-duty' (Whitbourne 2013). If this is the case – and we do, indeed, spend over fifty per cent of our waking hours absorbed in 'unfocused' thought (Kilingworth and Gilbert 2010: 932) – it is clearly to be expected that this will include time spent driving, especially if our day includes a long journey. However, this degradation of the daydream to something so mundane and unexceptional would seem to depend upon its changing nomenclature. While, in the realm of popular psychology, the term may be a convenient catch-all for all 'absent-minded musing' and 'internal mentation' (Whitbourne 2013), other psychologists continue to distinguish between focused/sustained reveries and more generalised 'mind-wandering' (Thompson 2015: 350–6). Evan Thompson's explicit attempt to distinguish between 'mind-wandering' and 'mindfulness' – drawing on recent neuroscience as well as psychological studies – is of particular interest here since it suggests that what Bachelard and Bloch had in mind when they championed daydreaming as a positive cognitive activity was effectively a mode of meditation rather than an unfocused drift from external stimuli to internal preoccupations (Thompson 2015: 351). Given that my own focus in this chapter is on the extraordinary rather than the ordinary states of automotive consciousness that driving can give rise to, I shall, for the most part, be following Bachelard and Bloch in their characterisation of this fascinating interior/anterior cognitive state. Nevertheless this location of the phenomenon of daydreaming within the discourses of twentieth-century cognitive psychology and, in particular, the work of automobility/transport psychologists will, I hope, have provided some explanation as to why and how daydreaming while driving is not only possible but to be expected.

Six types of automotive reverie

As well as capturing the shape and character of an 'everyday' automotive reverie – in this case, a drive home from Christmas shopping during the late 1930s – the following extract from Jan Struther's *Mrs Miniver* (1989 [1939]) also introduces a motif – the colour coding of emotions in accordance with traffic lights – which complements my conceptualisation of daydreaming as two sets of traffic lights (see Figure 5.2) or (echoing William Empson[11]) 'six states of automotive reverie':

> The lights changed. She put the car into bottom gear, paused, then let in the
> clutch. It occurred to her as she did so that it was not only people's physical

reactions to those three colours that had become automatic but their mental ones as well. Red, yellow, green – frustration, hope, joy: a brand new conditional reflex. Give it a few more years to get established, and psychiatrists would be using colour rays, projected in that sequence for the treatment of melancholia; and to future generations green would no longer suggest envy, but freedom. In such haphazard ways are symbolisms born and reborn. (Struther 1989: 14–16)

In the same way that Mrs Miniver sees in the red, amber and green of traffic lights the frustration, hope and joy of an increasingly mechanised and regulated public, so too have I identified three sets of binaries – euphoria/frustration, enlightenment/delusion and utopia/death-drive – as indicative of the different types of daydreaming a motorist (driver or passenger) might engage in. As noted above, the reason I have figured these as binaries is precisely because the line between enlightenment and delusion, and between utopian and 'suicidal' reverie, is so frequently transgressed in the more sophisticated literary texts. Needless to say, this is a mutability that most of us will recognise from our own daydreaming, behind the wheel or otherwise: sometimes, as Bachelard and Bloch advocate, the daydream can be marshalled to deliver thoughts and visions of great clarity, insight and life-enhancing potential, while on other occasions it may simply indulge misguided desire and wish-fulfilment. Either (in the 'best-case' scenarios) we may progress from generalised feelings of well-being and contentment with our present/ future circumstances (euphoria), through a moment of enlightenment to a utopian vision of the future (personal and/or social), or (less positively) the euphoria may induce deluded fantasies which progress to an equally deluded utopian vision or, as the result of a 'reality check', are diverted to a 'catastrophic' ending figured as (symbolic) self/other annihilation. Alternatively, the reverie might begin with anxiety before – through a moment of clarity/enlightenment – tracking towards a more positive/utopian outcome, or – and probably more typically – the driver might become so stuck in his/her anxiety that no relieving daydream/ fantasy is possible. We will see examples of several of these alternative 'routes' through the automotive reverie in the textual explorations that now follow.

Euphoria

For Bachelard, daydreaming is synonymous with well-being and euphoria a natural consequence of the fact that the dreamer, interacting with the world as a 'phenomenologist of the imagination' (Bachelard 2014: 152–3) (see above), benefits from a 'dispersed ontology':

The dreamer's being is a diffuse region . . . This intermediary being deadens the dialectic between being and non-being. The imagination does not know non-being. Its whole being can easily pass for a non-being in the eyes of the man at work, under the pen of the strong ontology metaphysician . . . It is not without reason that people commonly say that the dreamer is *plunged* in his reverie. The world no longer poses any opposition to him. The I no longer opposes itself to the world. In reverie there is no more non-I. In reverie, the *no* no longer has any function: everything is welcome. (Bachelard 1971: 167 (italics in original))

For Bloch meanwhile, and as noted in the introduction to this chapter, the well-being of the dreamer depends less upon his intimate, phenomenological relationship with the external world but in his or her ability to direct and *utilise* his or her daydreams. Both men, as previously observed, believe that the dreamer has a 'cogito', but Bloch's is the more instrumental:

There is no spell in this condition, at least none which the dreamer has not voluntarily imposed on himself, and which he could not revoke. The waking dream-house is also furnished exclusively with ideas chosen by the dreamer himself, whereas the sleeper never knows what is awaiting him beyond the threshold of the subconscious . . . Because the ego itself then becomes a wishful idea for itself, one freed of censorship, it experiences the green light of release which appears to have come on from all other wishful ideas. The relaxation of the ego in night-dreams is merely a sinking . . . (Bloch 1986: 88 (my italics))

Whereas Bachelard's dreamers realise euphoria as a consequence of their 'dispersed ontology', then, Bloch's acquire theirs through the transcendence of an ego no longer tied to the backward and downward movement of the unconscious. Looking only ahead, the daydreamer inhabits a world where traffic lights are forever green, and who – at his most 'ambitious' – 'flies with outspread wings up to the Temple of Posterity' (Bloch 1986: 91).

In the course of this book, we have already encountered numerous textual examples of the euphoria that the experience of driving and passengering can induce if conditions are favourable. Motoring, from its earliest days, is seen to have alternately soothed and thrilled its passengers, lulling them into a state of tranquil well-being (see Kennedy 1919b) or rousing them to heady excitement, as in this extract from Mrs Aria's 'Woman and the Motor-Car' (1906):

As he [the chauffeur] spoke he turned into Cliff Road and changed to a greater speed. The sensation was exhilarating in the extreme, the rapid motion causing the salt air to fan our faces pleasantly. The afternoon was perfectly still, and the murmur of the sea came faintly to our ears as the echoes of the waves in a conch shell. (Mrs Aria 1906: 53–4)

For Mrs Aria, a young divorcée, the euphoria induced by flying along in an open-topped car as a passenger or, subsequently, learning to drive is implicitly sexualised. The novel sensation of being swept along by a powerful machine, combined by the attention of a 'handsome' chauffeur or driving-instructor, evidently inspired erotic daydreams in the female motorist, even allowing for the fact this text is a fictionalised account of the author's personal experiences:[12]

In a few minutes we were gliding through an unexpected avenue . . . here and there a straight, slim poplar stood apart, disdainful, reserved, and a patch of blue sky was visible through the green roof . . . He drove back while I leaned contentedly against the crimson leather cushions, watching the nervous grip of his sunburned hands. I longed to encounter some real difficulty, even danger, in order to see how he would emerge from the ordeal. That he would prove equal to any emergency I never for an instant doubted. (Mrs Aria 1906: 141–5)

The kinaesthetic and haptic pleasures (or occasional 'trials') of motoring are also, of course, integral to high-brow Modernist literature, as noted in Chapter 1 with reference to Woolf's 'Evening Over Sussex' (1942) and explored in the work of literary scholars and cultural historians such as Danius (2002), Duffy (2009) and Garrington (2015).[13] What makes Woolf's text so notable in this regard, however, is the way in which it draws a direct link between the visceral and the cognitive; following Bachelard, we may assume that it is the paradoxical yoking of speed, stillness and serenity that facilitates Woolf's highly intellectual daydream (which arguably combines a phenomenology of the external world with what Bachelard describes as the 'phenomenology of the imagination' (see above)). However, it is also the time spent bowling along in the open air that seemingly causes her to quit her intellectual reverie and dream, instead, of bacon and eggs (Woolf 1942: 14).

Once we enter the era of the covered car and the paved road (Urry 2007: 130), meanwhile, literary fiction quickly exploits the condition of euphoria/well-being associated with the car's protective shell. For Bachelard the shell-image is redolent not only with associations of our 'original home' (and, by extension, womb) (Bachelard 2014: 32), but also childhood daydreaming. Both Bowen's and Lehmann's novels feature episodes in which the female protagonists are seen enjoying the protection offered by their cars and its associated dream-space, and the motif recurs in a good deal of female-authored 'middle-brow' fiction from the mid-twentieth century including Struther's *Mrs Miniver* (1989), Bowen's later novels including *Eva Trout* (2011 [1968]) and Elizabeth Taylor's *A Game of Hide and Seek* (2011 [1951]). In every case, the intimate interior of the car is explicitly linked to the female traveller's romantic hopes and fears and is repeatedly figured as the space in which she both daydreams a utopian future and sees those dreams, which prove to be delusions, cruelly unravel. Taylor's novel is exemplary in this regard, using two such automotive reveries to book-end the dawn and the demise of Harriet's relationship with (her husband) Charles:

> Harriet loved this driving at night. This hastening through empty villages and then the deserted streets of the town, was the most undemanding pleasure, like watching a beautiful film without a plot.
> Only through the fan-shaped spaces on the wind-screen did the outside scene appear. The rest of the glass was pearly with rain and steamed, so that they seemed cut off from the world in the closest intimacy.
> 'Are you happy?' Charles asked.
> 'Yes, I do feel very happy.' (Taylor 2011: 86–7)

> She tried to look out of the window, but beyond the silver drops on the glass, which turned gold as they passed a lamp, she could see very little. A string of blurred lights went up and over the hill. The quiet avenues and crescents were darkened and rain-swept.
> Charles, who had so much to say in others' presence, now had nothing to say. His coat collar was up to his ears, his hands were deep in his pockets, he sat hunched up in the far corner, away from Harriet. 'Marriage does not solve mysteries,' she thought. 'It creates and deepens them.' The two of them being shut up physically in this dark space, yet locked away forever from one another, was oppressive. Both were edgy.
> 'Coming on faster now,' said the driver, over his shoulder.
> 'Yes,' they both tiredly agreed.
> 'Shouldn't wonder if it went on all night' . . .
> She loved the sensation of being driven at night and was reluctant to leave this musty car. 'Wake up!' Charles said crossly. (Taylor 2011: 146–7)

In such texts the euphoric dream-space of the car is seen to facilitate reveries of *dis*illusion (arguably an enlightenment of sorts), as well as those of (deluded) fantasy. However, even on those occasions, such as here, when the revelation is of a sobering nature, the protective shell of the car, together with its easeful, forward-propulsion, clearly plays a crucial role in enabling the protagonist to confront the uncomfortable truths that have been welling up inside her. Although such scenarios bear scant resemblance to Bloch's characterisation of the daydream as an unstoppable flight towards a utopia, a dawning moment of realisation will often impact positively on the future too. At the same time, I would argue, that the moment of disillusion throws a shadow over our consciousness, daydreaming – as I am defining it here – ends. The reflection that ensues turns its attention from (im)possible futures to the recent past and strives, in the manner of Didion's Maria Wyeth (see Chapter 4), to take control of it. This is the distance, if you like, between imaginative and critical thinking; at times it profits us to invent, at other times, to analyse – and driving, I contend, facilitates both.

Anxiety

For Ernst Bloch, anxiety is the 'first and fundamental negative expectant emotion' (Bloch 1986: 109) and, for that reason, I have elected to make it the descriptor for this subsection rather than terms more commonly associated with automotive angst, namely 'frustration' or 'rage' – the latter being the altered state of consciousness now most commonly associated with car driving. This assumes that anxiety is, as far as 'negative expectant emotions' are concerned, an umbrella concept that incorporates all the rest, and it is true that when I conducted my own auto-ethnography of a 'road trip' in 2012, 'anxiety' was my preferred means of grouping the complex array of negative emotions that driving throws up when, for whatever reason, we are no longer moving towards our destination at the speed, or in the manner, we expected (Pearce 2012: 99–100).

For my purposes here, indeed, Bloch's figuring of anxiety as an 'expectant emotion' works well alongside a theory of driver frustration/ road rage that focuses on the (thwarted) *act of driving* rather than attendant social, cultural and psychological issues. In other words, although all theories of road rage recognise the significance of roads, traffic, other drivers and cars in their analyses, the common factor in virtually all such incidents – the fact that the progressive, future-oriented passage of the car and its driver has been threatened or interrupted – is easily overlooked or minimised. Thus, while I acknowledge that road rage – together with the less extreme expressions of anxiety that drivers demonstrate in stressful situations – is a complex psychological matter which defies a single explanation, I hope that this focus on the consequences of our comfortable, soothing, protective and – above all – *forward-moving* dream-machines being stopped in their tracks will lend further weight to this particular hypothesis. By recognising (automotive) anxiety to be, at least in part, a consequence of the euphoria driving otherwise promises and/or delivers, we can also better understand the fantasies/ performances to which it gives rise; for while such, frequently colourful, outbursts are clearly not to be confused with daydreams as I have chosen to define them here, very often the driver is described as acting out a role unlike his/her normal self (Katz 1999: 66–71): a consequence, perhaps, of his or her daydream-self being rudely awakened. For Bloch, indeed, anxiety is ultimately 'the content of [a] wish' which has been 'annihilated' (Bloch 1986: 82). When we consider the vast spectrum of things a driver might be looking forward to at any given time – from the most basic bodily comforts (Woolf's 'eggs and bacon', for instance) through to Bloch's own 'world-extending' fantasies – we begin to see what it means to have that promised (and often taken-for-granted) future delayed, postponed or, indeed, 'annihilated' by an actual or threatened event (see Figure 5.3).

In his defining study of late twentieth-century driver behaviour, psychologist Jack Katz does indeed recognise the significance of having one's progress interrupted, explaining it as disruption of the transcendence of time and space that driving otherwise offers:

> How does becoming angry when driving bring previously tacit, transcendent dimensions of action into vivid corporeal awareness? First of all, driving is itself essentially a means of transcending space, of getting from here to there.

Figure 5.3 'M25 Jam' (2007), Peter Bassett © Fotolibra (FOT484622).

When traffic or a rude driver cuts one off, the experience is of falling out of a flow and being stuck or held back . . . In some instances of becoming angry, drivers are clearly frustrated in their attempts to 'get there' *and they imagine clear pictures of themselves as they once were or might soon be in other places.* (Katz 1999: 34–5 (my italics))

This acknowledgement of the driver's vivid 'anticipatory consciousness' (they are already picturing things they might shortly be doing) explains why any actual and/or symbolic act that disrupts the flow (like being 'cut off' by another vehicle or unexpectedly finding one's self behind slow-moving traffic), is likely to create stress in the majority of drivers regardless of whether they are technically 'in a hurry' or not. Through the simple act of getting behind a steering wheel and turning the ignition, a driver is instantly propelled towards future events whose imminence s/he can hasten with a press on the accelerator. The faster s/he drives, the sooner certain things will happen. The fact that nothing else in contemporary life delivers quite the same illusion of our ability to control time (in particular *to get ahead of it*) helps to explain why driving can be experienced as a reliever as well as a cause of stress. It also brings a whole different set of connotations to the concept of *drivetime*, as I return to in this chapter's conclusion.

For Katz, the driver's apparent ability to transcend time and space is, however, just one of many ways in which the 'metaphysical merger' (Katz 1999: 33) of human and car has succeeded in isolating drivers from their immediate social environment, rendering them hostile to anyone or anything that threatens their (hybrid) integrity. Staying with the particular threat posed to the driver's 'anticipatory consciousness' through actions and events that disrupt his or her progress, however, we are reminded that not all driver-anxiety commutes into anger that is directed at fellow motorists or is routed through a (temporarily) inflated sense of ego and entitlement. For some drivers (and passengers), the focus of anxiety remains firmly fixed on the future task/event that cannot be reached ('in time') because of the delay, and the angst – if it turns anywhere – is towards themselves. Both my 2012 auto-ethnography (Pearce 2012) and this book's Interlude capture this sort of anxiety; as I sit in traffic or worry about the delays I may encounter further along the route, I am seen to fantasise elaborate 'worst-case' scenarios, my mind returning to traffic jams I have encountered at particular junctions in the past, as well as focusing obsessively on the task/appointment I will miss (a phone call to an elderly neighbour, collecting the dog) if I do not get there in time. Once again, it would be wrong to describe such fretting as daydreams in the manner of Bloch and Bachelard, but its content is arguably too focused and well-developed to be seen as mere 'mind-wandering'. Following my earlier discussion, I would suggest that such fantasies conform to Bloch's theory that anxiety *forms itself* around 'the annihilated content of a wish' (Bloch 1986: 85) and the images and scenarios our minds conjure up at such times are precisely that: the things we hoped/expected to happen *not* happening – and their consequence. For subjects inclined to anxiety, such 'negative expectant emotions' can prove very unpleasant and 'bad car journeys' a cauldron for their manufacture.

Although published at either end of the 'motoring century', Ilya Ehrenburg's *The Life of the Automobile* (1999 [1929]) and Ben Elton's *Gridlock* (1991) share a common dislike and exasperation with the 'car-system' (Dennis and Urry 2009). That is to say, both authors review and satirise the impact of automobility beyond its immediate social consequence (for example, pollution and road-deaths) and marvel, incredulously, at how and why the post-industrial world has chosen to invest in a form of transport that is so dysfunctional and non-sustainable. That Ehrenburg had this vision at the time that the car population was miniscule compared to now and the longer-term consequences of the automobile revolution only just beginning to be felt, is remarkable, even if it also reminds us of the extent to which automotive enthusiasts have underplayed this 'other history' of the car. The 'traffic jam', possibly the most potent symbol of a failing automobile system, is a case in point here; although the problem of traffic congestion was virtually synonymous with the invention of the car, there is a tendency to think of it as a much more recent problem.[14]

Ehrenburg's story of a 'day in the life' of taxi-driver, Karl Lang, is memorable both as portrait of the extreme alienation of labour (Karl's job has robbed him of his ability to think) and of the extreme anxiety of the motorist caught up in traffic. While the latter is my immediate concern here, it is worth noting how Ehrenburg caricatures Karl, implying that the only way a driver could possibly disengage with the stress of being mired in traffic on a daily basis is to become an automaton himself (Ehrenburg 1999: 168–70). Very notably, there is no 'anticipatory consciousness' in Karl's world; as the narrator concludes, without sufficient time to think, it is pointless beginning, and the trade-off is that there is no anxiety either. This is in signal contrast to Karl's passengers or 'fares':

A fare got into Karl's taxi. He had no suitcase and no portfolio. But he breathlessly whispered: 'Kaiserdam 268'. He wasn't able to sit calmly. He drummed his fingers on the glass. He propped his legs against the wall. He was urging on the lazy car. He was the most ordinary of passengers. Round glasses. A beige felt hat. He wasn't old or young, rich or poor. He was one of four million.

The car stopped at a crossing. The road was clear. No cars, no pedestrians. The passenger banged on the window. Karl didn't budge. *Naturally the fare was in a rush. All fares are in a rush. That's what cars are meant for.* But there was a red light. Somewhere an invisible authority pulled a lever, and suddenly, as though riven [*sic*] to the ground, excited cars stopped at various corners of various streets. The engine panted impatiently. Its breath mixed with the breath of the passenger. Then the green light flared up and the car zoomed off. (Ehrenburg 1999: 172 (my italics))

The yoking, here, of the expectation of getting somewhere quickly – i.e. 'ahead of time' – and automobility ('that's what cars are meant for') echoes my own earlier point about the way in which just stepping into a car orients mind and body towards a future moment. While some of the modes of driving we have considered in this book – notably 'searching' and 'cruising' – may be seen to welcome such incursions of the 'synchronic' time of 'the moment' into the ('diachronic') time of the journey,[15] most of us will be familiar with the angst of Karl's passenger which stems from his understanding that the car, on this occasion, has been engaged to take him somewhere – 'Kaisersdam 268' – as quickly as possible.

So acute, however, is the anxiety the 'fare' suffers as a result of the taxi's failure to move quickly enough through the congested road system that he never makes it to his destination. The price for his anxiety – his failure to 'beat' or, at least, to *match* the clock – is to suffer a heart attack:

It started raining. The traffic-lights and the numbers wilted. Now a ruler slid across the windshield. It quickly wiped away the drops. It was fussy and exact: left to right, then right to left. A passenger's heart is not constructed as well. He took off his hat. He raised himself. He was very pale. Here was Kaiserdam! ... But how long this street was! Uneasily he peered at the numbers. Then, worn out, he closed his eyes. (Ehrenburg 1999: 172)

While the moral of this tale, from the perspective of Ehrenburg's text as a whole, is plain to see – the 'car-system' (Dennis and Urry 2009) destroys the lives of *all* its agents and users – in the context of my discussion here it also serves as a vivid illustration of the extent to which the function of the car has become bound up in our 'anticipatory consciousness' and the psychological consequences of those expectations being undermined.

Ben Elton's *Gridlock* (1991) also features an encounter between a driver (this time a private chauffeur) and an impatient passenger (Sam Turk, a top executive with 'Global Motors'), but one who responds to the stress of his situation rather differently:

Traffic jams are strange things, they resonate. As when a stone is dropped in a pond, the matter does not end with the initial plop . . . Traffic jams never actually end, they merely expand and contract, merging into one another, endlessly connected by frustration and grinding synchromesh. There is a little of the very first traffic jam in every one that has happened since.

Sam was caught up in the ripple effect. His car, like his industry, was at a standstill and he was getting impatient.

'Jeez,' he barked, lowering the electric window which separated him from the driver. 'I never seen [*sic*] the city like this before. It's Sunday goddamit, doesn't anyone in this damn country worship the lord anymore? What the hell's going on?' The driver explained that the traffic was particularly bad that day because there had been a huge protest rally in Hyde Park and the effects had fanned out across the city.

'A *protest* rally? What, like a hippy thing?' gasped Sam in astonishment. 'I don't believe this fucking country!' (Elton 1991: 37–8)

This episode – one of many in the novel to inflict 'poetic justice' on the 'car-system' and its representatives – parodies the frustrated motorist's instinct to lash out and/or vilify whoever or whatever gets in the way of his or her progress; the fact that, in this case, it is a protest rally against the government's plans for the nationwide expansion of the road network (which Turk and Global Motors naturally have a vested interest in) is what fuels the comedy. Placing the novel alongside Jack Katz's research (see above), it would appear, however, that there is nothing exaggerated in Sam Turk's response. Many of Katz's interviewees confess to episodes of frantic gesturing, as well as verbal abuse far more colourful than Turk's when consumed with road rage. For Katz, such behaviour is best explained as the subject's attempt to win back his or her agency and power by enacting the role of the 'avenging hero':

The trick is to call up moral energy to construct a drama of communal importance in the immediate situation, then to clothe oneself in the role of avenging hero. Once the situation has been given morally transcendent meaning, it does not matter that no one else is watching, since the relevant audience is universal and could never physically be in attendance anyway. (Katz 1999: 49)

What is especially interesting about this analysis in the context of my discussion here is that the frustrated drivers' performances may be thought of as the acting out of a daydream which extracts them from the frustration and humiliation of the intolerable present and relocates them in a new and, according to Katz, improved, future – even if they are still, in reality, running behind schedule and stationary on the tarmac. In more general terms, any outburst of anger may, of course, be likened to the release of a pressure valve, and thus be understood as a strategy for mitigating the sort of internalised stress that led to the death of Ehrenburg's 'fare'.

The fact that my two fictional examples focus on passengers rather than drivers is also significant inasmuch as much road rage theory, following psychologists like Katz and Van Lennep (1987), propose that drivers are more prone to anger on account of the fact they feel their vehicles to be an extension of themselves. As Katz observed, 'we will fail to appreciate fully the difference in the perspectives of the driver and passenger' unless we recognise the extent to which a driver experiences a threat to his or her car – by being 'cut off', for example – as a threat or violence to his or her 'phenomenological body' (Katz 1999: 33). The corollary to this, however, is that automobile passengers may experience equally acute stress and provocation, though of a qualitatively different kind, on account of their enforced passivity (see also Laurier and Dant 2011). While the cut-off or 'stalled' driver is still in touch with the power source that will, eventually, relieve him or her of their stress (the steering wheel is still in their hands, the accelerator under their feet), all the passenger can do is sit and wait, drumming his fingers on the window (Ehrenburg) or shouting at the driver (Elton).

The fact, meanwhile, that car passengers can and do get stressed despite the fact that they are differently positioned to drivers is arguably further evidence that slowing down, stopping and the attendant fear of 'being late' – when sat in a vehicle designed to get you to your destination 'ahead of time' – is the most fundamental cause of automotive angst. Other road users and unexpected road situations will, of course, play their part – and present themselves as the more likely targets for our rage – but there is nothing quite like the sensation of flying along a road sweetly, thinking about things to come and then being unexpectedly and abruptly *stopped*.

Enlightenment

For Bachelard and Bloch, enlightenment was, of course, the chief purpose of the daydream: a means, for Bloch, of creatively imagining a better future (the daydream 'builds castles in the air as blueprints' (Bloch 1986: 86)) and, for Bachelard, the result of experiencing more fully the 'wonder' of existence through a phenomenology that attends not only to the material world but also that of the imagination (Bachelard 1971: 153–4). For both philosophers, also, the enlightenment facilitated by the daydream is achieved, in part, through the dreamer's new ontological relation to the world, and each regards 'confidence' as key to the dreamer's success in securing his or her vision:

> Through imagination, thanks to the subtleties of the irreality function, we re-enter the world of confidence, the world of the confident being, which is the proper world for reverie ... Knowledge of the real world requires complex phenomenological research. The dream worlds of wide-awake, diurnal reverie are dependent upon truly fundamental phenomenology. And thus we have come to believe that it is through reverie that one must learn phenomenology. (Bachelard 1971: 14)

In a neat recalibration of a term – 'irrealisation' – which for automotive psychologist Van Lennep (1987) is one of the chief *dangers* of driving – Bachelard turns the tables on mainstream phenomenology and suggests that only those who yield themselves up to the 'dispersed ontology' of the dreamer will gain the 'confidence' to achieve true enlightenment. This is because it is only in the dream-state that the subject can transcend the dialectic between 'being and non-being' and fully grasp the uniqueness of that which presents itself to his or her consciousness (Bachelard 1971: 167).

For Bloch, meanwhile, the unique insight and, hence, 'confidence' (Bloch 1986: 110) of the dreamer depends upon a rather different restructuring of the subject's ontology. Instead of characterising the (day)dreaming subject as ontologically 'dispersed' and hence continuous with the (imaginary) phenomenological world with which s/he engages, Bloch invokes a vocabulary of flight, freedom, exuberance and general elevation to account for the empowerment, i.e. the daydreamer is one who soars *above* the phenomenological world and, from the perspective of distance, is able to 'solve' its riddle:

> The daydream can furnish inspirations which do not require interpreting, but working out, it builds castles in the air as blueprints too, and not always just fictitious ones. Even in caricature, the daydreamer is presented in a different light than the dreamer: he is then Johnnie Head-in-the-air, and thus by no means a sleeper at night with his eyes closed. Lonely walks or enthusiastic youthful discussion with a friend or the so-called blue hour between daylight and darkness are particularly conducive to waking dreams. (Bloch 1986: 86)

> 'The individual imagines he can see tangled plans, the clarification of which previously seemed impossible, disentangled before him as well as the way to being accomplished' (Lewin, Phantastica, 1927, p. 159ff.) ... Consequently, the ego in the waking-dream is found to be very animated, even striving. (Bloch 1986: 90)

As was outlined in the introduction to the chapter, this characterisation of the dreamer as an elevated, perspicacious and altogether 'god-like' figure is probably more typical of the mode and manner of enlightenment associated with motoring. That said, Bachelard's 'dispersed ontology' can usefully be invoked, in certain circumstances, to help explain the process of enlightenment associated with being kinetically *immersed* in speed, as may be seen in the textual examples to which I now turn.

Although Jack Kerouac's *On the Road* (2000) is a text I elected to discuss in the context of the state(s) of automotive consciousness specifically associated with our *flight from* certain material, psychological and existential circumstances, it also deserves to be considered here in the context of more hopeful, future-oriented dream-states. Alongside those episodes in the text which characterise Dean Moriarty's 'flights' across the North American continent as blindly and 'unthinkingly' focused on his destination in the manner of Virilio's dystopian vision (2008), there are others which show him and his companions entering into meditations or achieving states of enlightenment that accord with Bachelard's and Bloch's definitions of the daydream. Perhaps the stand-out example of this is the episode already discussed in some detail in Chapter 3, namely the journey that Dean and Sal make together from San Francisco back to Denver in the back seat of a Plymouth (Kerouac 2000: 18–19; text reproduced in Chapter 3). Apart from reinforcing my own point that passengering, as well as driving, can facilitate reverie, the episode also demonstrates that daydreaming need not be a solitary business; as Bloch himself observed (see above) 'enthusiastic youthful discussion with a friend' (Bloch 1986: 86) can also lead to the proverbial 'blue skies' thinking. What Bloch would have made of Dean and Sal's conversation is, of course, debatable, but the episode certainly serves as a vivid illustration of how (auto)mobility – complemented here, perhaps, by the use of certain drugs – can fuel the 'phenomenology of the imagination' as well as that of the empirical world. Although Dean's and Sal's visions are sourced to their childhoods, their meaning and interpretation in the present is very evidently focused on their future: that is, their search for 'IT' (Kerouac 2000: 189). Indeed, the way in which their ride in the back of the Plymouth stimulates their memories of passengering in their parents' cars when children also fits well with Bachelard's theory that the spaces-of-daydreaming in the past (notably, the house and its most intimate nooks and crannies) begets daydreaming in the present (Bachelard 2014: 30–2). By rediscovering the euphoria of being 'borne aloft' in the powerful cruiser, Dean and Sal relive their own dreams of flying and, in the process, achieve a triumphant transcendence and enlightenment in the present. Speed, distance and elevation – the illusion of flying over the land – are the key means to this sort of ecstatic vision, and resonate with Bart Kennedy's analysis of 'the magic of speed' quoted at the head of this chapter.

Speed, however – as discussed in Chapter 1 – is a culturally inscribed and profoundly relative phenomenon and we should therefore not be surprised to find Mr and Mrs Miniver enjoying a moment of structurally similar – if, admittedly, somewhat less ecstatic – daydream enlightenment on their drive up to Scotland:

> 'This' said Clem as they topped a rise, 'is where we passed those gypsies two years ago.'
>
> 'I know,' said Mrs Miniver. 'I was just thinking that. With the skewbald horse.' It was amazing, the number of little memory flags with which, on their minds' map, the road was studded. There were dozens of them now, and every year added a few more. There was one, for instance, near Colsterworth, where their first car (a two-cylinder roller-skate with overhead valves and partially exposed viscera, very sweet and willing but extremely second-hand) had dropped a push-rod; which, after a long search, they had recovered from a gutter a quarter of a mile behind . . . There were flags, too, at all the places they had stopped for a picnic; and one at the place they had seen a particularly fine double rainbow; and one at the place where, after rounding a sharp bend, they had come upon a man in a stationary car removing his false black beard. An enigmatic flag, that, five years old. (Struther 1989: 49)

For Mr and Mrs Miniver, as for Dean and Sal, the dream-space of the car begets previous daydreams (most notably, the fantasy of man in the stationary car being a spy) and, subsequently, leads Mrs Miniver to a moment of hazy, yet intense, enlightenment into the ability of memory to 'reverse' the onward march of time:

> Moving northward in space, thought Mrs Miniver, they had moved backward in time; reversed the irreversible, recaptured in late summer the feeling of spring. By what analogous mental journey, she wondered, what deliberate pilgrimage of the heart, could one – but she did not pursue that metaphor, it would give her the slip, she felt, like the man with the false beard. (Struther 1989: 50)

The vividness with which their past journeys may be recreated in the present enables Mrs Miniver to glimpse the simultaneity of past, present and future, and while she does not have the philosophical wherewithal to follow its implications through – or, indeed, bring it to bear upon her emotional life ('the pilgrimage of the heart') – it is a moment of enlightenment nonetheless. As for Dean and Sal, journeying backwards through time as well as forwards through space, creates a new and surreal perspective from which it is possible to grasp the complexity of our 'being' in time with new clarity.

Elsewhere in Kerouac's text, the means and manner of enlightenment are more akin to Bachelard's 'dispersed ontology' than the moments of epiphany illustrated in the previous extracts. The signal episode in this regard, already discussed in Chapter 3, is Dean's seventeen-hour 'streak' from Denver to Chicago. While there I reflected on the way in which the representation of Sal's reeling consciousness was reminiscent of Henri Bergson's theory of how perception and memory shadow one another in the present moment, with recently subjugated perceptions (now memories) ever-ready to spring back into consciousness when prompted to do so, it is clearly also possible to read the episode as an extended reverie or daydream (Sal, it will be recalled, tries to go to sleep but is unable to) in which his radically 'dispersed' ontological relationship to the time-space through which he flies makes him *part* of all he apprehends in just the way that Bachelard (see earlier quote) outlines:

> Now I could feel the road some twenty inches beneath me, unfurling and flying and hissing at incredible speeds through the groaning continent with that mad Ahab at the wheel. When I closed my eyes all I could see was the road unwinding in me. (Kerouac 2000: 213)

While Sal Paradise does not exactly register this 'dispersal' of being as a moment of pleasurable enlightenment or wonder ('All that old road of the past unreeling dizzily as if the cup had been overturned and everything gone mad. My eyes ached in nightmare day' (Kerouac 2000: 213)), it certainly bears all the hallmarks of an exemplary Bachelardian reverie. With mind and body shaken loose from the control of the quotidian 'cogito', the dreamer merges with everything s/he sees, thinks or senses and knows them with a new intensity: 'the dreamer's being invades what it touches, diffuses into the world' (Bachelard 1971: 167).

An important, but easily overlooked, difference between my reading of this text in Chapter 3 and what I propose here is that, by identifying Sal's reeling thoughts and visions as a type of daydream (even if, for him, they have the quality of nightmare), we are also acknowledging that it qualifies as an *altered*, rather than a merely *heightened*, state of consciousness. Bearing in mind the spirit of mind-expanding excess in which the novel was written, and has subsequently been received by many thousands of readers, it is, I believe, important that we draw upon theories like Bachelard's to appreciate what the text was attempting in those terms. It is, after all, a novel that flirts openly with the discourse of madness, and the intermittent use of the adjective – in the episode that the previous extract was taken from, for example, both Dean and the 'overturned world' are described as 'mad' – is surely meant to remind us that, in these moments of frenzy, both the story and its characters have moved beyond the realm of everyday consciousness. This fine line between enlightenment and madness is one to which I return in this chapter's concluding section on the 'death-drive'.

Delusion

When does a daydream become a deluded fantasy? Unfortunately there are no simple answers to this question in the work of either Bachelard or Bloch since, for them, the daydream is, by definition, a positive and empowering state of consciousness predicated upon well-being (Bachelard 1971: 153: '[There is] no reverie without well-being') and 'Hope' (Bloch 1986: 110). If we look to our own lives, however, I suggest that most of us will know and recognise the difference. Although the deluded fantasy resembles the daydream in all functional particulars – that is, it emerges out of a general sense of euphoria and constructs and/or embellishes narratives which will be realised in the future even if they are sourced in the past – it typically falters when trying to imagine a credible *outcome* to the ideal scenario. Given that all utopias, are by definition, beyond the reach of probability, the distinction between ones that are 'credible' and those that are not may seem spurious. However, it is arguable that one of the ways in which a delusion distinguishes itself from a daydream is that it struggles to 'journey to the end' (Bloch 1986: 95) of its own fantasy. As is illustrated in the texts that are the subject of this section, the happy ending is hard to come by, even in dreams, for those who know their current house is built on sand.

Written within three years of one another in the 1930s, Elizabeth Bowen's *To the North* and Rosamund Lehmann's *The Weather in the Streets* are two of the period's best-regarded 'middle-brow' romances, and the delusion they trade in is their heroines' misplaced love for a man they have no hope of marrying. In both texts the motor car figures prominently and becomes the 'scene' (Barthes 1990: 192)[16] of intimate romantic encounter, daydreaming and – in the case of Bowen's *To the North* – eventual psychosis. Like Taylor's *Hide and Seek* (2011) discussed earlier, the motoring featured in these novels is very much of its time, with the covered car presenting itself to novelists as a convenient and plausible location for clandestine romantic trysts and open-topped sports cars (like the one favoured by Emmeline) the means of passionate elopements. This also alerts us, of course, to the symbolic and metaphorical appeal of the car to the fiction writers of the period, a feature which cautions against any simplistic use of the texts as historical windows onto automotive consciousness (Pearce 2014: 79–80). As will also be seen in the discussion the 'death-drive' which follows, driving, from its earliest days, was seized upon as a compelling trope with which to encapsulate – and, typically, lambast – those species of mental illness (neurosis/hysteria, obsessive-compulsive disorder, mania) associated with the 'modern age' (Kern 2000:

125–6). In other words, the representation of drivers (women, in particular) seemingly losing their minds through an 'addiction' to speed were convenient poetic devices for exhibiting such neuroses rather than narratives based on scientific evidence that driving contributed to mental illness.

Inasmuch as *To the North* and *The Weather in the Streets* follow remarkably similar narrative trajectories – a young woman falls in love with a man she shouldn't and, against her better judgement, enters into a secret affair with him which is destined to end badly – it is not surprising to discover that they make similar use of the car, both as a plot device and a symbol, especially at the beginning of the romance. In both texts, for example, the car is the space in which the 'heroines' drift into euphoric reverie consequent upon their first, 'fatal' attraction to the 'hero'. However, their contrasting treatment of the episode is useful in drawing out the different forms such daydreaming can take.

In Lehmann's text, Olivia's first extended reverie follows the party at which Rollo first notices her and offers to drive her home in his car. In the intimate, sexually charged space of the car, Olivia is nevertheless shown to follow a vivid sequence of observations, most of them deriving from her childhood, which have nothing to do with Rollo or the present moment:

> Down into the valley. Far below to the left, a sprinkling of late lights still spoke in the mist, from village windows. On the right, the beech coppice ran down steeply to the road: when Kate and I used to come on our bikes with a picnic tea, and sometimes the Martins came; or Marigold was allowed to meet us, riding over on her pony. We cut our initials with a penknife, each choosing a different tree, and said we'll come back to look in twenty years . . .
>
> Round the corner on the hill known in the family circle as The Bad Turn: perennial object of foreboding and suspicion to Mother, though innocent still of disaster. Down, past the first cottages, round past grandpapa's houses – those triple-fronted stucco eyesores. In the middle top window a light – the usual light that burned all night – the window of the youngest Miss Robinson . . .
>
> He drew up close to the fencing, under the laurel hedge; switched off the headlights.
>
> 'There . . .' She waited a moment. 'Good-night, Rollo, thank you so much for bringing me . . . It was a lovely evening . . .'
>
> He sat still and said nothing. He took out his case and lit a cigarette with deliberate movements. Then he said:
>
> 'When shall I see you again?' (Lehmann 1981: 128–30)

As well as endorsing Bachelard's theory that the spaces of past daydreams beget new ones (Bachelard 1971: 30–2) and the general significance of childhood to the practice and content of daydreams, the episode alerts us to the ways in which intense emotions – love and sexual desire in particular – are apt to realise themselves in their attachment to or projection onto things other than the love object. This accounts for why 'the world' appears magically transformed to those in love and why the practice of daydreaming is so integral to the early stages of a love affair. We get to know we are in love not only by thinking, obsessively, about the beloved, but also – following Bachelard – by exploring our new ontological relationship to the world which is, itself, transformed as a result of our capacity to see it with fresh eyes. In our deepest, most complete reveries (and the textual representation of Olivia's here is several pages long), we often draw intently upon the past in order to reorient our future course.

One important contrast between the two novels vis-à-vis their representation of automotive consciousness is that Olivia is a passenger and Emmeline a driver. The symbolism of this – Emmeline is notionally the 'author of her fate', Olivia the passive victim – is also figured in the daydreams of the two protagonists taking on a slightly different complexion. While Olivia's passengering mind is free to roam widely across her phenomenological imagination – including, as we have seen, into the depths of the past –Emmeline's is typically more focused on the phenomenological *present*: the world as 'seen from the car' (Kennedy 1919b):

> Emmeline, who was liking life better than ever, took no chances – crawled sedately west for a little, in second gear, down the Euston Road, in the lee of a lorry clattering with steel girders. Leaving the hoarse dingy clamour, the cinema-posters of giant love, she turned into Regent's Park, swept round under lines of imposing houses and, out of the park again, mounted to St John's Wood . . . The glades of St John's Wood were still at their brief summer: walls gleamed through thickets, red may was clotted and crimson, laburnum showered the pavements, smoke had not yet tarnished a leaf . . . Someone was giving a party: more gold chairs arrived . . . Emmeline wished them joy – but it depressed Cecilia to hear the music of parties to which she was not invited. (Bowen 2006: 115–16)

Emmeline's euphoria takes its cue from the world she sees and senses from the driver's seat of her open-topped car. Like Olivia, she is, however, seen projecting her new-found joy onto all that she encounters, and although, once again, her (prospective) lover is not the focus of her thoughts, his presence is felt in everything she casts her eyes upon. For both characters, moreover, the 'slow', 'soft' (Lehmann 1981: 125) and steady (Bowen 2006: 115) progress of their vehicles may be seen to embody, and facilitate the rapturous, 'forward-springing' (Bergson 2000: 48) direction of their dreams, dreams, alas, that – in both cases – are shortly to be exposed as delusions.

While the car contributes crucially to the plot of each romance, it is necessary that I move directly to its role in what is the focus of my reflection here, namely the protagonists' deluded investment in their relationships even when it is clear that the dreams on which they have been built will never be realised. A significant contrast once again emerges in that, in Lehmann's text, the car is figured as a space which *protects* the daydream and sustains the illusion, while in Bowen's it quickly establishes itself as a space in which delusion is exposed and confronted. This, I would suggest, is consistent with a more overtly symbolic use of the car in Bowen's novel. From the beginning of the story, Emmeline's car – rather like Gatsby's in Fitzgerald's novel (2008) – is laden with signifiers of its ultimate demise, while Olivia's (that is Rollo's various vehicles) serve to contextualise the development of the relationship in realist terms and, indeed, capture the way in which car journeys fuel and sustain our fantasies.

In their depiction of the heroines' weekends away with their lovers, both texts make particular use of the car as a space of 'innocent' daydream (Lehmann) and *dis*illusion (Bowen). As Olivia 'floats out of London' in Rollo's car, high on champagne, the world as viewed from her passenger's seat 'dazzles' with her projected love and desire:

> He called for me with the car on Saturday morning . . . We drove to his club to get some money . . . It was such heavenly day. We seemed to float out of London on the sun – champagne again, I suppose. We had no plans except to head for the coast and wander till we found somewhere we liked. It was one of those days when all of the landscape seems built up of intersecting planes of light and shadow; the tree-trunks' silvery shafts wired with gold and copper, violet transparency in between the boughs. The hills looked insubstantial, as if you could put your hand through them. The damp road flashed kingfisher blue . . . (Lehmann 1981: 168–9)

Although this euphoria is subsequently dampened – circumscribed by doubt and paranoia – when Olivia and Rollo leave the car to go for a walk on the Dorset coast, Olivia's reverie is magically restored as soon as she re-enters the car: 'Back in the car again, leaning against him, the rug tucked round, I felt better' (Lehmann 1981: 170). Similarly, while a breakdown (in heavy rain) dispels some of the car's protective aura on their second weekend away (Lehmann 1981): 189–90), it is restored during their summer expedition to Austria (Lehmann 1981: 224–5). Thus, taken together, this is a novel which makes a strong case for the way in which the closed car, in particular, represents a singular – perhaps unrivalled – tryst in the modern world. It is therefore not surprising that when Olivia reflects, lyrically, on the time (i.e. temporality) of 'the affair' in an aside located near the beginning of the novel, she does so in imagery that equates it with the space-time of the car:

> It was then the time began when there wasn't any time. The journey was in the dark, going on without end or beginning, without landmarks, bearings lost: asleep? . . . waking? . . . Time whirled, throwing up in paradoxical slow motion a sign, a scene, sharp, startling, lingering as a blow over the heart. [. . .]
> There was this inward double living under amorphous impacts of dark and light mixed: that was when we were together . . . Not being together was a vacuum. (Lehmann 1981: 144 (ellipses in the original))

Affairs, like car journeys, may thus be seen to represent temporary and intermediate states of being; sharply illuminated in the recollections and fantasies of the lovers concerned, they remain (largely) invisible to rest of the world.

By contrast, Emmeline and Markie's motoring weekend is an unmitigated disaster. Markie, who is unable to drive himself, forces Emmeline to take him back to town from their cottage on the coast for a 'decent meal' even when she is exhausted ('I'm so tired, Markie. I'd hate to drive any more' (Bowen 2006: 251)), and their journey there and back is silent and estranged. Similarly, on the their first weekend away – to Paris – the lovers' taxi-ride to their hotel is explicitly contrasted to the preceding aeroplane flight across the channel where Emmeline – soaring high above the earth – was possessed by 'momentary coldness and clearness of feeling' (Bowen 2006: 171). In the taxi, however, confusion reigns and, in a prefiguration of the relationship's demise, Emmeline is brought face to face with the irrationality of her decisions and the implausibility of her future:

> Oppressed by once more plunging into this shadowy network when she had lately been seeing so clear a plan, perplexed by some new view of life that, not quite her own, leant double strangeness to everything, Emmeline sat silently in the taxi beside Markie. They crossed the river and swerved up the left bank to their hotel. (Bowen 2006: 173)

I observed at the start of this section that delusions distinguish themselves from daydreams, in part, by their inability to follow their fantasies through to a credible 'happy ending'. The distinction between the 'probable' and the 'possible' is helpful here inasmuch as the utopian objective of the daydream (if we follow Bloch) needs to be at least a *possibility* if it is to inspire us (1986: 86–7). In these two 1930s novels, by contrast, we encounter fictional representations of young women who indulge in reveries to which there *can* be no happy endings. Yet such is the yawning need to simulate that closure that Emmeline uses her car to deliver an alternative resolution in death (Bowen 2006: 295–306) even if, as observed previously, it is an ending so laden with symbolism that it is arguably not 'about' driving at all (Pearce 2014: 78–80, 93). Lehmann's text, by contrast, which forfeits closure for realism (neither Olivia nor Rollo die but are forced to live with the 'death' of their love instead),[17] arguably provides us with greater insight into why driving – or, in this case, passengering – can sustain delusional fantasy so successfully; as well as representing the quintessential 'time out of time', the car – as discussed in Chapter 1 – preserves the illusion of futurity through its comforting and utterly reliable forward progress: 'He put in the clutch and softly, smoothly drew away . . .' (Lehmann 1981: 125).

Utopia

For Bloch and Bachelard there is no daydream without utopia. Although Bachelard may not employ exactly this conceit to communicate his vision, there can be no doubting that both philosophers share the same intent. For while Bloch's implication – especially in the context of *The Principle of Hope* as a whole – is the more explicitly political, both men share the belief that the whole purpose of the daydream is to arrive at a new (and newly *hopeful*) apprehension of the world. In other words, both Bachelard's 'cosmic reverie' (Bachelard 1971: 14, 173) and Bloch's 'world improving dreams' (Bloch 1986: 92) have utopia (personal and/or social), and nothing less than utopia, as their destination. This, arguably, is also what classifies their shared project as a commitment to altered rather than merely heightened states of consciousness; there is, for both, a defining imperative for the dreamer to 'journey to the end' (Bloch 1986: 95) of their vision.

For the driver, too, the destination can often be seen to define the journey. As we saw in Chapter 3, this fixation on the point of the arrival at the expense of the journey was, for Virilio, precisely what has de-natured (auto)mobility and undermined our ability to inhabit either the landscape or the temporal moment through which we pass: 'it is the fleeting desire to go right to the end as fast as possible that produces the opening out [*écartement*] of the travelling the tearing apart [*écartèlement*] of the landscape' (Virilio 2008: 105). But we have also seen in Chapters 2 and 4 examples of driving-events which have very little concern for their destination and – either in the drivers' willingness to stop the car whenever the fancy takes them or to drive with no thought of stopping at all – figure automotive consciousness as a means of dwelling in the automotive present in a profound and purposeful way.

In this section I return to an exploration of driving scenarios in which destination *does* matter, but in a very different way to the fulfilment of the blind 'will to flight' outlined by Virilio. In the context of our wider discussion of automotive reverie, and the trajectory of the daydream in particular, I propose a model of utopian destination-oriented travel in which the objective matters less in and of itself than as an integral part of the daydream, in other words a model which understands the destination as a process of 'becoming-toward' (Trigg 2012: 141, discussed in Chapter 1).

While, once again, it is important to distinguish between the poetic/narratological device and a documented account of driver-experience, the texts I have surveyed for this project include several memorable portraits of beautiful, distant cities (and, in some cases, whole countries) appearing on the driver's (or passenger's) horizon. In every case, the city figures not as a destination per se but as part of the future that the travellers are driving, and dreaming, themselves towards. On some occasions, as in the following extracts from *On the Road* and *The Great Gatsby*, the wonder of the location lies in the fact that it is new, unknown and, for those for who travel towards it, completely outwith their previous experience:

> Now I could see Denver looming ahead of me like the Promised Land way out there beneath the stars, across the prairie of Iowa and the plains of Nebraska, and I could see the greater vision of San Francisco beyond, like jewels in the night. (Kerouac 2000: 15)

> Over the great bridge, with the sunlight through the girders making a constant flicker on the moving cars . . . The city seen from the Queensboro Bridge is always the city seen for the first time, in its first wild promise of all the mystery and the beauty in the world. (Fitzgerald 2008: 54–5)

This is a vocabulary that resonates with Bachelard's own and, regardless of what other symbolism adheres to these 'new Jerusalems', they appear to exhibit the 'truly fundamental phenomenology' which '[absorbs] the real world in the imaginary world' (Bachelard 1971: 14) in an enduring poetic image. Even as the narrator describes the newness of what he or she sees, so too do they demonstrate their ability to grasp the wonder that is held out towards them: 'The image brings us an illustration of our astonishment' (Bachelard 1971: 153–4). The fact that these visions, combining the phenomenology of the external world with that of the imagination, are achieved from and through the perspective of a moving vehicle would matter less to Bachelard, but both passages suggest that it the mirage of these glittering metropolises moving ever closer that is the key to their mystery. Even as the traveller moves toward the city, so, too, does the city move towards him; each mirrors the other's 'becoming-toward'.

Elsewhere in my archive are examples in which the distant utopia, though still framed in the time/space of the future and the traveller's own 'becoming-toward', is also recognisable as home. This is especially true of the non-fiction prose (autobiographies, motoring articles, travel guides) from the early part of the twentieth century which figure Scotland as what I have described elsewhere as a 'destination home' (Pearce 2000: 162–78). Although only some of these hopeful travellers are Scottish-born, they have identified with its dramatic landscapes, its history and culture, as the 'home of the heart' and hence, in their journeys north, project their best hopes and dreams upon it. In this regard, it is both the fantastical object of one of Bloch's 'world-improving dreams' (Bloch 1986: 92) and that which inspires it.

A recurrent motif in many of these texts – so common, indeed, that it is probably best thought of as a convention – is a moment of pause and wonder when Scotland first comes into view. During the first half of the twentieth century, the most popular route north to Scotland from London and the South-East was via the Great North Road, whereupon travellers either branched west towards Appleby to pick up the A6 or continued north-east to Edinburgh via Carter Bar (see Grieves 1999: 61 for a period photograph). As Chris Cooper (2013: 8–17) has detailed in his own latter-day tribute to this route, the Great North Road was steeped in romance for early motorists. This was partly on account of its associations with the old coaching routes, but also the simple fact that, if followed to its end, it would take motorists all the way to Scotland and 'The North'; in other words, it was a tangible link or spatial-temporal corridor to a land that was – and, indeed, still is – swathed in discourses of romantic otherness.

Several of the writers we have already encountered, such as H. V. Morton (2008: 3–4), purposefully enhance that otherness by adopting a 'long-view' of the land that now stretches before them, prolonging, if you like, its 'becoming-toward' status. For Mr and Mrs Miniver, meanwhile, the viewpoint at the summit of the road between Bowes and Brough (they, too, are taking the westerly route north) does this job for them:

> They were climbing steadily now; and presently the bones of the earth began breaking through the grass in rocky scars and outcrops; and higher still there were no fields at all, only bare moors. At the summit of the road, half-way between Bowes and Brough, they stopped, according to their

invariable custom, and got out to stretch, smoke, and enjoy the view. They
were standing on the spine of England, nearly fifteen hundred feet above the
sea. Yorkshire lay behind, Westmoreland in front . . . The silence, after the
monotonous hum of the car, was almost startling. The air was knife-keen and
fresh as lettuce. It seemed a far cry from the lush, matronly, full-blown landscape of the south through which they had set out that morning. (Struther
1989: 49–50)

The fact that the land Mr and Mrs Miniver see stretched out before
them is, for the moment, England and not yet Scotland does not mitigate
their pleasure; indeed, it arguably enhances it by remaining part of their
'becoming-toward' reverie. This is not Scotland, but it bears a semblance
of Scotland in its Northerness and hence serves to fuel their 'positive
expectant emotions' (Bloch 1986: 110). As for the motorists in *On the
Road* (2000) and *The Great Gatsby* (2008), the utopia towards which
Mr and Mrs Miniver travel very much depends upon their 'anticipatory
consciousness' (Bloch 1986).

A similar, if even more ecstatic, utopian vision presents itself to Alec
Maclehouse and his companion on their one-day flight to Edinburgh
from London in 1930 (see extract quoted in Chapter 3). While, previously, I discussed Maclehouse's essay as a consummate expression
of 'motoring for motoring's sake', I present it again here as another
instance of the way in which the 'becoming-toward' quality of motoring
is instrumental in characterising the final destination *as* a utopia. This
is encapsulated in Maclehouse's friend's rhetorical question, 'doesn't it
suggest infinite possibilities?' (Maclehouse 1930: 65); rather than a holy-
grail or pot of gold at the end of the rainbow, Maclehouse's Scotland *is*
the rainbow: a place of potential that will sustain the travellers' dreaming rather than put an end to it. In this regard, it is a vision that can also
be contrasted with Kerouac's characterisation of Mexico in the final part
of *On the Road* (2000) as 'IT'. Mexico – and, in particular, Mexico City
– as we saw in Chapter 3 serves as a fixed and final destination for Dean
Moriarty and his fellow travellers; it is the 'great road south' which
slows Dean's driving to a crawl and eventually to a halt (2000: 273–4).
And although it does deliver its moment(s) of insight and enlightenment
because of this, it is also, very markedly, the road on which the dreaming
stops. Utopia is, ultimately, a figment of our anticipatory consciousness and depends upon the condition of 'travelling-toward' remaining
forever visible on the horizon.

Death-drive

Janice Galloway's short story, 'Nightdriving' (1992 [1991]), features, in its final section, this heart-stopping account of a driver's late-night journey home:

> It's not my car but someone lets me use it if I promise to be careful coming home late. The road I have to travel is treacherous and twists through coun- tryside so there are no lights to mark the edges, just the solid dark that rises with the hills on either side. There are never many cars. You see headlamps float over dips in the darkness and know there must be a road beneath: an unseen path below the rise and fall of the beams in the blackness on either side. And sometimes you see nothing. Not until they slew from nowhere, too close from a corner that didn't exist before, a hidden side-road or farmhouse track . . . The road looks new. It looks like nowhere you have been before.
>   And you remember.
>   You keep driving and remember.
>   The city road is a narrow stretch with hills that rise on either side, steep like the sides of a coffin . . . Between them green and brown, the husks of broken cars: a v-shaped glimpse of somewhere else so far away it seems to float. It's distant and beautiful and no part of the rest: no part of the road I am travel- ling through, not Ayrshire, not Glasgow. It comes and goes behind a screen as I drive towards it, a piece of city waiting in the v-shaped sky if this is my day to make a split-second mistake. And I know too it's simply the way home. I accelerate because it is not today. I am still here. Driving. (Galloway 1992: 126–7)

Working with the same iconography – the beautiful, distant city – as the 'becoming-toward' utopias in the previous section, Galloway's story adds the further twist, both thrilling and sobering, that this driving-event – hers, ours – might be the last. The fact that it is also just a regular journey home is, of course, what gives the story its existential meaning, a reminder that the moment of death lurks, unseen and neces- sarily unanticipated, on the dark verges of everyone's consciousness. Meanwhile, although for Galloway driving was most likely no more than an especially vivid and evocative narrative trope through which to explore this conceit, in the context of this book it may be seen to figure – as the dark twin of utopia – the furthest reaches of automotive reverie. For none of us can escape the fact that all car journeys are, indeed, circumscribed by the possibility of a (fatal) accident; I know that I never get into my car without this thought igniting, for a short instant, my consciousness. What I am interested in here, however, is the way in which such awareness unconsciously impacts upon the reveries and daydreams which we nevertheless continue to pursue and which this chapter has shown to be part of normative driver behaviour.

Circumscribed by the possibility of our mortality, does it follow that the automotive reverie is inspired and directed by that same trajectory? Does the true meaning, and value of the automotive reverie lie in the fact that it allows us to confront, explore and, ultimately, embrace *this* possibility while ostensibly pursuing an earth-bound happy ending for our dreams? Both A. B. Filson Young and Bart Kennedy, as well as Ernst Bloch himself, certainly glimpsed something of this covert and subliminal objective in their essays on motoring, and I shall return to these texts at the end of this section. Prior to this, it is, however, necessary that I briefly mention some rather more typical and notably less elevated representations of the existential 'threat' posed by driving by twentieth-century writers and commentators.

The fact that cars can and do account for the many thousands of deaths worldwide every year[18] has been integral to those discourses that posit automobility as a 'bad' thing. These very material, life-shattering consequences of motoring may nevertheless be seen to have been widely exploited by literary and film representations of fatal motoring events where – as demonstrated by Ehrenburg's *The Life of an Automobile* (1999) and Bowen's *To the North* (2008) – the tragic accident is typically symbolic of something other than the dangers and consequences of widespread automotive transport. In both these texts, for example – as in the case of Fitzgerald's *Great Gatsby* (2008) – the wrecking of the car and death of its passengers is very obviously a metaphor for a more all-encompassing personal and/or social malaise. In other words, death-by-car is a convenient means of exacting poetic justice on malign or regrettable contemporary trends (be this capitalist greed, female neuroses and/or mechanisation itself). Historically, such discourses were quickly looped back into the public information campaigns which attempted to shock drivers into a recognition of the dangers of motoring; indeed, the message implicit in many of the posters linked to such campaigns was not only that driving was dangerous, but that it was a social evil (Jeremiah 2007: 147–8).

Iain Borden discusses the different ways in which the car-crash has been figured in the history of film in his own chapter on the altered states of consciousness associated with driving. Drawing a particular distinction between the 'external' and 'internal' worlds such driving-events are used to signify, he cites Bruce Conner's 'A MOVIE' (1958), Peter Weir's *The Cars That Ate Paris* (1974) and, of course, Jean-Luc Godard's *Week End* (1967) as examples of films that use car crashes to highlight 'a general social or even global condition' (Borden 2013: 209). The fiction writing of the early-twentieth century arguably attempts something similar but through comedy and satire. As will be evident from the previous chapters of this book, literature abounds with driving-events which end badly, but in the period 1918–45 there appears to have been a peculiar penchant for stories centred on the pathological obsession of vulnerable and deluded characters for cars and/or motoring which lead, inevitably, to a horrible accident (fatal or otherwise). Ehrenburg's 'Charles Bernard' (1999 [1929]) may be seen as a prototype for this sort of 'revenge comedy', but the two texts I have selected to demonstrate the genre here are Nigel Balchin's 'The Enthusiast' (1959 [1954]) and an extract from Evelyn Waugh's *Vile Bodies* (1959 [1930]), both reproduced in John Welcome's *Best Motoring Stories* (1959).

Balchin's story is particularly poignant because its autistic central protagonist, Uncle Fergus, is used to poke fun at the way in which some people develop passionate obsessions for inanimate objects as the result of their inability to pursue meaningful human relationships. Fergus, the 'hero' of Balchin's text, dotes on his pre-First World War 'monster' of a car in the manner of a wife and surrenders both home and possessions to maintain 'her' even when he can no longer afford to (Balchin 1959: 20–1). The drama of the story nevertheless centres on Fergus's rare opportunity to take the car for a 'long spin' when the story's intra-diegetic narrator (his nephew) needs to get to Bristol. Having exited London in a sober and steady manner, Fergus is unable to withstand the temptation of the open road and the taste of speed – a common factor in most texts of this kind – sets him, and his nephew, on a 'drive to the death' (Balchin 1959: 24). The fact that death, on this occasion, is averted does not obviously mitigate the comic contempt in which Fergus is held (especially when placed alongside his characterisation in the early part of the story). The inability to withstand the seductive thrill of speed is portrayed both as a psychological weakness and also as a pitiful folly of the 'modern age'.

Similar sentiments underline Evelyn Waugh's satirical portrait of Angela Runcible in *Vile Bodies*. Attending a motoring 'race meet' with friends, the seemingly 'silly' and neurotic Angela – having already enjoyed too much champagne in the beer tent – inadvertently ends up participating in the race through a mix-up in the 'pits' and, drunk on a mixture of alcohol and speed, is witnessed hurtling towards probable death as her car leaves the track. The fact that she narrowly escapes this fate does nothing to lessen her ridicule. Indeed, the pathetic figure she cuts at the story's end – at first catatonic, then markedly 'insane' – is arguably crueller. Angela Runcible is a young woman whose neurotic disposition makes her susceptible to any readily available stimulant – champagne, fast cars – but, unable to handle either, she is duly punished:

They reached London by luncheon time the next day, and learned that Miss Runcible had been found early that morning staring fixedly at a model engine in the central hall at Euston Station. In answer to some gentle questions, she replied that to the best of her knowledge she had no name, pointing to the brassard on her arm, as if in confirmation of this fact. She had come in a motor car, she explained, which would not stop. It was full of bugs which she had tried to kill with drops of face lotion. One of them threw a spanner. There had been a stone thing in the way. They shouldn't put symbols like that in the middle of the road, should they, or should they?

So they conveyed her to a nursing home in Wimpole Street and kept her for some time in a darkened room. (Waugh 1959: 51)

Looked at in the round, these whimsical, satirical representations of the automotive 'death-drive' may be welcomed by some as an antidote or corrective to the glamorisation and/or eroticisation of car crashes featured in the films discussed by Iain Borden (2013) and Amit Thakkar (2014).[19] However, so evident is it that they are using their protagonists' susceptibilities to comment on the social and psychological ills of the 'modern world' that it is important not to confuse them with critiques of driving per se. While plenty of drivers, now as then, enjoy the adrenalin rush associated with speed, its characterisation as an obsession and/or addiction is scientifically unproven and hence the aspect of driving whose connotations have been most obviously appropriated by writers and artists for symbolic, and often sensational, purposes.

A small selection of texts, however, seek to understand, on their own terms, the relationship between the embodied experience of driving and the reveries we pursue while at the wheel. One of the most evocative of these is Filson Young's mystical reflection on 'The Road to Holyhead' in the concluding chapter of *The Complete Motorist* (1904). Here he writes:

If, winged with the modern magic, you use the Holyhead Road you cannot fail to be cheered by a great company that keeps with you throughout the miles. I speak not of the trees, but of those more constant flankers of a main road, the telegraph poles and wires ... And fast as you fly, the messages of good or evil news, of fortunes won or lost, of lives begun and lives ended, are flying faster along the wires ... For all the company that marched through Dunstable in double ranks on each side of the road ... only two keep faith with the road. These are the two that, when the last miles have been entered and the journey has resolved itself in a dream of miles and speed and a wind laden with honey and roses, go with you down the long straight ribbon over Anglesey to where the sea plunges under the cliff and the gulls cry about the lighthouse. For the wires are the Holyhead wires, although you could not distinguish them among the throng at St. Albans; and the wires dip under the sea and go to their promised land; but the road? – The road to Ireland, for all its earnestness and splendid purposes pauses forever on the edge of Wales, and resigns its charge to the waiting ships ... (Filson Young 1904: 327–8)

Once again, this is a text whose iconography reproduces that of the utopias we considered in the previous section, but – in contrast to Janice Galloway – Filson Young sees his vision through to the *true* 'end of the journey' (Bloch 1986: 95) where the road ends and the driving (i.e. the 'becoming-toward') stops. If this appears an unnecessarily solemn interpretation of the text's ending, it is surely one of which the author put his readers in mind in this observation a few pages earlier:

> And so I doubt not that when some of us who have fallen into this bondage [i.e. love of motoring] lie a-dying, the last image of the world present to our minds will be the picture that thousands of miles have photographed on our memory; of the road stretched white and narrowing, of the trees hurrying to meet us, of the snug homesteads left behind in the dusk, of the eternal Unknown that lies just beyond the turn of the road. (Filson Young 1904: 323)

In the 'winged flight' of the motor car, then, and the long, white ribbon of road fringed with telegraph poles and wires on which it travels (see Figure 5.4), Filson Young discovered an experience which embodied, and an image that captured, our journey through life. Profound and all encompassing, this is a phenomenological apprehension of the world – part observational, part imagined – fit to accompany us to our deaths and, by corollary, to bring the anticipation of that death to bear upon all our journeys.

So compelling is this conceit that, although fortuitous, it was not entirely a surprise when I chanced upon an almost identical trope, and sentiment, expressed by Bloch in *The Principle of Hope*. In the section of his book in which he explores his philosophical model of 'anticipatory consciousness' in terms of 'wishful images', Bloch posits 'the lure to travel' as one of the most archaic expressions of our desire for the 'not-yet-conscious'. However, as will be seen in the following extract, the utopian framework of the journey also carries within the shadow of our 'final journey':

> But the journey pursues a wishful image of beautiful otherness at least on this distant point, and one which is a foreign country ... Which is in fact also why post-festum the travel-image may remain so closely related to art ... [and] ... the gathering transformation towards the final journey. The often reported procession of images at the hour of death, or even possibly in old age, therefore not only has people, figures, objects on its concentrated route ... but also travel-images – even embellished again post-festum with utopian festiveness. And this last spice was perhaps already at work in the first sight of uncommon objects, burning and concealing, or conversely intensifying the real state of the matter. (Bloch 1986: 374)

Figure 5.4 'Telegraph wires at night', Gordon Crosby, *Autocar*, 8 March 1929. Courtesy of the National Library of Scotland.

It nevertheless requires a final visit to this book's most faithful travelling companion, Bart Kennedy, for a closing image that will convert the road schemas of Filson Young and Ernst Bloch into a recognisable driving-event. Reflecting on the world as 'seen from the car' while touring a mountainous district of the British Isles, Kennedy expresses his impatience to get to the end of a road which is very evidently '*the* Road':

Time passes, and then out in the distance far ahead of you there come faint tracings of outlines that are set up high. As the car glides along, these outlines become clearer and sharper. They are the outlines of mountains, rising in the distance. You are passing now over a plain, and there comes to you a longing to enter into these mountains. You would like the car to go still more swiftly. You feel an impatience; but soon this feeling passes. You sit back and wait.

Great are the mountains now . . . And around them mists are wreathing. Soon you will be threading your swift way amongst them . . .

You are going up now. Going higher and higher. The car is going more slowly. Up and up. Higher and higher. And now you are merging again into the fuller light of the sun.

Here again is the sea, and yonder is the sun – a globe of golden shining. Your car goes on. (Kennedy 1919b: 125)

Although, like Galloway, Kennedy's narrator manages to steer his way clear of his final destiny on this occasion there is no doubting that for him, as for us, it forever lurks around the next corner: a reminder that the 'becoming-toward' pleasure of our automotive daydreams is in touch with *this* knowledge as well as its more earthly utopias.

Conclusion

It will be remembered that the challenge I set myself in the opening paragraph of this book was to demonstrate, by means of close readings of a wide range of literary and other texts from across the 'motoring century', that the practice of driving is not only paradigmatic of the way we think, but also a means of facilitating and structuring the different modes of thought we are engaged in when sitting behind the steering wheel of a car and/or lounging in the passenger seat.

In this final chapter I have focused, in particular, on the way in which driving may be seen not only to prompt but also direct the narrative of our reveries. For apart from providing drivers and passengers with a space both temporally and spatially 'closed off' from the distractions and demands of everyday life, the forward motion of the car – what Dylan Trigg (2012: 141) has characterised as the condition of 'becoming-toward' – typically propels our thoughts towards resolution, be this in the form of a personal and/or worldly 'utopia' or a transcendental expression of the death-drive. Not all reveries achieve this conclusion, of course, and one of my subsidiary arguments here (via discussion of the 1930s romances of Elizabeth Bowen and Rosamund Lehmann) has been to suggest that our more obviously deluded fantasies reveal themselves as such through their inability (following Bloch 1986: 95) to 'journey to the end' of the dream in question. And while it is, of course, arguable that all daydreaming or reverie may incline towards this sort of narrative shape and/or compulsion, my own experience certainly bears out the hypothesis that the 'becoming-toward' nature of driving – especially when thought of in terms of the integrity of individual driving-events as proposed in Chapter 1 – enhances the process. In favourable circumstances, the domestic car – and possibly the HGV lorry – is, indeed, the archetypal 'dream-machine' and hence of particular significance if, like Bloch and Bachelard (and *unlike* a good deal of contemporary psychology), we value the role of reverie in our cognitive lives.

In the section on 'anxiety', meanwhile, this chapter – by bringing together Jack Katz's (1999) work on the psychology of 'road rage' with literary texts from either end of the twentieth century – proposed that the *interruption* to our automotive reveries occasioned by traffic congestion (along with other unexpected and untoward events such as breakdowns or taking the wrong route) is surely a major factor in the stress/distress experienced by drivers and passengers on such occasions. Katz's research is especially interesting here, since his conclusions suggest that 'road rage' is, itself, a species of reverie: the means by which the driver 'acts out' or performs his or her version of events, thus regaining control over the situation (Katz 1999: 49).

This discussion of what happens to the driver's consciousness when the 'becoming-toward' motion of the car stops prompts further consideration, also, of the concept of 'drivetime' itself inasmuch as it reminds us of the extent to which motorists have become increasingly invested in a mode of transport – or rather the sensation/illusion provided by a mode of transport – that promises to 'beat the clock'. Once they are travelling at speeds in excess of – I would suggest – 60mph, drivers and passengers typically relax in the (embodied) knowledge that they are moving quickly (or, at least, quickly enough) to reach their destination in 'good time' and are hence in control of their fast-paced days (and lives); by corollary, when the travellers' speed is brought significantly below their expectations, they are prone to suffer the profound existential angst of time, itself, rushing by *without them* in the most distressing of ways. Driving-events such as these may, indeed, be considered the dark underside of 'drivetime' as discussed in Chapter 4; instead of time spent in the car gifting motorists a 'time-out-of-time', traffic jams and other delays can plunge them back into a world where the clock appears to be ticking down to a deadline that (as for the 'fare' in Ehrenburg's story (1989) anticipates their own death. The fact that the everyday act of driving can be the occasion of such opposite experiences of temporality is, of course, a further explanation for the hold the car has had over us as a means of transport.

Earlier in the book, meanwhile, I investigated the ways in which driving facilitates and structures thought in terms of 'searching', 'fleeing' and 'cruising'. Heading out on a motoring excursion where driver and passengers *expect* to stop (Chapter 2) – perhaps frequently – lends itself to a very different mode of automotive consciousness again: one, indeed, that is historically much more in tune with other modes of automobility such as cycling and walking. What the literature, typically from the early part of the century, tells us about this sort of driving is that it combines the opportunity for the sort of reverie we have considered in this and the previous chapter with an interest in the phenomenological world as 'seen from the car' (Kennedy 1919b) – or, indeed, when the car is stopped. This contrasts, again, with cruising (Chapter 3) – a practice I have characterised as an opportunity for self-reflexive meditation and problem-solving that many display *minimal* interest in the perceptual realm. The chapter on 'fleeing' (Chapter 4), meanwhile, responded to Baudrillard's (2010) and Virilio's (2008) indictment of (fast) driving as an expression of the 'annihilation' of thought through an exploration of two classic 'road trip' texts – Highsmith's *Carol* (1990) and Kerouac's *On the Road* (2000) – which both prove and disprove their thesis. My own argument – that it is the psychology and intent *which we bring* to a driving-event that will ultimately determine its existential status – appears borne out in the investigation, as well as identifying a close connection between the sort of 'thought-less' driving experience that Baudrillard and Virilio describe and motoring's long history as a *sport*. For every driver who looks forward to getting into their car in order to speculate and remember, there is another who is equally keen to 'switch off' and forget.

As noted in the Preface, *Drivetime* has explored these variables of automotive consciousness from a purposefully historical perspective, taking the 'motoring century' – 1990–2000 – as its limit point. Along the way, I have, nevertheless, speculated on the implications of automobility's eventual demise for the provision of 'thought-space', as well as the privileged access it has granted us to locations that would otherwise remain off limit. In this last regard, I have seen it especially important to recognise that, as the century advanced, the access, liberation and personal protection provided by the car was as, if not more, important for lower-income and /or minority groups (Gilroy 2001; Garvey 2001; Dunn 1998) than the middle classes. While the latter are able to travel the world by other means, for many millions of others the world over, the car remains the only means of tasting those pleasures.

Readers of this book will not have escaped the fact that for me, personally, the prospect of a 'car-less' – or, indeed, a 'driverless-car'

(Laurier and Dant 2011) – future presents itself as a cause for nostalgia and concern: where will I do my thinking if 'drivetime' is no longer available to me? Given that Bull (2001: 199), following Sennett, has likened the 'sanctuaries' provided by cars to latter-day cathedrals in this regard (see Chapter 1), I can only hope that the unique spatiality/temporality – not to mention the cognitive focus – currently afforded by driving will become available by other means. This may well not be a mode of transport, of course; indeed, it may not even be a technology. However, in the light of both my own 'life in cars' (see Young 2014) and the literary representations of automotive consciousness that this book has surveyed, I find it hard to imagine that the 'cathedral' of the future will not involve mobility of some kind.

Notes

1. Gatsby's car: see https://silverbirchpress.wordpress.com/2013/05/17/what-type-of-car-did-gatsby-drive/ (last accessed 25 October 2015).
2. Gordon Crosby (1885–1943) is widely recognised to be the leading automotive painter and illustrator of the early twentieth century. See note 30 to Chapter 1; see also Jeremiah (2007: 69–70) and Garnier 2009 [1978]).
3. I discuss the dramatic ending of Bowen's novel – wherein Emmeline and Markie are killed in a fatal crash during her 'insane' flight North – elsewhere (Pearce 2014: 78–98).
4. Driving/passengering: the states of consciousness I consider in this chapter embrace the experiences of both drivers and passengers, but I endeavour to use either or both terms advisedly throughout.
5. Like Bachelard, I have elected to use the terms 'reverie' and 'daydream' interchangeably. However, although they also figure as synonyms in the *OED*, it is worth noting that contemporary psychology, which tends to focus on the more banal and everyday expressions of 'mind-wandering', favours 'daydream' (see note 7).
6. Placing Bloch in terms of either his philosophy or his politics is no easy matter; although springing from a Marxist base, his work is clearly inspired by a transcendental (and humanist) vision, while his critique of Freud betrays a powerful fascination with the workings of the unconscious. See the Translators' introduction to Bloch (1986).
7. Although the three volumes of *The Principle of Hope* were first published in their entirety in 1959, they were written during the Second World War (1938–47) which accounts for their frequent asides to the 'dark days' through which humanity is currently living.
8. See Whitbourne (2013), 'Why and How You Daydream': https://www.psychologytoday.com/blog/fulfillment-any-age/201301/why-and-how-you-daydream (last accessed 29 October 2015). Whitbourne presents the view now popular in both psychology and neuroscience that mind-wandering or daydreaming is intrinsic to our 'default network system' and hence an

unremarkable feature of the human mind that needs to be 'managed' rather than celebrated.

9. By the 1930s, road traffic accidents in the UK had already risen to staggering proportions. Jeremiah (2007: 146) cites T. C. Foley (1934) who estimated that twenty persons were killed and 590 injured every day on British roads at that time.

10. Groeger (2000: 63–4) lists the most important cognitive psychologists working in the field during the 1990s who have argued for 'automaticity' in driving. More recent work in the field includes He et al.'s 'Mind-wandering Behind the Wheel' (2011) and Charlton and Starkey's 'Driving Without Awareness' (2011).

11. This phrasing is a pun on Willliam Empson's celebrated work of literary criticism, *Seven Types of Ambiguity* (1973 [1966]).

12. As Mom discusses in *Atlantic Automobilism* (2014: 170–6), there was a huge boom in 'sub-literary' fiction on automotive themes in both Britain and America in the 1920s and 1930s. In America, the genre was dominated by the Williamsons – Alice and husband Charlie – and the chauffeur figured prominently in many of these adventures, erotically and otherwise.

13. Danius's *The Senses of Modernism* (2002), which includes discussion of speed and automobility (pp. 124–38), was a ground-breaking text in this regard. See also Garrington (2015: 119–23) on 'motor kinaesthetics'.

14. In Britain the situation on Britain's arterial roads reached a crisis point in the 1950s (Jeremiah 2007: 166–7; Merriman 2007: 65–6). Gloucester was one of the nation's most notorious bottlenecks as captured in this video: https://www.youtube.com/watch?v=CDtjscPwrKY (last accessed 30 October 2015).

15. Synchronic/diachronic: deriving from the work of linguist, Ferdinand de Saussure, 'diachronic' analysis is concerned with evolution and (historical) change over time, while 'synchronic' analysis focuses on a particular moment of time. See Hawkes (1977: 19–28, 46–7).

16. See *A Lover's Discourse* (Barthes (1990: 192): 'The first thing we love is a scene. For love at first sight requires the very sign of its suddenness.'

17. Readers unfamiliar with the text should, however, be aware that Markie *nearly* dies in a car crash but later disputes that it was a 'death wish' – voluntary or involuntary – that caused him to go off the road (Lehmann 1991: 344–5, 380–1). It should also be noted that the final conversation of the novel focuses, in particular, on the lovers' *drives* together.

18. See comparative statistics for road traffic accidents in Britain and America from 2001–10: http://www.unece.org/fileadmin/DAM/trans/main/wp6/publications/RAS_English_Flyer_2012.pdf (last accessed 30 October 2015). The statistics for Great Britain – for the year ending June 2014 – record 24,580 persons being killed or seriously injured which includes 1,760 fatalities. Although these figures are significantly down on the figures recorded in 2006–7 despite a year-on-year increase in motor traffic, these remain sobering statistics.

19. J. G. Ballard's *Crash* (2008 1973]) and the 1996 film (dir. David Cronenberg) inspired a wave of publications on the significance of the car crash in contemporary culture including Brottman (2002) and Vidal (2013) as well as discussions in Borden (2013) and Thakkar (2014).

References

'A motor-tramp in North Wales' (1919) *The Car*, No. 914, 26 November, p. 36.

Addison, C. (2002) 'Dangerous and irrepressible: cars and driving in post-apartheid South Africa', in P. Wollen and J. Kerr (eds), *Autopia: Cars and Culture*. London: Reaktion Books, pp. 219–26.

Adey, P. (2010) *Mobility*. London and New York: Routledge.

Adorno, T. (1976) *Introduction to the Sociology of Music*. New York: Continuum.

Archer, N. (2013) *The French Road Movie: Space, Mobility and Identity*. New York and Oxford: Berghahn Books.

Aria, Mrs (1906) *Woman and the Motor-Car: Being the Autobiography of an Automobilist*. London: Sidney Appleton.

Atwood, M. (1997 [1971]) *Surfacing*. London: Virago.

Augé, M. (1995) *Non-Places: Introduction to an Anthropology of Supermodernity*, trans. J. Howe. London and New York: Verso.

Auster, P. (2006 [1990]) *The Music of Chance*. London: Faber & Faber.

Bachelard, G. (1971 [1960]) *The Poetics of Reverie: Childhood, Language and the Cosmos*, trans. D. Russell. Boston: Beacon Press.

Bachelard, G. (2014 [1958]) *The Poetics of Space*, trans. M. Jolas. New York: Penguin Books.

Bakhtin, M. (1984 [1929/1963]) *Problems of Dostoevsky's Poetics*, trans. C. Emerson and M. Holquist Minneapolis, MN: University of Minnesota Press.

Balchin, N. (1959 [1954]) 'The Enthusiast', in J. Welcome (ed.), *Best Motoring Stories*. London: Faber & Faber, pp. 13–26.

Ballard, J. G. (2008 [1973]) *Crash*. London: Harper Perennial.

Banham, R. (1973 [1971]) *Los Angeles: The Architecture of Four Ecologies*. Harmondsworth: Pelican.

Barbalet, J. M. (1999) 'Boredom and social meaning', *British Journal of Sociology*, 59 (4): 631–46.

Barthes, R. (1990 [1977]) *A Lover's Discourse*. Harmondsworth: Penguin.

Baudrillard, J. (1994 [1981]) *Simulacra and Simulation*, trans. S. F. Glaser. Ann Arbor, MI: University of Michigan Press.

Baudrillard, J. (2010 [1986]) *America*, trans. C. Turner. London and New York: Verso.

Bennett, B. (forthcoming) *Revolutionary Films: A Cinematic History of Cycling*.

Bergson, H. (1959) *Oeuvres*, ed. A. Robinet. Paris: Presses Universitaires de France.

Bergson, H. (2000 [1908]) 'Memory of the present and false recognition', in R. Durie (ed.), *Time and the Instant: Essays in the Physics and Philosophy of Time*. Manchester: Clinamen Press, pp. 36–63.

Bergson, H. (2010 [1896]) *Matter and Memory*, trans. N. M. Paul and W. S. Palmer. Digireads.Com (facsimile edition).

Bloch, E. (1986 [1959]) *The Principle of Hope*, Vol. 1, trans. N. Plaice, S. Plaice and P. Knight. Cambridge, MA: MIT Press.

Böhm, S., Jones, Land, C. and Patterson, M. (eds) (2006) *Against Automobility*. Oxford: Blackwell Publishing/Sociological Review.

Borden, I. (2013) *Drive: Journeys Through Film, Cities and Landscapes*. London: Reaktion Books.

Bowen, E. (2006 [1932]) *To the North*. New York: Anchor Books.

Bowen, E. (2011 [1968]) *Eva Trout*. London: Vintage.

Bracewell, M. (2002) 'Fade to grey: motorways and monotony', in P. Wollen and J. Kerr (eds), *Autopia: Cars and Culture*. London: Reaktion Books, pp. 288–92.

Brentano, F. von (2002a [1888–9]) 'Descriptive psychology or descriptive phenomenology: from the lectures of 1888–89', in D. Moran and T. Mooney (eds), *The Phenomenology Reader*. London and New York: Routledge, pp. 51–4.

Brentano, F. von (2002b [1888–9]) 'Psychology and the empirical standpoint', in D. Moran and T. Mooney (eds), *The Phenomenology Reader*. London and New York: Routledge, pp. 32–4.

Brottman, M. (ed.) (2002) *Car Crash Culture*. London: Palgrave Macmillan.

Bull, M. (2001) 'Soundscapes of the car: a critical ethnography of automobile habitation', in D. Miller (ed.), *Car Cultures*. Oxford and New York: Berg, pp. 185–202.

Carrabine, E. and Longhurst, B. (2002) 'Consuming the car: anticipation, use and meaning in contemporary youth culture', *Sociological Review*, 50 (2): 181–96.

Charlton, S. G. and Starkey, N. J. (2011) 'Driving without awareness: the effects of practice and automaticity on attention and driving', *Transportation Research Part F: Traffic Psychology and Behaviour*, 14 (6): 456–71.

Chopin, K. (1994 [1899]) *The Awakening*. London: Women's Press.

Clarke, D. (2007) *Driving Women: Fiction and Automobile Culture in Early Twentieth-Century America*. Baltimore: Johns Hopkins University Press.

Clarsen, G. (2008) *Eat My Dust: Early Women Motorists*. Baltimore: Johns Hopkins University Press.

Conner, B. (dir.) (1958) *A MOVIE*. US: Independent short.

Cook's Tours (1861) *Cook's Scottish Tourist Official Directory. A Guide to the System of Tours in Scotland, under the Direction of the Principal Railway, Steamboat, and Coach Companies*. Leicester: T. Cook, Printers.

Cooper, C. (2013) *The Great North Road: Then and Now*. Old Harlow: Battle of Britain International.

Cresswell, T. (2006) *On the Move: Mobility in the Modern Western World*. London and New York: Routledge.

Cresswell, T. and Merriman, P. (eds) (2011) *Geographies of Mobilities: Practices, Spaces, Subjects*. Farnham and Burlington, VT: Ashgate.

Cronenberg, D. (dir.) (1996) *Crash*. Canada: Movie Network/Telefilm Canada.

Cross, A. (2002) 'Driving the American landscape', in P. Wollen and J. Kerr (eds), *Autopia: Cars and Culture*. London: Reaktion Books, pp. 249–58.

Cross, A. (2004) *An English Journey*. Film and Video Umbrella. London: John Hansard Gallery.

Danius, S. (2002) *The Senses of Modernism: Technology, Perception and Aesthetics*, Ithaca, NY and London: Cornell University Press.

Dant, T. (2004) 'The driver-car', *Theory, Culture and Society*, 21 (4–5): 61–79.

Dant, T. and Martin, P. J. (2001) 'By car: carrying modern society', in J. Grownow and A. Warde (eds), *Ordinary Consumption*. London: Routledge, pp. 143–57.

Davidson, I. (2012) 'Automobility, materiality and Don DeLillo's *Cosmopolis*', *Cultural Geographies*, 19 (4): 469–82.

Davies, B. (1929) 'Sightseeing in a hurry: Part II – visiting as much as possible of Central Europe in a limited space and time', *The Autocar*, 28 January, pp. 104–6.

Davis, S. C. H. (1929) 'Motoring for motoring's sake: a rapid trip from Glasgow to London in the teeth of a great gale', *The Autocar*, 29 March, pp. 650–1.

Davis, T. (2008) 'The rise and decline of the American Parkway', in C. Mauch and T. Zeller (eds), *The Road Beyond the Windshield: Roads and Landscapes in the United States and Europe*. Athens: Ohio University Press, pp. 35–58.

Dayton, J. and Faris, V. (dir.) (2006) *Little Miss Sunshine*. UK: Fox Searchlight Pictures.

Deleuze, G. and Guattari, F. (1992 [1987]) *A Thousand Plateaus: Capitalism and Schizophrenia*, trans. B. Massumi. London: Continuum.

Demaus, A. B. (2006), *The Halcyon Days of Motoring*. Stroud: Sutton Publishing.

Dennis, K. and Urry, J. (2009) *After the Car*. Cambridge: Polity.

Didion, J. (2009 [1979]) *The White Album*. New York: Farrar, Straus & Giroux.

Didion, J. (2011 [1970]) *Play It As It Lays*. London: Fourth Estate.

Doan, L. (2006) '*Primum mobile*: women and auto/mobility in the era of the Great War', *Women: A Cultural Review* 17 (1), pp. 26–41.

Doel, M. (1996) 'A hundred thousand lines of flight: a machinic introduction to the nomad thought and scrumpled geography of Gilles Deleuze and Felix Guattari', *Environment and Planning D: Society and Space*, 14 (4): 421–39.

Duffy, E. (2009) *The Speed Handbook: Velocity, Pleasure, Modernism*. Durham, NC: Duke University Press.

Dunn, J. A. (1998) *Driving Forces: The Automobile, Its Enemies and the Politics of Mobility*. Washington, DC: Brookings Institution Press.

E. J. B. (1919) 'A beautiful corner of North Wales', *The Car*, 906, 1 October, p. 161.

Edensor, T. (2003) 'M6 – Junction 19–16: defamiliarising the mundane road-scape', *Space and Culture*, 6 (2): 151–68.

Ehrenburg, I. (1999 [1929]) *The Life of the Automobile*, trans. J. Neugroschel. London: Serpent Books.

Elton, B. (1991) *Gridlock*. London: Macdonald.

Empson, W. (1973 [1966]) *Seven Types of Ambiguity*. Harmondsworth: Pelican.

Featherstone, M. (2004) 'Automobilities: an introduction', *Theory, Culture and Society*, 21 (4–5): 1–24.

Filson Young, A. B. (1904) *The Complete Motorist*. New York: McClure, Phillips & Co./London: Methuen (facsmile reproduction, Nabu Public Domain Reprints).

Fitzgerald, S. (2008 [1925]) *The Great Gatsby*. Oxford: Oxford University Press.

Fleming, I. (2012 [1955]) *Moonraker*. London: Vintage Books.

Forster, E. M. (2012 [1910]) *Howards End*. London: Penguin English Library.

Friese-Greene, G. (2007 [1925]) *The Open Road: A Cinematic Postcard of Britain in the 1920s*. BFI DVD.

Galloway, J. (1992 [1991]) *Blood*. London: Minerva.

Garnier, P. (2009 [1978]) *The Art of Gordon Crosby*. London: Hamlyn.

Garrington, A. (2015 [2013]) *Haptic Modernism: Touch and the Tactile in Modernist Writing*. Edinburgh: Edinburgh University Press.

Garvey, P. (2001) 'Driving, drinking and daring in Norway', in D. Miller (ed.), *Car Cultures*. Oxford and New York: Berg, pp. 133–52.

Gibson, J. J. (1982 [1938]) 'A theoretical field-analysis of automobile driving', in J. Wilson, E. Reed and R. Jones (eds), *Reasons for Realism: Selected. Essays of James J. Gibson*. Hillsdale, NJ: Lawrence Erlbaum Associates.

Gilroy, P. (2001) 'Driving while black', in D. Miller (ed.), *Car Cultures*. Oxford and New York: Berg.

Godard, J.-L. (1967) *Le Week-End*. France: Comacico/Lira Films.

Gombrich, E. H. (1980 [1960]) *Art and Illusion: A Study in the Psychology of Pictorial Representation*. London and Edinburgh: Phaidon Press.

Grieves, R. (1999) *Scotland's Motoring Century*. Paisley: XS Publications.

Groeger, J. (2000) *Understanding Driving: Applying Cognitive Psychology to a Complex Everyday Task*. Hove: Psychology Press.

Halicki, H. B. (dir.) (1974) *Gone in 60 Seconds*, US: Halicki Junkyard & Mercantile Co.

Hawkes, T. (1977) *Structuralism and Semiotics*, New Accents Series. London: Methuen.

He, J., Becic, E., Lee, Y. C. and McCarley, J. S. (2011) 'Mind-wandering behind the wheel: performance and oculomotor correlates', *Human Factors: The Journal of the Human Factors and Ergonomics Society*, 53 (1): 13–21.

Heitmann, J. (2009) *The Automobile and American Life*. New York: McFarland & Co.

Highsmith, P. (1990 [1952]) *Carol*. London: Bloomsbury.

Hislop, D. (2012) 'Driving, communicating and working: understanding the work-related communication behaviours of business travellers on work-related car journeys', *Mobilities*, 8 (2): 220–37.

Hissey, J. J. (1902) 'The Great North Road', *The Car*, No. 6, 2 July, p. 188.

Holmes, J. C. (1952) 'This is the Beat generation', *New York Times Magazine*, 16 November, p. 10.

Horton, D., Rosen, P. and Cox, P. (eds) (2007) *Cycling and Society*. Aldershot: Ashgate.

Humphreys, R. (1999) *Futurism*. London: Tate Gallery Publishing.

Husserl, E. (2002a [1900–1]) 'Introduction to the *Logical Investigations*', in D. Moran and T. Mooney (eds), *The Phenomenology Reader*. London and New York: Routledge, pp. 65–77.

Husserl, E. (2002b [1964]) 'The phenomenology of internal time consciousness', in D. Moran and T. Mooney (eds), *The Phenomenology Reader*. London and New York: Routledge, pp. 109–23.

Hutton, G. (2011) *Old Glencoe and Ballachulish*. Glasgow: Stenlake Publishing.

Huxley, A. (1959 [1925]) 'Lord Hovenden' [*These Barren Leaves*], in J. Welcome (ed.), *Best Motoring Stories*. London: Faber & Faber, pp. 13–26.

J. L. C. (1905) 'London to Liverpool and back: a lady driver's journey on a De Dion', *The Autocar*, 8 April, p. 490.

Jeremiah, D. (2007) *Representations of British Motoring*. Manchester: Manchester University Press.

Katz, C. and Mom, G. (2014) 'Why not now? The electric vehicle as a vehicle of tomorrow', *Mobility in History: The Yearbook of the International Association for the History of Transport, Traffic and Mobility*, 5 (1): 51–63.

Katz, J. (1999) *How Emotions Work*. Chicago and London: University of Chicago Press.

Keir, D. and Morgan, B. (1955). *Golden Milestone: 50 Years of the AA*. London: Automobile Association.

Kennedy, B. (1919a) 'The magic of speed', *The Car Illustrated*, No. 904, p. 115.

Kennedy, B. (1919b) 'Seen from the car', *The Car Illustrated*, No. 905, p. 125.

Kern, S. (2000 [1983]) *The Culture of Time and Space: 1880–1918*. London: Methuen.

Kerouac, J. (2000 [1957]) *On the Road*. London: Penguin.

Killingworth, M. A. and Gilbert, D. T. (2010) 'A wandering mind is an unhappy mind', *Science*, 330: 932.

King, D. B. and Wertheimer, M. (2007) *Max Wertheimer and Gestalt Theory*. New Brunswick, NJ and London: Transaction Publishers.

Kirsch, D. A. (2000) *The Electric Car and the Burden of History*. New Brunswick, NJ and London: Rutgers University Press.

Koocamorph1 (2010) 'Los Angeles freeway traffic', https://www.youtube.com/watch?v=_d_Q8Fipc2A (last accessed 20 November 2015).

Kore-Schröder, L. K. (2007) '"Reflections in a motor car": Virginia Woolf's phenomenological relations of time and space', in A. Snaith and M. Whitworth (eds), *Locating Woolf: The Politics of Space and Place*. Basingstoke: Palgrave Macmillan, pp. 131–47.

Koshar, R. J. (2008) 'Driving cultures and the meaning of roads: some comparative examples', in C. Mauch and T. Zeller (eds), *The Road Beyond the Windshield: Roads and Landscapes in the United States and Europe*. Athens: Ohio University Press, pp. 14–34.

Kurmann, R. (2010) 'Northbound I-110 Harbor Freeway in Los Angeles, CA', https://www.youtube.com/watch?v=l11yudAIxcc (last accessed 20 November 2015).

Laurier, E. (2004) 'Doing office work on the motorway', *Theory, Culture and Society*, 21 (4–5): 261–77.

Laurier, E. (2011) 'Driving: pre-cognition and driving', in T. Cresswell and P. Merriman (eds), *Geographies of Mobilities: Practices, Spaces, Subjects*. Farnham and Burlington, VT: Ashgate, pp. 69–82.

Laurier, E. and Dant, T. (2011) 'What we do whilst driving: towards the driverless car', in M. Grieco and J. Urry (eds), *Mobilities: New Perspectives on Transport and Society*. Farnham and Burlington, VT: Ashgate, pp. 223–44.

Laurier, E., Lorimer, H., Brown, B., Jones, O. et al. (2008) 'Driving and passengering: notes on the ordinary organisation of car travel', *Mobilities*, 3 (1): 1–23.

Lehmann, R. (1981 [1936]) *The Weather in the Streets*. London: Virago.

Levitt, D. (1909) *The Woman and the Car: A Chatty Little Handbook for All Women Who Motor or Who Want to Motor*. London and New York: John Lane, The Bodley Head (facsimile reproduction, Nabu Public Domain Reprints).

'Los Angeles area freeways – 1975' (2008) https://www.youtube.com/watch?v=w9wpmYam56Q (last accessed 20 November 2015).

Maclehouse, A. (1930) 'A Highway of Romance', *SMT*, 4 (2): 59.

Marinoff, L. (2010 [1941]) 'Persistence pays', *Times Higher Educational Supplement*, 1 April, pp. 46–8.

Marion, J.-L. (2002) *Being Given: Toward a Phenomenology of Giveness*, trans. J. L. Kosky. Stanford, CA: Stanford University Press.

Mauch, C. and Zeller, T. (2008) *The World Beyond the Windshield: Roads and Landscapes in the United States and Europe*. Athens: Ohio University Press.

Maxwell, S. (2001) 'Negotiating car use in everyday life', in D. Miller (ed.), *Car Cultures*. Oxford and New York: Berg, pp. 203–22.

Merleau-Ponty, M. (2002 [1945]) *Phenomenology of Perception*, trans. C. Smith. London and New York: Routledge.

Merriman, P. (2004) 'Driving places: Marc Augé, non-places and the geographies of England's M1 motorway', *Theory, Culture and Society*, 21 (4–5): 145–67.

Merriman, P. (2007), *Driving Spaces: A Cultural-Historical Geography of England's M1 Motorway*. Oxford: Blackwell.

Merriman, P. (2012) *Mobility, Space and Culture*, International Library of Sociology. London and New York: Taylor & Francis.

Miller, D. (ed.) (2001) *Car Cultures*. Oxford and New York: Berg.

Mitchell, W. J. T. (1995) 'Gombrich and the rise of landscape', in J. Brewer and A. Bermingham (eds), *The Consumption of Culture 1600–1800: Image, Object, Text*. London: Routledge, pp. 103–18.

Mom, G. P. A. (2004) *The Electric Vehicle: Technology and Expectations in the Automobile Age*. Baltimore: Johns Hopkins University Press.

Mom, G. P. A. (2014) *Atlantic Automobilism: Emergence and Persistence of the Car*. London and Oxford: Berghahn.

Moran, D. and Mooney, T. (eds) (2002) *The Phenomenology Reader*. London and New York: Routledge.

Moran, J. (2009) *On Roads: A Hidden History*. London: Profile Books.

Morrison, B. (2014) 'The proud highway of second thoughts: review of Neil Young's *Special Deluxe*', 19 November, http://www.theguardian.

com/books/2014/nov/19/special-deluxe-neil-young-review-proud-highway-thoughts (last accessed 26 November 2015).

Morrison, K. A. and Minnis, J. (2012) *Carscapes: The Motor Car, Architecture and Landscape in England*. New Haven, CT: Yale University Press.

Morton, H. V. (2008 [1929]) *In Search of Scotland*. London: Methuen.

Morton, H. V. (2013 [1927]) *In Search of England*. London: Methuen.

'Motoring in Arran' (1929) *The Autocar*, 8 November, p. 1001.

'Motoring in West Somerset' (1919) *The Car*, No. 904, 17 September, p. 101.

Muir, E. (1996 [1935]) *Scottish Journey*. Edinburgh: Mainstream Publishing.

Mullarkey, J. (1999) *Bergson and Philosophy*. Edinburgh: Edinburgh University Press.

Murphy, T. D. (1908) *British Highways and Byways from a Motor Car: Being a Record of a Five Thousand Mile Tour in England, Scotland and Wales*. Boston: L. C. Page & Co.

Murray, L. and Upstone, S. (2014) *Researching and Representing Mobilities: Transdisciplinary Encounters*. Basingstoke: Palgrave Macmillan.

Nabokov, V. (2000 [1955]) *Lolita*. London: Penguin.

Narozky, V. (2002) 'Our cars in Havana', in P. Wollen and J. Kerr (eds), *Autopia: Cars and Culture*. London: Reaktion Books, pp. 169–76.

National Geographic (2010) *Drives of a Lifetime*. Washington, DC: National Geographic.

Orwell, G. (2002 [1937]) *The Road to Wigan Pier*. London: Penguin.

Osmond, D. (1929) 'As in the beginning: a blasé motorist rediscovers the pleasures and joys of motoring', *The Autocar*, 15 February, p. 32.

Otoiu, A. (2002) 'Automobile metempsychoses in the land of dracula', in P. Wollen and J. Kerr (eds), *Autopia: Cars and Culture*. London: Reaktion Books, pp. 199–208.

Parker, I. (2002 [1999]) 'Traffic', in P. Wollen and J. Kerr (eds), *Autopia: Cars and Culture*. London: Reaktion Books, pp. 296–306.

Parker, Sir G. M. P. (1919) 'The wings of the wind', *The Car Magazine*, 1 (1): 7–14.

Pearce, L. (1994) *Reading Dialogics*. London: Edward Arnold.

Pearce, L. (2000) 'Driving north, driving south: reflections on the spatial/temporal co-ordinates of home', in L. Pearce (ed.), *Devolving Identities: Feminist Readings in Home and Belonging*. Aldershot and Burlington, VT: Ashgate, pp. 162–78.

Pearce, L. (2012) 'Automobility in Manchester fiction', *Mobilities*, 7 (1): 93–113.

Pearce, L. (2013) 'Autopia: in search of what we're thinking when we're driving', in J. Stacey and J. Wolff (eds), *Writing Otherwise: Experiments in Cultural Criticism*. Manchester: Manchester University Press, pp. 92–105.

Pearce, L. (2014) 'A motor-flight through early twentieth-century consciousness: capturing the driving-event 1905–1935', in L. Murray and S. Upstone (eds), *Researching and Representing Mobilities: Transdisciplinary Encounters*. Basingstoke: Palgrave Macmillan.

Pearce, L. (2017) '"Driving as event": literary excursions in automobility', *Mobilities* [under review].

Pearce, L. (2016) 'Love's schema and correction: a queer twist on a general principle', *Journal of Popular Romance Studies*, 5 (2). Online journal.

Perry, F. (dir.) (1972) *Play It as It Lays*. US: Universal Pictures.

Petit, C. (dir.) (2008 [1979]) *Radio On*. BFI DVD.

Petit, C. and Sinclair, I. (dir.) (2002) *London Orbital*. UK: Film Four/ Illuminations Films.

Phillip, A. (1919) 'Late autumn touring', *The Car*, No. 910, 29 October, p. 235.

Polanksi, R. (dir.) (1974) *Chinatown*. US: Paramount Pictures.

Pooley, C. (2010) 'Landscapes without the car: a counter-factual historical geography of twentieth-century Britain', *Historical Geography*, 36 (3): 266–75.

Pooley, C. (2013) 'Uncertain mobilities: a view from the past', *Transfers*, 3 (1): 26–44.

Pooley, C. (forthcoming) 'Cities, spaces and movement: everyday experiences of urban travel in England *c.*1840–1940', *Urban History*.

Pooley, C., Turnbull, J. and Adams, M. (2005) *A Mobile Century? Changes in Everyday Mobility in the Twentieth Century*. London and Burlington, VT: Ashgate.

Priestley, J. B. (1984 [1934]) *An English Journey*. London: Heinemann.

Proust, M. (1941 [1913–27]) *Remembrance of Things Past*. London: Chatto & Windus.

Redshaw, S. (2008) *In the Company of Cars: Driving as a Social and Cultural Practice*. Aldershot and Burlington, VT: Ashgate.

Rubin, M. K. (2009) 'Alice Ramsay's historic cross-country drive', Smithsonian. com, http://www.smithsonianmag.com/womens-history/alice-ramseys-histo ric-cross-country-drive-29114570/?no-ist (last accessed 20 November 2015).

Sachs, W. (1992) *For Love of the Automobile: Looking Back into the History of Our Desires*. Oxford: University of California Press.

Scharff, V. (1991) *Taking the Wheel: Women and the Coming of the Motor Age*. New York: Free Press.

Schnapp, J. T. (1999) 'Crash (speed as engine of individuation)', *Modernism/ Modernity*, 6 (1): 1–49.

Schwarzer, M. (2004) *Zoomscape: Architecture in Motion and Media*. New York: Princeton Architectural Press.

Scott, D. (2012 [1917]) 'Motoring at night', in *A Number of Things*. London and Edinburgh: T. N. Fowlis (facsimile reproduction), pp. 41–9.

Seiler, C. (2008) *Republic of Drivers: A Cultural History of Automobility in America*. Chicago and London: Chicago University Press.

Sennett, R. (1990) *The Conscience of the Eye: The Design and Social Life of Cities*. London and Boston: Faber & Faber.

Sheller, M. (2004) 'Automotive emotions: feeling the car', *Theory, Culture and Society*, 21 (4–5): 221–42.

Sheller, M. and Urry, J. (2000) 'The city and the car', *International Journal of Urban and Regional Research*, 24 (4): 735–57.

Shirley, R. (2015) 'Speed and stillness; driving in the countryside', in C. Berberich, N. Campbella and R. Hudson (eds), *Affective Landscapes in Literature, Art and Everyday Life*. Farnham and Burlington VT: Ashgate, pp. 69–81.

Sinclair, I. (2003 [2002]) *London Orbital*. London: Penguin.

Solnit, R. (2001) *Wanderlust: A History of Walking*. London: Verso.

Stacey, J. and Wolff, J. (eds) (2013) *Writing Otherwise: Experiments in Cultural Criticism*. Manchester: Manchester University Press.

Stocks, J. W. (1902) 'From Land's End to John O'Groats', *The Car*, No. 11, 6 August, pp. 367–9.

Stradling, S. (2002) *Persuading People Out of Their Cars*. Paper presented at ESRC 'Mobile Network' conference.

Stradling, S.G., Meadows, M. L. and Beatty, S. (2001) 'Identity and independence: two dimensions of driver autonomy', in G. B. Grayson (ed.), *Behavioural Research in Road Safety*. Crowthorne: Transport Research Laboratory.

Struther, J. (1989 [1939]) *Mrs Miniver*. London: Virago Press.

Tarantino, Q. (1992) *Reservoir Dogs*. US: Miramax Pictures.

Tarantino, Q. (1994) *Pulp Fiction*. US: Miramax Pictures.

Tart, C. (1990 [1969]) *Altered States of Consciousness*. New York: HarperCollins.

Taylor, E. (2011 [1951]) *A Game of Hide and Seek*. London: Virago.

Thakkar, A. (2014) 'Crash and return: "choque", allusion and composite structure in Alejandro González Inárritus "Amores Perros" (2000)', *Quarterly Review of Film and Video*, 31 (1): 11–26.

The Shell Poster Book (1998) London: Profile Books.

The Smiths (1986) 'There is a light that never goes out', *The Queen Is Dead*. WEA.

Thompson, E. (2015) *Waking, Dreaming, Being: Self and Consciousness in Neuroscience, Meditation, and Philosophy*. New York: Columbia University Press.

Thorold, P. (2003) *The Motoring Age: The Automobile and Britain 1896–1939*. London: Profile Books.

Thrift, N. (2008 [2004]) 'Driving in the City', in *Non-Representational Theory: Space, Politics, Affect*. London and New York: Routledge, pp. 75–88.

Times Motoring Correspondent (1929) *The Art of Driving*. London: Times Publications.

Trigg, D. (2012) *The Memory of Place: A Phenomenology of the Uncanny*. Athens: Ohio University Press.

Urry, J. (2004) 'The "system" of automobility', *Theory, Culture and Society*, 21 (4–5): 25–39.

Urry, J. (2007) *Mobilities*. Cambridge: Polity.

Urry, J. (2011) 'Does mobility have a future?', in M. Grieco and J. Urry (eds), *Mobilities: New Perspectives on Transport and Society*. Farnham and Burlington, VT: Ashgate, pp. 1–20.

Urry, J. (2013) *Societies Beyond Oil: Oil Dregs and Social Futures*. London: Zed Books.

Van Lennep, D. J. (1987) 'The psychology of driving a car', in J. Kockelmans (ed.), *Phenomenological Psychology*. Dortrecht: Martinus Nijhoff.

Vidal, R. (2013) *Death and Desire in Car Crash Culture: A Century of Romantic Futurisms*. Oxford and Bern: Peter Lang.

Virilio, P. (2008 [1984]) *Negative Horizon: An Essay in Dromoscopy*. London and New York: Continuum.

Volti, R. (2006) *Cars and Culture: The Life Story of a Technology*. Baltimore: Johns Hopkins University Press.

Waugh, E. (1959 [1930]) Extract from *Vile Bodies* ['Agatha Runcible's Motor Race'], in J. Welcome (ed.), *Best Motoring Stories*. London, pp. 27–51.

Weir, P. (1974) (dir.) *The Cars That Ate Paris*. Australia: MCA.

Welcome, J. (ed.) (1959) *Best Motoring Stories*. London: Faber & Faber

Wharton, Edith (2008 [1908]) *A Motor-Flight Through France*. New York: Atlas & Co.

Whitbourne, S. K. (2013) 'Why and how you daydream', https://www. psychologytoday.com/blog/fulfillment-any-age/201301/why-and-how-you-daydream?collection=131155 (last accessed 21 November 2015).

Wilenski, R. H. (1930) 'The road beautiful: a plea for wider vision', *SMT*, 4 (2): 37–41.

Williams, H. (1991) *Autogeddon*. London: Jonathan Cape.

Williams, R. (1977) *Marxism and Literature*. Oxford: Oxford University Press.

Williams, R. J. (2002) 'Pleasure and the motorway', in P. Wollen and J. Kerr (eds), *Autopia: Cars and Culture*. London: Reaktion Books, pp. 281–7.

Windmer, E. L. (2002) 'Crossroads: The automobile, rock and roll and democracy', in P. Wollen and J. Kerr (eds), *Autopia: Cars and Culture*. London: Reaktion Books, pp. 65–74.

Wollen, P. and Kerr, J. (eds) (2002) *Autopia: Cars and Culture*. London: Reaktion Books.

Woolf, Virginia (1942 [1927]) 'Evening Over Sussex: reflections in a motor car', *The Death of the Moth and Other Essays*. London: Hogarth Press, pp. 11–14.

Woolf, Virginia (1978 [1927]) *To the Lighthouse*. London: Dent.

Wordsworth, D. (1981 [1803]) *Recollections of a Tour Made in Scotland*. Edinburgh: Mercat Press.

Young, N. (2014) *Special Deluxe: A Memoir of Life and Cars*. London and New York: Penguin (Viking).

Žižek, S. (2014) *Event: Philosophy in Transit*. London: Penguin Books.

Zuckerman, W. (1991) *End of the Road: From World Car Crisis to Sustainable Transportation*. White River Junction, VT: Chelsea Green Publishing.

Index